AF485635

JUDE'S ALMOST DAILY BLOG BOOK 3

Jude's Almost Daily Blog Book 3

By: Jude Stringfellow

Copyright © 2024 by Jude Stringfellow.

This is a work of fiction. Names, characters, places and incidents either are the product of the author's imagination or are used fictitiously, and any resemblance to any actual persons, living or dead, events, or locales is entirely coincidental.

Dedication Page

This book is dedicated to my good friend and former co-worker, *Julie Szabolcsi-Anderson*. (Woot!) She's an amazing person with a great talent for music, art, and so many other crafts and fun stuff. She's one of those people who you meet and you just know you're gonna be friends forever! (...and it didn't hurt that she loves Scotland as much as I do!)

Thank You Page

There are so many people who deserve a big thank you for being part of this particular book. Some of you were in the book because I wanted to put you in it; some of you are in the book because you deserve to be in it. Thank you to each and every one of you who is mentioned and if I had to change your name to protect someone else, hey, it is what it is.

Thank you, Tex. You keep me thinking, you keep me listening, learning, and growing. Thanks for reading the book too; it means a lot to me.

Thank you, Jesus for literally always being there. You deserve not only the praise and the honor, but you deserve even more. I can't wait to see you!!

Disclaimer Page

As usual, my disclaimer will read (and say) that this is not a truth-telling, tell-all where I name names and give out minute details about everything. So many things in this book are either tongue-in-cheek worthy, or they're just stories I thought I would tell you. I'm not gonna say I lied; that would be a stretch, but I'm certainly not going to say I'm always telling the truth either.

The book is to be enjoyed. Enjoy it. Don't worry your pretty little head about facts. They'll take care of themselves I'm sure. Now, that being said, there are some blogs that are more serious than others; and you'll be able to tell which ones I'm trying to get your attention on, and which ones you're supposed to giggle at while you read. I do cover a few heavy-hitting topics such as mental health, self-worth, love, death, and true relationships. I think if you're old enough to read this book by yourself you can figure it out.

As usual, I did go through the book and try to fix as many errors as possible. I even used GRAMMARLY!! But, as you can imagine, there are times when you just can't fix every mistake. The book is as flawed as the rest of us. I did use several royalty-free photos from Canva.com. I didn't have to give them credit, but feel that I should. There are paid or Pro photos/graphics as well. I choose to use the free ones when I can. There is a subscription for it.

ENJOY!!

PART 1

Tomboy, That's Me!

Today, if a little girl told her mom she wanted to run with the boys, play in the creek, climb trees and go hunting (huntin') her own mother may call a counselor and ask if her daughter is a candidate for a gender transformation surgery. Parents today think of sexual roles as being so severely drawn that kids can't be kids anymore. They can't explore their likes or dislikes without there being a real crisis! Stop already! People, please, just know that you're gonna be fine. Kids are just normal if and when they step out of the box that maybe a stranger-than-should-be society has placed them into. Let a kid dance to his or her own drummer now and again. Thank God, I'm old! I didn't have to worry about anyone calling me names or thinking I was weird because I could swallow a tadpole or swing out into the lake and drop off the rope upside down!

Well, I did get called names, but the names I was called were "*Tomboy*" or "*Smarty-pants*". The latter was shouted out to me at various times because, not completely unlike Hermoine Granger, I seemed to make an annoyance of myself when I knew the answers. I always knew the answers. Why did I always know the answers to whatever the teacher was asking? Hell, that's easy, I read the required assignment when I was told to. I was called a Tomboy because by the time I was four, I could climb any tree, hop a fence, rein in a horse, chase down a goat, and if I needed to, yeah, I could swallow a tadpole that I caught myself right out of the creek that ran next to the school. Why would I do that? Because most of the boys were too chicken to do it, but I could! They were still faster than me, and they could hit the ball further, but I didn't mind going over the fence that had the big ol' sign on it warning everyone that it was Federal property, and no one was allowed to "*Trespass*"; whatever that meant. We didn't really care much about such things.

In school, I wanted to play the saxophone, not the stupid flute. I ended up with the flute, but I wasn't happy about it. I wanted to play baseball, but they wouldn't let a girl on the team. I played on the church team though. I wanted to run track, and I did. I also lifted weights, swam, and jumped about 100 fences to get from the high school to my house without having to take the streets when I missed the bus. I didn't really like riding the bus anyway. If I walked home I could keep in shape, play with dogs I didn't really know and meet folks who were staring at me from their living room windows...."*There she is again!*" Little wave.

When I was four I used to climb over my friend's fence because his backyard abutted the main street I needed to go up to get to the library. I lived at 2212 N. Mueller, and the Bethany Library was at 3501 N. Mueller. All I had to do was hop over the Willis' back fence and go straight up Mueller, and that is exactly what I did. Rain, sleet, snow, heat, it didn't matter. I wanted to "read". I was four. I wasn't really reading, but I thought I was. On the way to the library, I'd have to pass a cop that always placed himself at 30th street and Mueller. The police station was next to the library, and still is in the city of Bethany, Oklahoma. The cop would wave at me, and he'd call the library to let them know I was coming. They'd usually end up calling my mom sometimes, even before I arrived! It was such a great little system. I never knew how she knew to pick me up a couple of hours later so I didn't have to walk back after dark. Smart woman, that one!

My uncle had horses. I rode my uncle's horses. I didn't bother saddling them. I just climbed up and held on. There were more horses behind the church, too. I left church services and rode those horses. The owners weren't necessarily churchgoers, I guess. Somehow, Mom always found out where I was, and there she was at the fence line, just waiting on me, sometimes without a smile on her face. My friend's dad went huntin', and he taught me how to shoot a gun before my daddy did. My daddy was actually rather surprised that I already knew how; Mom wasn't thrilled about that either. She didn't really smile all that much when it was just me and her; she was usually dragging me home from somewhere I wasn't supposed to be. At least she understood that I was normal for a Tomboy type, and she didn't have my head examined. She did, however, get a switch after me now and again.

My Grandma on my daddy's side was a GIRLY GIRLY GIRL. Oh my goodness, you never saw such a sight as my gloriously made-up, coiffured, and lipsticked young Granny. She was only 15 when she had my daddy, so when the kids came along, she wasn't more than 35-40, far too young to call herself a Granny. She wanted us to call her Olivia. That wasn't going to happen. My mom would have shot blood out of her eyes and mine if I had done that.

My mom's mom was 43 when she had my mom, so by the time we came along, she was already older, and I don't think I saw her made-up except at her funeral. I wasn't really sure who was in the coffin, to be perfectly honest with you. She was 99 when she died; my younger, girly-girl of a granny died at age 68, I think. Crazy! My Grandma Edwards, mom's mom, was a stout, hard-working farmer type, and she would have none of the mischiefs I brought to my own mom. I think I know why my mom was so lenient with me. She was raised with a heavy hand. Dad never saw a hand when he was growing up. He was born, hit the streets, then joined the Navy.

Tomboys are tough. We skinned our knees, broke bones, even toppled over a few times, and ended up worse for wear, but we didn't cry about it. We couldn't really take the time to cry about anything, we had things to do. We had places to go. We had things to see and things to create...mostly havoc. I was raised in the city part of the city of Bethany, not the rural section, but you know I didn't hang out under the street lights long. I headed off to the outer skirts with the livestock, with the wildlife, and where the creek met the river. I may ride my bike five or six miles in one direction when I got old enough to reach the pedals. I wanted the boy's bike, but Mom put her foot down on that one. Mine had flowers on the seat. She was determined to make me her little pumpkin...Well, OK, but I took to hanging upside down so often I had to wear shorts under my dress.

To be honest with you, I don't think I wore shoes unless I was going to school or church. I didn't wear them to the store. I didn't wear them to eat at a restaurant. You didn't have to back then. I know I didn't wear them when I drove my car. Mom finally told me once that if I wore another hole in my socks, I had to buy them myself. OK. Socks are cheap. Oh wait, did you think I ran around town barefoot? No!! I'm not a hillbilly!! LOL...more of a Tomboy or maybe, OK yeah, a bit of a redneck. I still don't wear shoes unless I'm working or going out in public. They make you do that now. When I come home, the shoes come off. I've bought a great many pairs of socks in my life. I don't really care if I match them or not. Mostly not.

I think I grew up OK. That may be up for debate, but I think I'm good. I don't have an identity crisis. I don't think I'm a man trapped in a woman's body. I don't even want to be a man. I just like outshining them now and again because I can. I still can't lift as much as one; I can't outrun one. I can't hit the ball further, and no, I can't out-drink one because (a) I don't drink alcohol, and (b) I'd end up peeing myself if I tried. I'm still pretty much a smarty-pants, though...I still read everything I'm told to, and just for the heck of it, I read so much more than I'm told to. Yep...Little Miss Know it All; well, not all, but you know...stuff.

Me on my cousin Gene (Age 5)

The Gray Man

This film may have been released as a DVD or in theatres in 2007, but it was filmed almost entirely in June 2005! My son Reuben is in this movie, and I want to see it. It was so funny, too, the way he was hired for it. Reuben attended Putnam City High School in Oklahoma City through the Putnam City School District. He was a senior in 2005, and during the month of March, just 8 weeks before he was to graduate, we found out that his counselor had screwed up his credits - - not Reuben; a kid can't do that despite what appears on paper - the counselor has to approve everything a kid picks and chooses. Of course, a kid is going to seek the easy route; of course, a kid is going to try to get out of the things he or she has to take to graduate if he or she can be an office aide every semester!

The office absolutely loved it when Reuben was there - the boy was MADE to run errands. He'd make it a game and time himself as he would blast down the halls, literally ramming into people he liked, tackling friends in the name of having to get there! The boy was excited, to say the least. HOWEVER, you can't be an office aide every semester and get credit! That's something his counselor should have put a stop to. So, he didn't qualify to actually graduate in 2005....this was an absolute disaster!

I had already opened my home school for the girls, and they were under a strict curriculum, but I decided to add Reuben as a student for the 1.5 credits he was missing. If I could get him those credits before June 30, 2005, I could see him graduate, and he would have a real diploma issued by the home school, yes, but it would be official, signed by his principal, me, and an officer of the district itself. What to do? OK...I gave the boy an 8-week crash course in POETRY....yes, you heard me, POETRY for 1 full credit. He had to read it, analyze it, write it, research it, and read it out loud to an audience.

It wasn't as difficult for him as I first thought, and as a reward for the boy, I actually published 4 of his poems in a book I wrote called *"Periwinkle,"* so now he's even a published poet. For a half-credit course, I thought about drama since he failed it in his freshman year. Same trappings - I would have him read about it, write about it, and maybe put on a little play for me - but then I found out that they were filming *WISTERIA*, a feature film just 30 miles from where we live. I took him there to WATCH them film - no idea they'd hired him on the spot.

We were watching, just watching, when someone suggested that he fill out the necessary forms and take a headshot just in case the director needed a big country boy for the background. All of the extras in the film were from Oklahoma - it was perfect. Well, they did hire him that day, but not for the role of a town dweller or country boy - he is the *"young cop"* under credits. He's the taller one, the thicker one, the one tackling the bad guy. He's in about 9 scenes, I think; I haven't seen the finished product, but we were filming every day for 2 weeks, and he was used in all of the street scenes as well as the courthouse scenes. The one I really wanted to see, but it was edited, was where the director tells Reuben to chase the bad guy (stunt man). He used the quote, *"tackle his ass"*....OH MY GOSH, did he really say that to a 6A state-qualifying high school Defensive End? FLASH! BAM! DOWN!

"OK," said the director, *"that was...that was....good. This time, let's give the guy a little more room to try, and I don't know...run. Could you be a little less aggressive and maybe not smile so much? You're a*

cop; he's a bad guy." What can I say? The boy was thinking of football. It was hilarious! I couldn't stop laughing, and there was no way I could have approached the director in time to correct his error; he was too far away. I could hear him through a box, but I couldn't even have waved him down - the boy was GONE the second the stuntman broke out of the barn! It took 4 or 5 takes, and the stunt man was laughing his butt off with each new and developed try - I just wonder which take they used...and if the boy is smiling or if they finally convinced him that he was a cop rather than a lineman. It took a bit of work.

So, there he was in the country tackling the man, on the streets holding people back from the courthouse, in the courthouse as a guard, and opening doors. That much, I know. At the time he was filmed, Reuben's hair was all the way to his shoulders, and the hair/makeup artist was so sure he wouldn't want her to cut off his golden red locks to make him look like the 1929-1935 era New York City beat cop that he was portraying - but he was all over it. *"I just saved myself $15!"* was his answer.

He didn't have to go get his hair cut! The fact that the role of an extra in this particular film didn't pay a single penny meant NOTHING to Reuben. He was having the time of his life. You should have seen his face when I mentioned that he actually got to eat for free as well - it was catered by the company...WHAT? Oh, that was all she wrote! "*Hell Yeah*!" was all I heard for weeks...free food, chasing people, tackling them in cornfields, beating people up on the streets, and driving old Model-T cars? Could it be this much fun and still be legal? You just had to be there.

We were there in the 90-degree weather, filming 12–15-hour days. Reuben wore a wool suit the entire time. Because I was his personal assistant, I had to wipe his sweaty face constantly! Can you imagine what my position

20

that pays if the extra isn't paid anything? He did, however, have the best (bar none) personal assistant on the set. Even the stars complained about it. *"I wish my mother was here to bring me drinks and wipe my sweat"* was a great quote from my good buddy Vyto Ruginis (Star Wars and many drams as well as commercials. Google Vyto!) Yes, doesn't everyone wish their personal assistant would run up to them between takes and wipe their sweat, feed them granola bars, give them drinks, and ask them if they need a pee break? I even straightened his clothes, tied his shoes, and brought him back to the 1930s by removing his wristwatch and telling the director so he could edit accordingly. I'm nice like that.

I want to see this film now. I could care less about the terrible, twisted man that it features - a gross and disgusting man, this Albert Fish. He's one of the worst people I have ever read about - not joking. I may only watch it for Vyto's parts and, of course, the *"Young Cop"*. I swear if they didn't give him credit, I'd be all over them....hahaha..not really, but a P.A. has to have their client's back, right? Should I get my boy an agent? Suffice it to say, he earned half credit for baking in the sun for weeks filming the movie. I just can't wait to see it!!

Reuben in 2005 – Putnam City Pirates

My Diatribe

Oh yeah, it's true. Ima gonna bombast anyone who tries to take a single word, poem, blog, book, or creative idea that I came up with and then try to either say it is their work or that it's good, but could be better if we just...you know, changed it. No. You do you. I'll do me. Just today, minutes ago, I received an email from a literary agent in New York asking me to allow her to use my image, my work(s), and my influence to get her a better position within her publishing house. She was literally trying to stroke my ego by dropping my name, saying she's my agent, she could boost herself inside the house she is already a part of - lies. It's so openly and blatantly false I wondered if she really thought that little of me, to think I wouldn't see through her deception, or if she just wasn't all that good at hiding it. Either way, the answer is no. I'm good.

Her approach was interesting, and I'll even give her a bit of credit for using my skills and talents as a way to find a special soft spot in my heart, but baby, this ain't my first rodeo, and I've been kicked a few times by the one horse I trusted; you aren't going to get into my business by telling me how pretty I am, how good I write, how talented I seem to be, and how my influence in the world of words can be a benefit for more than just myself. No, you can go out there in the big bad open market and find yourself another skinny fish, one who hasn't been used to scavenging for food, one who hasn't been tricked by stink bait, and maybe one who would follow your lure just because it's pretty and flashy. This catfish has been feeding off the mud long enough to know what dirt looks like -- I'm good. I'll let God send me food. His promises don't come dangling on an invisible line with a reel at the end. (and remember, catfish have teeth)

My daughter Laura felt the crash and the crush of the media lures years back when she was singing both on the side and professionally. She was approached a number of times by those agents, producers, publishers, people who wanted her sooooo badly, you know, the type. Somehow, because of how they work and who they know, they end up backstage after a show and ask you to give them a call - - promising the world, saying it will be the best decision you ever made. Tell that to Taylor, Rhianna, Billie, and Katy -- maybe they should have stuck their foot out and stepped as hard on those types of would-be predators as my Laura - - BAM!

She turned down the very producers who ended up fronting and pushing a world-known artist just weeks later; it funny how the songs they gave Laura to practice ended up with this new woman, and she claims to have written them. That was one of their assurances; you can say you wrote this or that song when, in reality, they don't let you write a word of any of the songs you sing - - they allow you to think you write with their people, but they change your words, often at the last minutes saying it just wasn't feeling right. They nod and ask you if you understand? You understand, right? Of course you do; you may understand too well, but realize a day late that you're signed on, and you won't be swimming in the pond freely for a minute.

My diatribe to the music industry, and I suppose now the writing industry is this: NO. You can't take our work and claim it is yours. You can't say we are represented by you unless, of course, we are represented by you. Now, if you want to write a blog about me, about us, about Laura, about anyone really, and you want to tell the truth, tell people your opinion, you can do that. You can praise, you can criticize, you can trash me, I don't care - - it won't change my style, my thoughts, my writing, my mind, or anything else - - but hey, here's a thought; tell the truth. Don't go after someone who needs money, needs to be saved, needs to be helped along, and make them a half-baked offer that barely gets them back on track, keeps them afloat just enough so they'll bend over backward to do your bidding, and then you try and ask them to thank you massively online and when being recorded. Stroke. Stroke. Be honest. What in the world is wrong with that? Oh, well, I just said it - - the world.

Laura still sings every single day. She's not recording at this point, but she's not wearing some ridiculous costume, being flown around the world, fed drugs, and lured into dens of filth just to be a product for a named label either - - nope, she's playing games with friends, eating what she wants, sleeping where she wants, dancing, writing - - more writing than she to actually. She's not rich, but she's happy - how do we gauge success anyway? No one is asking her to cover up her imperfections or asking her (telling her) she'll be CGI'd to make her appear more commercially acceptable - - she's a catfish like her momma, happy being free and avoiding shiny objects. A bit for the wiser, that one.

This world has enough liars without becoming a part of their schemes. No, thank you, I'll take the lumps and even the hardships over pretty dressings and easy money; I get to keep myself in the process. That's a bit more rewarding -- you understand, right? Of course, you do. Maybe all too well.

Laura with Leaf (Leopard Gecko)

Italian Cream Cake (Because I Can)

You know me, I don't (and can't) play the guitar to save my life. I mean, if my life were literally depending on it, I would at least have the wherewithal to grab the damn thing by the neck and use it as a beating tool to find myself either space, time, or both. I just can't expect my fingers or thumbs to do the things that some people can do with their eyes closed, making the most unique sounds that God has ever created. It is what it is, but there is something I can do, and I don't know that I've ever tried to do it with my eyes closed, but if push came to shove and there was no other way, I could if I needed to, make and bake an Italian cream cake! I'm really very good at it!

There are times, and today was one of them when I'll just be sitting at my computer thinking about remodeling a home I don't own. The strong and urgent sensation that I need to bake just creeps right over me and through me. I have a few go-to recipes that seem to stave off anything too serious, but today it was one of the ultimate comfort foods; Italian cream cake. I think I put my first one together when I was in grade school. I didn't actually enter the State Fair with it, but I lied and told people that I did. I never said I won any ribbons; I just said I entered it into the competition. God only knows why my mom let me get away with such nonsense. She couldn't bake, that's probably it right there! LOL...sorry, Mom. She's a great artist, though! She makes her recipes out of oils, pastels, pencils, and watercolors.

The Italian cream cake is one of those over-the-top eggy types, and you have to blend it using a hand mixer to make it fluffy and smooth. You add the coconut to stiffen it up a bit and, of course, for flavor and texture. The recipe calls for buttermilk and at room temperature. I didn't have buttermilk. I have not been able to find it either, thank you very much. I can make it, but I didn't take the time to do that today. I used whipping cream and regular milk, let it set out for an hour, and added a bit of vanilla. It's all good. No, really, it is ALL very, very good.

I don't need or want to bake a round cake here at my house since it's just Laura and I living here. We don't need to be fancy. I cut the recipe back enough to fill up a 9x9 Pyrex, and since I had a bit left over, I made a couple of good-sized cupcakes as well. I just took them out of the oven and put them straight into the freezer so I could ice them and drop a few pecans on top. That's gonna be really nice - - I don't really have to have a reason to celebrate when I bake. I just bake. It's the same thing that some people do when they walk into a room and pick up their Gibson or their Fender. I have a Yamaha guitar that I call Wally. I do actually pick him up and play chords, so he's not lonely. I offered him a bite of my cupcake - - he declined.

For me, baking is not just a thing to do. I consider it a release of stress, pressure, happiness, joy, sorrow, and even mental anguish if I had any, but I don't really have anything like that - - maybe it's because I bake. I am quite sure there must be a solid connection between anxiety and blending eggs into Stevia. I don't use sugar when I bake. I haven't used granulated sugar for more than 2 years. I get the same results, and no one knows the difference. I don't have to freak over the calories, which means I can have two pieces of Italian cream cake if I want to! (I mean, let's get real, I could eat the whole thing if Laura wasn't here to help). I think I'll grab a friend or two to share it. If you're gonna sing a song you wrote or recite a poem you wrote, you'll want someone else to like it too, right? Yeah! I'm the same when it comes to food. I have to share. (I have a few good friends, you know; I keep them happy)

Here's the recipe I used. I don't know that I found it anywhere; it's just the one I use. (Remember, this is for a 9x9 glass dish, not a 3-tier round)
Preheat the oven to 350. You don't want the top browning before the middle.

Cream together in a mixing bowl (I use a hand mixer)
4 eggs
1 cup of Stevia
3/4 cup of butter
1 tsp of vanilla
1 cup of buttermilk (I used whipping cream and Lactaid)
Add the following:
1-1/2 cups of all-purpose flour
1 tsp baking soda
1/2 tsp salt
3/4 cup of flaked coconut

BLEND with a hand mixer until it is really smooth.
Pour it into a 9x9 (sprayed with oil) glass dish. Bake for about 35 minutes, but check it a few times. You'll know it's ready when the sides and top are golden brown. You can lightly touch the top, and it doesn't give, and you can check it with a toothpick in the middle. If the toothpick comes out clean, it's done.
The icing: (ONLY apply when the cake is cool)
2-1/2 cups of powdered sugar (I don't use Stevia for this)
8 oz of cream cheese
1/4 cup of butter
1 tsp of vanilla

BLEND IT AND MAKE IT CREAMY. (add coconut if you want)

When the cake is done, you can wait to cool it or stick it in the fridge or freezer for a few minutes. Add pecans to the icing if you want, or just spread the icing and then add the pecans. If you do make a round cake, this recipe will make a two-tier only, and the pans need to be sprayed and use a little flour on them to help get the cake out before icing it.

Photo Credit: Canva.com (royalty-free)

The Nose Knows

I don't know how many men tell me they can't smell worth a darn. I'm usually not surprised these days, but for years, it just sort of struck me as being so very odd that a man couldn't smell what I was definitely smelling, be it good or bad. I now relive in my mind the many times I would curl my nose upon stumbling into a bad smell, only to see my son, my dad, my son-in-law, just about any man, calmly walking through the musk, the mold, the sewage, whatever putrid odor was invading my obviously more sensitive nostrils. *"You can't smell that?"* I would ask. To my chagrin, most of the time, they would look blankly at me and ask, *"What? What am I supposed to be smelling?"* Sometimes, one or the other will say, *"Oh, I can't smell anything, never could really."* It just makes me wonder about...you know, men.

Women can smell just about anything. I say, women, I should say THIS WOMAN can smell just about anything. My two daughters are far superior to me in that department. Laura can't even go into a craft store or an all-natural food store because of the herbs and various spices being wafted about. She really should be able to somehow harness that ability, maybe see if she could put a freakin' Bloodhound out of work. I don't know if that could be a thing, but if it could be a thing, she would be really good at it. She's really great at sniffing; I'm really good at detecting. I see it, smell it, feel it, know it, and I'm on it. I have a keen way of not being able to let something go if it's gotten up under my nose and/or spirit. Nope, if it's locked on my radar, I will have to hunt down the source, be it a smell or a hunch about something else. We (women) just have a knack, I guess - - some better (or worse) than others.

I think I lost a boyfriend over it once. I'm not kidding you. I was making dinner when he came in from the outside world, and as he passed by me to wash his hands, I asked him how his mother was. He hadn't told me he had been to see his mom, but I could definitely smell her Charlie by Revlon perfume on him. It's not as if she took a bath in it either; it was just casting a very faint hello at me as he passed. He said she was fine, but all that evening, he was upset that I knew he had been at his mom's when he hadn't told me. I don't think it was guilt because I couldn't care less if he was at her place. We got along. It was just that he wasn't comfortable with me knowing something without him having revealed it. Oh well, I guess that's something he never would have learned to live with. I know a lot of things. I've been deducing and thinking thoughts for over 1580 years now...I'm not even a Highlander!

Some people play guitars. Some people know Math. Some people have zero issues with typing over 100 words per minute, and they never check to see if they've misspelled something. I am not one of those people, but I can look a man in the eyes and see what I need to see, know what I need to know, and I suppose to some, that means I'm a mind reader. Nope, just really good at reading faces, bodies, words, and signs that you're throwing out there, buddy! I'd say it's a gift, but it could just as well be a curse, I suppose. It all depends on the situation.

I was talking about Laura replacing a Bloodhound, I watched a YouTube true crime show last week where a particular Bloodhound was given the scent of a man the cops believed was the killer or could be with the killer at the time someone was killed. The dog was given a relatively old scent; it had been picked up with a sniffing machine in an abandoned car that was left for over six weeks in a parking space about two miles from where the deceased was found. The dog picked up the scent and ran with it. By saying he ran with it, he pulled the handler's arm so hard the man fell on his face, lost the dog, and had to run to keep up. After a few hundred feet, the cop's partner took off in the patrol car to follow the dog.

The dog ran about two and a half miles before cutting through woods, up a path, through a gate, and into a family holiday party in the back garden of the man's mom and dad. The dog, who had never met the man, sat beside him and stared into his face. For his part, the man was unsure what was happening. He petted the dog on the top of the head and said something like, "*Hey boy, where'd you come from?*" when the police partner(s) showed up and arrested him on suspicion of murder. Good dog, indeed.

The man confessed to having been with the killer and even assisting his friend in disposing of the body. The man did, in fact, drive the car with the body in the truck, and the killer walked to the area to start digging the grave. The absence of the killer's scent made it that much more possible for the dog to find his mark. I'm not saying Laura could do something that extraordinary, but it does remind me of just how marvelous God is and how He decides who and what will be gifted and just exactly how they will be. I'm not sure a Collie, German Shepherd or Great Dane could have completed the task. I just don't know, but what I do know, and what I have known for years, is that I am able to read patterns, gestures, expressions, emotions, and such - - and in reading, I can also detect when someone is both lying or about to lie. That's when I start sighing. I hate it. I hate that, I know. I hate that I can't accept this from others and I hate that I tell them what I can't allow. If I tell the truth, and I do, I expect the truth to be told to me.

I have to admit that I have lied in my lifetime. I usually have an out, too, a way for others to be able to not tell me what they are thinking and still hold my heart or my friendship. I ask them to pinky-swear with me and to agree that if they can tell me the truth, they will. If they can't do so at this time, they will consider doing so when they can. I just can't take a lie. Put me off and agree to tell me more later, but never, please, never lie to me. It hurts too badly. Have you seen those people who can hear a song once and play it on the piano? I'm not like that. Have you heard of those who can see something and then draw it out perfectly, either using a pencil, pen, chalk or whatever medium? I am not that person, either. I can write a poem on a dare. I can create a story, a tale, even the basis of a good novel, so maybe smelling good things and smelling really bad things isn't my only useful talent! I hope not.

I am Sooooo Not Techy

If you know me at all, and some of you do, you'll know that I type well enough. I can spin a good tale, but I am the worst when it comes to making things work in terms of tech. I just don't have that gene. I have the creative gene in spades. I can whip out a poem in minutes if you want me to, and as long as I have pen and paper, I can show it. Having said that, if you want me to connect something with a cord or wire to something else that deals with or eventually causes something entirely different to do whatever it's supposed to do because it's supposed to do it -- you're out of luck. That's not my forte.

Let me explain this week's trauma drama when it came to technology and I am having another row. My computer, the one I'm sitting at this very moment, decided (all on its own, mind you) not to send a signal to my monitor. I swear, my monitor didn't do a damn thing to the computer. There was no reason for this disruption. It was as if the CPU had heard me talking about replacing it, and it just threw a hissy fit. I know my smartphone can hear and see everything I say, maybe even what I'm thinking, but the CPU should not be in the same class of intelligence. The CPU is an H.P. Elite desk, and I think I got it about four years ago. Because I don't ever really spend a great deal of money on anything electronic, I wasn't too surprised that after four years it decided to stop working.

My monitor, which is a Dell, told me in no uncertain terms that it was not receiving a signal and that it was going into power saver mode. I get that. Everything needs to sleep now and again. I did what all people who are like me do in these situations; I found a kid to fix the problem. The problem with that plan is that my kid is 33 now. She's no longer protected by the tech fairies, and she can't find a simple solution. She unplugged everything, she plugged it back in, we turned everything off, and restarted it. There was no signal. There was seemingly no change. OK, I have six monitors. I'm a trader. I have tech at my disposal; I just don't know how to fix it or make it do things.

When the second monitor did the same thing, and it wasn't a Dell, I decided to bring in the big guns. By the big guns, this time, I mean I took the computer to work with me to have the highly skilled and professional electronic know-it-alls take a crack at it. I didn't want you to think that I shot a hole through the CPU in a sort of *"Bubba Shot the Jukebox"* way. No, I called Jon and Tom at work, and they were more than willing to assist this particular damsel in her connectivity sort of distress. They are, in fact, experts.

You know what happened. Everyone knows what happened. The same silly thing that always happens when this sort of thing happens. You take your car to the mechanic, and it no longer makes THAT sound. You take the computer to the I.T. gurus, and it not only fires up but also runs faster than it has in months. Thanks, guys, that was great! What did you do? Their answer? They plugged it in and turned it on. No! No! I won't accept that. I didn't accept that. We unplugged everything. We replugged everything. We turned everything on and then off again. We did that! It has to be something else. Well, it was something else.

I took the CPU back home, and I found that old and ancient kid that I store in the other room for emergencies such as this. She was reluctant to assist after hearing that they were able to fire the thing up without any issues. Neither of us could put a fingertip on whatever the issue could be. We dedicated an entire three more minutes to the matter. First, we unscrambled the twisted and spaghettied wires and sorted those out to make them resemble something usable. Then we used our brains to be sure we were putting the suitable plugs into the right places, but these plugs had been in the right places because my computer and monitor had been friends for a long time. Then Laura, the kid I'd stuffed away, told me that she had an idea. This could be good, this could be bad, but whatever; neither of us had anything to lose.

Laura took a swab and cleaned off the connectors. Oh....well, OK. There's that. You know, like when your battery and the cable get gross in the car? Yeah, that. So, after she cleaned the various points of connectivity for every cord and/or wire possible, she shoved the connections with a bit of force to be sure they were secure. We crossed our fingers, prayed, and we turned on the CPU. (I will say that Laura also noticed that I had the CPU upside down, but if that was the problem, it could and should have shut off ages ago. It's been upside down apparently for a minute) BAM! Connection!! What? Yep! That's so me. That's my life. Dusty and needs a good cleaning from time to time, but is still willing to shine when appropriately treated. I'd say I'm so embarrassed, but I'm not. I'm happy.

There were about six days between the time the problem started, and we got it fixed, so I wasn't blogging. I wasn't searching the internet unless I was using my phone. I wasn't in my room wiling away the hours in the hardcore study for Series 66, and I wasn't researching things for the murder book; again, if I wasn't using my phone. It did give me lots of time to sit with the dog and just read my Kindle. Oh, the Kindle!! I love that thing. My birthday came and went, and my son took me to dinner. I'll tell you about that in another blog. I had a great week. There may be something to just unplugging yourself from the world every now and again. Try it sometime. It felt really good!

I know what you're thinking....six monitors? Yes. It really cuts down on the toggling. Call me crazy, but it is a conversation starter.

It's the Little Things That Makes Me Sing

I don't know if everyone knows, but I'll go ahead and mention it; I'm unemployed at the moment. I'm not one of those proud people who can't tell anyone they aren't working. In fact, it's quite the opposite. When I'm not employed, I tend to use my time wisely enough by producing works of writing. When I was unemployed last year, I wrote a book in just under a full month. I published it and started a new job; then, due to the ever-increasing unethical behavior of many of the people who own their own businesses, I was released when I refused to hide money. Well, there you go - - unemployed.

Because it was in the middle of spring, I decided I would change gears and do something really cool. I decided to learn how to become a Claims Adjuster. I mean, I already had the license; I may as well use it, right? So, I began studying, and before long, I was engrossed in not one, not two, not even three, but about eight different companies that all wanted me to train under them so that they could eventually hire me, deploy me, send me out to do work for their carriers (insurance companies who pay them). Well, training takes time. I decided to file for unemployment, hunker down, and just sail through summer without going anywhere or buying anything, and so far, it's been working! YEA!

I did get around to writing another book, too, and then after that was a success, I decided to put a second blog book together. I had already written the blogs; I just needed to format, add photos, make a cover, and BAM! Another book!! Oh, but wait, there is MORE...yes, more. I wrote a poetry book 17 years ago, or rather, I wrote many poems and stuck them together 17 years ago, and I'm redoing that project now as well. I'm adding about 30-40 more poems to it, and I'm changing the name and the cover. You name it; it's all being changed. It will be up in about two weeks.

When you're on unemployment, the other side, your employer, has the opportunity to appeal the decision of the state to pay you. He/she/they shouldn't do that; it's not fair, and it only shows the world how very ugly and unwilling you are, but he did it. He appealed, and I was supposed to have a hearing on the matter last month. Well, I had the right to ask for a continuance, so I did. Booyah! Then, the state was super awesome and decided to postpone our hearing until right up to the minute (a few weeks) from when I will no longer have unemployment. It's a moot point for him, but one I really was very happy to see NOT come to fruition. God is too great.

I was literally in the closet praying about it because I knew I didn't do anything wrong. I hate it when I'm 100% correct, and someone gets the upper hand just because they have money or status. It's not right. Well, there I was praying, and the phone rang. It was the appeals court, and the clerk was telling me at 2:05 p.m. that the employer did not register by the 2:00 p.m. deadline, so the point was, in fact, moot - very moot. I win. God wins!! I don't win. I am blessed to be receiving whatever they pay me so I can pay my bills, study, and wait to be hired by the right company. Yes, I have time to edit my new murder mystery, too! God is so very, very awesome. That employer needs to realize that he was never in control of me; I won't lie to him or anyone else, even if it means I lose my job. (It's not the first time.) He also needs to realize that he pissed me off, and I killed him off in the next novel. It happens.

The way a deployment works is simple; first, we wait for a catastrophic event to take place, and when it does, the Independent Adjuster firms call us. We are the independent adjusters who are on their standby rosters. They tell us there is an event, and we choose if we want to go. We work the claims literally 7 days a week, and often 10-12 hours a day. We are paid well, but we are not writing, and we are not studying; we are working. Deployments can last from three to twenty weeks, and sometimes they go longer. The claims aren't always settled immediately, so you can come back years later and clean up some of the claims that never got settled.

As a newbie without experience, this is my first waiting period, and I'm pretty sure I'll be picked up soon. Today alone, I was contacted by four of the 1238 companies I am registered with. I think I'm really registered with 17, but I thought 1238 looked good for dramatic reasons. I'm sitting here with my 10 state licenses, and my CCC One training, my Auto Certificate from State Farm, and I'm ready to hit it...by hit it, I mean I will be deployed literally from my desk at home, but I'll be closing the door so my daughter doesn't come in and tempt me with her nonsense - - too often.

Me, the Comedian

About the time a certain creative and ruggedly handsome songsmith from Edinburgh was being born, I was doing an excellent bit myself in Hollywood as a stand-up comedian. I laugh now about it for a few reasons. First, no one really does it anymore straight out of high school like I did. I was actually just barely old enough to be in the bar in Oklahoma, and in California, where I was at the time, I was too young. (and there I was up on their stage performing.)

I look back at my young and adventurous self, and again, I have a chuckle or two because I was literally unstoppable about getting up on stage to say whatever the hell I had in my head to say. I rarely depended on a skit or routine. I just winged it; said what was famous for the time, the day, that hour, you know, if something was happening right in front of me, I'd go off and talk about it. I used to ask the audience what they wanted to talk about and then proceeded to make up stuff so I could continue to involve them in the performance. Gosh darn, I wish we had smartphones back then.

When I say I was unstoppable, I mean I would literally jump and volunteer to go so no one had to feel nervous or giddy. I was never nervous or anxious about being heard, which probably isn't something that currently surprises anyone who knows me. Being a comedian helped in a few ways with any of the negative feelings I may be experiencing. I'd simply showcase it, involve the others, and dismiss it as if it was something that needed to be packed away - - or scorched. I loved the physical aspect of it, too. The gesturing, acting, moving about. If there was a pole near me, either on stage or just off of it, I would run up to it, throw myself onto it, spin around, and stick my legs out before turning upside down and wrapping one or both around the pole while I continued the skit. (Yeah, it was a fun time to be alive...and thin.)

The drinking age in my state, the state of Oklahoma, was 18 at that time. Everyone I knew was drinking. I made a lot of money off those people, too. I would get three or four of them rounded up to play poker, and since I didn't drink, I'd wait them out, bet heavily throughout the night, bluff my way out of every hand, and take home the money. I could get them to show their cards; that was helpful. I'd bet them I could tell them what they were holding. When I couldn't actually do it, I'd ask them to prove it - - and they would.

I remember when I worked at the Improv in Los Angeles, I had to find my own way there and back, but it wasn't a problem for me. I worked for three separate studios in their transportation departments. I could take home something as long as I brought it back. I owned a really cool Karmann Ghia, but why pay for gas when the studio can? I was never a headliner but moved up the ranks to third or fourth most of the time. You'd go in on an open mic night, do your bit, get votes, and the next week, if you came back, you went on in the order they told you to go on -- I loved that. I used it to gauge whether or not what I was doing was funny enough to make the next leap. It was.

I didn't resort to being sexual; that was what I used to not be. I would take a broom, mop, and bucket with me on stage and talk and joke while I swept the floor, claiming the last guy was so filthy I felt as if I needed to clean the place up a bit before I got started. It always worked. The Bee Gees worked too - - I know every word to every song, I think, and I did then as well. I'd pull out a lyric and challenge someone to finish it - - they couldn't because they were into acid rock, even classic, but not the Bee Gees. I'd make up some lie about being from Scotland and continue the rest of the skit in that accent. Loved it. (The Bee Gees were born on the Isle of Man, not Scotland)

I didn't start out as a stand-up. I tell people who choose to listen that I actually started out as a sit-down comedian. I began the first day of Kindergarten; the class was my audience. No, I wasn't the class clown; I was the class comedian - - a huge difference. I thought for years I would make my living up on stage, and I did for 3 years, but it never really paid, so I had other jobs as well. When I worked in L.A. I also worked the studios, taking vehicles back and forth. I also babysat a mansion, and from time to time, usually three days a week for three hours a day, I would answer the phone at California Student Loan Finance Corporation. I still can't get that out of my head sometimes when the phone rings.

"Hello, California Student Loan Finance Corporation, this is Jude; how may I help you?" takes a little time to say, but it gives the caller time to get their stories straight, doesn't it? You can't exactly say you've reached the wrong number when someone makes you wait that long. The CSLFC was just a few blocks east of Twentieth Century Fox studios on Pico Blvd. I would walk to their offices, and one day, I came across a big, giant, never-seen-before snail - - the joy! I picked it up and carried it to work with me. He died a few days later since I didn't know how to properly care for a snail, but he'll be the first one, I'm sure, to greet me at the gates of Heaven - - with an instruction manual. I'll have to read it and agree that I was woefully negligent before he'll let me pass - - Jesus, you know, forgives -- not necessarily the escargot.

ZuPoo vs. JudePoo

It seems that every year, some new "*guru*" with that obligatory young, liberal, and hipster look comes along and tells all of us that we should stop all the unnecessary dieting and we should give up our gym memberships because all the workouts, the time spent running on the treadmill and doing so much cardio is just not what we need to do. Our belly fat, they tell us, is only there because we allow it to be. We did it ourselves, and we're the only ones who can remove it.

I'm not saying that the good folks behind the latest "*fat burner*" pills called ZuPoo are saying we're never to pick up another barbell or that we're not supposed to juice the greens again, but they sort of kind of said it in their advertising. They have some guy with a three-day beard looking all sexy in his loose-fitting sweats, pushing his agenda, or their agenda, and I decided to look a little closer at it....and at their agenda, too.

According to the internet, which all of us know is always correct, (right?) the ingredients found in the ZuPoo product are as follows (not in any percentage order): Magnesium, Cascara Sagrada, Fennel, Apple Cider Vinegar, Ginger, Cape Aloe, Burdock Root, Bentonite, Milk Thistle and Cayenne. REALLY? We already knew that these ingredients could do the job of moving our bowels. It doesn't take a rocket scientist to go through the list and literally say "*yep*" each time we run into a supplement that another company used to claim the very same thing!

How many of us have done the whole apple cider vinegar lemonade thing? How many of us tossed a bit of cayenne into the stew to bring up our temperature a little so we could burn a few more calories? We all do it. Well, here's my take on it. I have a take, you know, because I'm not paying $25.00 a bottle for a 30-day supply of something that generally takes 3-6 months to see the results I'm looking for. NOPE.

I went on Amazon, and I bought the same ingredients in powder form (except the Apple Cider Vinegar. I can pour that into the mix), and I'll make a shake out of it so I can drink it once a day and be done with it. I'll even add psyllium husk as well as turmeric because I'm really just that cool. I'll add it to a juice I would have juiced, such as carrot or cucumber with an apple, and there you go - - one healthy holy-moly 8-10 ounces of colon cleanser to chase the devil right out of you.

I may have to sideline it with a good dose of Milk of Magnesia, but it can be done. I'll post the results as I get them, and that way, you'll know if I'm just a raging lunatic or if maybe I'm onto something. The ingredients cost me $36.00 and will last more than 120 days. I think the smallest bag of powder for the bunch was the fennel, and you only use a little of it anyway. I think I'll get 120 days out of the powders. Even if I only had 60 days, I'd be on top, but I think I can get at least 120.

My Bad (My Mistakes)

As a writer, I write. As an author, I auth, but I don't like correcting my mistakes. I mean, yeah, I do it, but I don't like it. I don't (a) like to admit that I make mistakes, (b) like to find them, and (c) like to correct them. When I write, I type. I also write it out in longhand in some ways, but not the entire book; what I do is write out the plots, the twists, my storyline, or my thoughts in longhand, and then I type them up on my keyboard into the computer using Word. I paid for Word. I think it should correct my boo-boos.

I wrote five novels last year, starting with January's release (or early Feb.) of "*Of Kilted Pleasure*," and then I decided to get the ball rolling on the Nick Posh thrillers, so I wrote "*Murder Book*" for an April release I think. Next came "*Edinburgh*," another romance book that takes place in Scotland, but it is a modern romance, whereas "*Of Kilted Pleasure*" is a Highland Romance that takes place in the 18th Century. "*Edinburgh*" wasn't finished until July, which makes you wonder what I was doing in May and June! I was studying to become a Claims Adjuster.

In August or early September, I released the sequel to "*Murder Book*," which is titled "*Pinball*." That's a roller-coaster book, for sure. Then, just before the year ended, I released another book, this time a drama/romance titled "*Bay Sorrel Ranch* ."BSR takes place in Oklahoma, and it is set in modern times. It's a drama novel, but it has twists and peaks in it. There's a romance, there's a murder, there's an investigation, there is some travel, and yeah, there is sex. Not gonna lie about it.

When I write, I write. I make tons of mistakes, but I don't immediately find them. If they have red or blue lines under the words, I see them, but if they don't, I don't. It's a fact. I paid for editing with "*Of Kilted Pleasure*," and that didn't happen. I've made that mistake before, and again, before, it didn't happen. I don't know why I thought paying for editing the next time would make a difference. It did not. I didn't realize I had made over 30 mistakes in the book until it was released, and I bought a copy and read it!! (and then subsequently corrected it)

So, what I did with the next 4 books, having published "*Of Kilted Pleasure*" through a house and having self-published the others, was to write the books, go through them before I have them published, and I did try really hard to make the corrections before sending them up to be published - - until it didn't work. I literally thought I sent up the right file for "*Bay Sorrel Ranch*," the one with the corrections, but NOPE, I did not. I sent up the one with the 84 mistakes. When I sent it out, it was published, and when I bought it and read it, I found 84 mistakes. I have since (yesterday) corrected them and resubmitted the book.

It really isn't hard to make the mistake I made in sending up the wrong file to be published. I named it too close to the one that didn't have the corrections, and when I should have deleted the other file, I didn't. I sent it up to be published. Wow!! So, that's a good lesson for me to learn -- when I write a book, I correct it. When I make changes and save the file, I should permanently delete the last one. I keep thinking maybe I will need it, but I should just delete it. I also saved it 5 times on my computer on my desktop, in documents, in downloads, and on two different flash drives. JUST INCASE!!

So, what I'm going to do now is to go through all the files I have on my computer for all the books I've written. I'll save ONLY the corrected versions and delete the others. I'll save the corrected versions on all the platforms, but only the corrected versions. Maybe my new book, *"1211,"* will not suffer the same fate - - maybe my readers won't suffer the same fate. The good news (and it's not really that great of news) is that I haven't sold many books, so it won't make that big of a difference. If anyone wants to exchange their book with mistakes for one without mistakes, I can probably do that, or they can keep it as a collector's item!!

I did have to change the cover for *"Bay Sorrel Ranch,"* too, since it had a nasty back cover that was off-center, and the photo needed attention. I corrected it. It should be up on Amazon in a week. We'll hope the others don't get sold, or if they do, someone will reach out to me complaining, and I can change books for them - - that's the hope. If it doesn't happen and they want to give me a poor review, well, I can't stop that. I know I make mistakes; at least, I admit it when I do.

Right now, I'm watching old movies to get ideas to describe things in my book *"1211"* since it takes place in 1930. I'm watching old movies and looking at the dresses, the men's clothes, the cars, the street signs, the house decor, and so forth. I want it to be detailed and authentic. I'll end up screwing up and adding something from the '40s probably, but hey, we make boo-boos from time to time - - if we didn't, we'd be robots, and there's no fun in that.

All of my books are available on Amazon.

Pinball (54% Done)

When I think about it, and you know I do, being more than 50% finished with a book means I'm on the back end. I'm leaving the forest rather than running into it. I'll still deal with the various trees, creeks, animals, and whatnot, but I am wrapping it up even as I'm making things make sense to the reader.

I love introducing new characters. A lot of the characters I write about will only be seen or heard in the chapter in which they are first discussed. You may never see or hear from them again, but they needed to be there when they were made public. You can't magically have something happen; people make the world go around, and you need to connect an event with a person, not just have something happen. Readers let you know fast if they are unhappy with your characters. My characters tend to have feelings, emotions, and backstories. I'll go back into the chapters and develop them even further during the fluff and stuff stage.

Right now, I'm sitting at 54% finished if I am aiming for an 86,000-word book. I have just under 47,000, and things are heating up!! People are dying, people are being caught, people are running away, and others are simply taking their tea by the shores of the Great Lake, Lake Michigan. They have no idea what's going on right behind them. These are blissful moments to be cherished.

I wrote four chapters today and only hinted at a little lovemaking. There hasn't been any real sex in this book except when the bad guy does the self-loathing thing, and I won't discuss that here; you'll have to read the book. I'm not happy about needing to write it, but it is a

50

symptom of one of the manic disorders that the guy has, so yeah, it was needed. There will be sex, though. I'm going to write it tomorrow, actually. This will be, as you may have suspected, between Nick and his fiancé or the woman he considers to be his wife, Elaine. They're really very much in love. I like them a great deal. They have a child together; he's adorable.

I'm on Chapter 18 now, so I've got about 12 more to go. I keep my books around 30-32 chapters; I think Murder Book has 35, but this one will probably end up with about 30 unless I have to add something that makes it all make sense. I do that, too. I'll throw in a chapter for the purpose of tidying up a few loose ends. Before I write the book entirely, I write out what I think the chapters will have, and I try really hard to keep the book on track - I'm not saying it always works. I need to go back over my Murder Book notes and see if I need to add things to this book that I forgot to include in the other. I do that, too.

Right now, I'm closing in on one of the killers. I think one will get away and live to tell about his exploits in another book - - maybe two....maybe three. I'll introduce other bad guys, more good guys, women and children, clerks, and doctors. I'll add police, librarians, and maybe even a Thanksgiving Dinner. You just may have to read a bit more to find out. Someone in my neighborhood today asked me if I saw the OU game yesterday, and I have to admit, I'm a fan, but I don't spend time watching games anymore. I write. I don't watch television, I write. I could think of something to do other than write, but that doesn't make me anywhere near as happy as writing does, so I like to write.

I'm hoping to be hired this week by either an insurance firm where I can be an investigative claims analyst or with an attorney where I'll do the same. I kind of hope it's the insurance company as the attorney is an individual guy, and you never know what can happen if he dies -- I'd be out of work. I need more security than that, but I do like the guy. I like both of my would-be potential bosses. I even wrote one of them into the book - - I told him I would. He's a bad guy - - he loves it. OK, well, that's it, and I'll catch you later after I've tucked Nick and Elaine into their bed for a romp or two; maybe they'll bring little Alistair a kid sister or a little brother. He may like that.

Murder Book (Half Way There)

I am telling you what!! You just don't know your characters until they do something that shocks you and makes you laugh. There I am, writing and thinking this book needs a bit of umpf when out of the blue, my main character ends up bedding his new partner's mother!! WHAT? It's OK, don't freak out, I don't go into any accurate sexual details. The main character is about 40 years old, and the partner is about 32 or so; his mom was young when she had him, so she's only 10 years older than the man she finds irresistible. He is compelling, c'mon, he's Nick Posh!! Who wouldn't be attracted to a man with Native American and Scottish blood running through his veins? I know I would be attracted...which may be one reason why he's my main character in the next 20+ books I'm writing. No brainer.

There we have it; there is something going on in the book that may interest and keep a few readers. The book is about murder, I get it, but you can't have a good book without interesting subjects, interesting people, good food, you know, the whole enchilada. Come to think of it, maybe Nick will make enchiladas for his Scottish friends since he was born and raised in the Southwest! Yeah, I can do that. Right now, the two men are fussing over the book itself. It has the names of the people who were killed and the names of the people who will be killed. Nick hasn't yet found the connection to tie the author of the book in with who the murderer(s) are, but it's only halfway written. I have an entire fiasco to go!

Writing can be both exciting and entertaining. I find that when I'm writing, I'm not looking at the clock; I'm not really eating like I should be. I stopped in the middle of it and took a shower, walked the dog, and went to the store. Then I didn't even remember where I was, so I started reading the last several pages only to surprise myself. I have no idea what I'm putting on the pages half the time until I go back and read it. There's suction from my brain to my fingers, and my eyes and mind don't get to see it or read it until I put the brakes down a bit and go back over the last few pages. I also read and re-read the notes I write to be sure I'm hitting on them and adding them into the mix. I do forget to do that, and then the great notes I really thought I had to have in the book end up being ready for the sequel.

All that being said, it's time to walk the dog and get the kitchen clean again so I can make something for dinner. I've decided to eat today. After I do that, I'll likely read another Sherlock Holmes story or two in order to release the points in my brain that want to do something monotonous and boring. I need the enlightenment of Sir Arthur Conan Doyle to rescue me. He has no idea how influential he can be. I wonder now if I'll ever get around to telling Eoghan that his mum and his employer and partner had a thing. I don't think they'll have another; I think it was just a thing they did and have between them. Telling Eoghan could upset him and even cause a rip between himself and Posh. Best, perhaps, to let adults be adults and not involve the kids - - yeah, he doesn't need to know. Here is a sample of that chapter:

"A tinge of awkward embarrassment rushed through the dark pigment of the man's face, burning only slightly down the back of his neck as he allowed his mind to imagine a thought. What would it be like to take the mother of his new partner only meters away from the man she had birthed? A man Posh had come to admire and even trust over the few weeks they had known one another. Posh wasn't sure if his mind could imagine the right superlative to address the stage Queen, but she deserved a response."

Murder Book
A Nick Posh Thriller
Jude Stringfellow
Murder Book
Jude Stringfellow

Edinburgh (The Book) Literally Blowing Through it

This is the most fun a girl can have; let me just say that. I'm past the 1/3 point of the book, and I think I started on Monday. I'll need to go look. Yes, I made the cover for the book first on the 21st, which is a little odd, but that's OK. I'm a little odd, too. I made the cover first, and now I'm on the 13th chapter, 4 days later. I started writing the book on August 22, which is a great day to do anything. The 22nd of every month is my favorite day. I was born November 22, my best friend was born June 22, my son was born March 22, and my daddy was born April 22. My nephew was born on August 22, and that's the day I met Jeannie (my best friend). Robin and Maurice Gibb were born December 22, so I gave Faith (my dog) the same birthday since she was born near that day. I like the 22nd. It's a great day.

So, here I am, in my office, sitting at the desk typing. I have decided that two chapters a day are a good amount, but tomorrow being Saturday, and then again on Sunday, I could see myself cranking out 3 or even 4 chapters each day. I assume there will be about 30 chapters. I assume there will be about 86,000 words. There will need to be about that many words because I've already made the dang cover and I don't want to have to do that again. Depending on the thickness and the page count, you have to adjust the spine width. It's good the way it is. I need to go see if I made it a 5x8 or a 6x9. It's a romance book, so I should have done the 6x9. Goodness, now I'm second-guessing myself.

After checking, I found that I did make it a 5x8 book, so that's going to be changed. I want the romance novels to be 6x9 and the murder books to be 5x8. I know, it's the craziest thing, but I like that. My Blog Books are also 6x9; it seems to be a favored size these days. Speaking of the Blog Books, I had to redo the cover on the 2nd book because I made a boo-boo and created it with a PRO or paid cover photo. Oops!! I changed it, and it's available now on Amazon. That only took 2 weeks to get the cover correct. Geez, Louise, it wasn't easy. When I got it in the mail, I didn't like the thickness of it, so I changed the size of the font and the spacing. It went from 262 pages to 317. OK, enough about that; this blog is about the new book.

One of the best things about writing a romance novel is writing the sex scenes. No, really, it's hilarious fun. You get to be so free and say what you want to say. You can create character flaws; you can be a real jerk about it. You can be humble and easy-going, or you can rip the wallpaper off the wall in a heated moment. It's all up to you; you're the author!! To get me going on what it is, I want to say I typically read other works from authors. I think I go way overboard with the wording so I can do exactly what they did, but pull out before I completely make a mess of things. OMG...did I just say that? Geez...again, yeah, no. Sorry!! LOL

I sort of do a food-porn thing at one point, making innuendo and using double-speak to make a few points; it's fun. I re-read it and laughed myself silly over what just came out of my keyboard. I can be so blunt sometimes. Other times, I can be so sweet and forgiving, even affectionate. I love writing. It really, really is the best job out there. I hope I can sell enough books to make it a full-time gig - - oh wait, maybe I should put a lot more sex in the book...yeah, that's the ticket. I'm good. I'll just write and be myself and see what happens. It's good now. I don't want it to be something someone reads to use as an example of someone going too far.

There will be at least two more ooh-la-la scenes in the book. One will be real, and one will be a reflection of what happened in the character's life before she moved to Scotland. Oh, and there will be excerpts from writings that are steamy because the ladies have a Pyrate Night in the book that requires erotic reading, drinking, fun games, and no men allowed... Those are the rules!! Just the gals, swinging from a pole, smoking cigars, and trying to outdo each other using their favorite weapons...a pen or a keyboard. Actually, in the book, it's going to be only pens. They have to write it out - - there's something about writing it out that makes it so much more personal. I think so, anyway.

That's it for today. I'll write more on Sunday to say I'm 1/2 way through the book. I think I will be. Let's see, I'm at 30,450 words now, that's 35%. With 7,500 words tomorrow and the same on Sunday, that will be roughly 45,000, so yeah, that will be over 1/2 way there. Boom! I love it. I love it. The real character of the book, the star character, is the City of Edinburgh. I'll describe her, talk about how she has existed, how seductive she can be, and how strong of a fortress she has been for so many centuries. She is my long-lost hope -- I will end up living there at least 1/2 the year after I write enough and sell enough books to afford it. She is not cheap!! Nope, she is one expensive and high-maintenance lady.

Edinburgh
Jude Stringfellow

Sex! Do I Have Your Attention?

I've always been a writer, even before I could write. That's not a funny statement either. I told stories before I could write them down, and to me, that's the same thing. I told stories and tales, but I wouldn't take credit for them because I knew they were made up, so I said my dog Rover told me things. I thought that would cover any and all strangeness attached to those tales and/or stories. I know, right? I know what you're thinking, "*Jude, you really had a dog named Rover?*" Yes. Yes, I did.

After I was about five and I was able to legibly write my own name, which was, at the time, Judy Stringfellow, I was given my very own Metropolitan Library card. I was allowed to check books out and bring them home with me. Again, at the time, no one told me that I was limited to only two books at a time. My mom OBVIOUSLY put the other dozen or so books I wanted on her account, and then as I read them, I would walk them back to the library one at a time. I was five. The library was about one mile from my home down one road; Mueller. I was five! You can't do that in 2023, folks. Kids would never walk their books back, would they? NOPE!

I'm still writing, and I'm writing more now than I ever have. I write in my journal every day and go through a 250-page journal every six weeks. How many books have I actually written? Geez! I have written five or six that have been published and several more that have not. I have this one book that I wrote in the '80s that is really nothing more than a trashy sexual experiment of erotica texts and prose; no, you can't read it; it even makes me blush. I wrote it in the same style as I would a journal, just

60

one sordid story after another, and my friends and I would read a passage or two when we had drinking nights -- except, yeah, I didn't really drink. I was the designated driver, so there's that.

During "*Pyrate Nights*," or nights when the girls would literally swing from the rafters, the poles, or any apparatus we could find (monkey bars at the local school), the girls and I would write these types of sexual tales with the sole purpose of making the others blush and/or spit their drinks out of their mouth; it was a true challenge of which I have to admit, I took things very seriously. I wanted to win. It was sort of, somewhat, a wee bit, in this vein of thought, that I decided to spice up my first romance novel. I did go a bit far, yes, I'll admit it. I did cross a line or two, but in all fairness, it was a fantasy of the fictional character, not a reality, and therefore, I think maybe I'm given some sort of leniency. I also pre-empted myself and confessed to my mother that I wrote it and that I was publishing it, but I also dedicated the book to her, so there's another brownie point -- maybe!

OK, but as a Christian, you may ask, how can you (I) write such things and not feel the least bit guilty for it? Well, let's discuss that for a second. You're here, I'm here, and people had sex to make that happen. No. Don't argue with me. Your parents had sex, and my parents had sex. We were born, and we learned to read, and we learned to write, but we also learned about sex. We learned when to have it, who to have it with, what the ins and outs (no, I didn't just say that, sorry) about sex is, and we learned that sex is not always kept neat and tidy in its little box. If you're having sex in a little box, I can tell you right now, it won't be neat, and it won't be tidy. We are not non-sexual beings. God made us humans. We are to be responsible with our bodies and, yes, with our minds. I'll admit my shortcomings (no, I won't pun that one); He knows me. I don't have sex with anyone except my brain....which often causes my face to smile.

This month, I will celebrate (that's not the best word choice) the 24th anniversary of my chosen celibacy. I choose not to be actively sexual with my body; I still exercise and activate my mind. Apparently, I activate and exercise my keyboard as well, and that's not a bad thing. I think we all think, and I know we all know. The ONLY reason I'm celibate is I'm not with someone. I'm not with someone because I choose not to be, and I choose not to be because the choices are really just not that pleasing to me. I watch. I observe. I witness. I investigate. I don't like what I see or find. I would much prefer to be single, alone, happily not engaging if engaging means I would have to put up with what I see, hear, find, witness, and observe.

I've said it before, and I'll say it again. If GOD and GOD alone want me to be a wife, I'll be a wife. I won't date anyone. I will not date anyone at all. I may marry someone, but I will not put myself through the whole *"getting to know you"* process and then realize that I would really rather not have put myself through that process. Nope. If God wants me to be a wife, He will make it happen. He will choose the man. He will put it together. He will line it up and cause it to be; until then, I'm counting the days until we just all go home. I'm so tired of the way people treat other people; especially the ones they SWORE to love, honor, cherish, and be faithful to. I can't stress that enough. God knows. If HE wants me to be married, HE will have to do the heavy lifting!

Sex takes place in my new book; c'mon, it's a romance novel. It goes without saying that sex takes place in the book. I'm mentioning it because my mom will want a copy, and my sisters, my brother, my nieces, and my nephews want a copy, too. My kids, of course, will wish to copy, but so will their friends, cousins, neighbors, co-workers, etc., and then there's my preacher. Yeah, he needs to know I sin in my head. I'll text him and tell him, but he probably figured it out already. I'm pre-empting again because when they pick up the book for the first time and start reading the very first chapter, they may see steam coming out of their eyes and nose before they get to the fourth or fifth page. OH MY GOODNESS! She said THAT!!!! (Yes, I did, Rover did not mention these things to me...ever.)

Why did I do that? Why would I go that far, too far, and hope it would be OK? I guess because we all think it. I've always been that girl who says what she thinks, and even when people stare wide-eyed at me with their jaws on the ground, I'm the one saying, *"You know you thought it too; I just said it* ."It's sort of always been that way. We have different personalities, and believe me when I say that I'm not overly sexual with my friends and family; I'm really not. I have to have a pen in my hand before I really get gritty; not that I have sex while I'm holding a pen, that could possibly be dangerous.

I hope you enjoy the book - - my realtor told me she had to read the first chapter a couple of times before moving on to the second chapter. That told me all I needed to know. The book may sell a few copies. I hope so. I want to buy that flat in Edinburgh...and write the sequel.

Chapter Nine was a Surprise, But a Good One

Earlier today, I was questioning myself on how I was going to handle this chapter because I knew it would require me to think like a man and have the restraint and maturity of a philosopher to describe what takes place within the body of a young lad when he comes across his first naked or semi-naked woman whom he has been crushing on secretly.

That is what happens in Chapter 9, and to say I had been putting it off for a while for fear that I may not be as sensitive as perhaps I needed to be would be more or less accurate. Today was the day! I managed. I just reread the chapter, and honestly, I did a great job. (She laughs because that sounded really arrogant for about a second until I realized that I'm the only one who can decide if I did or didn't give it my utmost! I'm the writer)

Chapter 9 is done. The characters of Aria Cambell MacFarlane and Ewan Williams Hastings are now formally acquainted. They will soon become fast and vast friends; this will lead to the utterly obsessive behavior of one of the characters, this behavior involving what we would clearly observe today as stalking behavior. We will see that the two are inseparable when the world, time, space, and society have only their separation in mind. We will find in time, in future chapters, that the two bodies will find reasons to unite. We will learn that the word "*love*" means more to some than it does to others.

The writing for Chapter 9 was a bit interesting on its own. I read through the 200+-year-old books written about the Borders of Scotland and the people, of course. I came across a tale, a story, about a man finding his son after many years of being apart from one another. The son had raced off from his homestead with a few shillings in his pocket and had not been seen for several years. No one was able to comfort his family as to what may have become of the man until some years later. Quite without ceremony, the father runs into a doctor who thinks out loud that the man before him resembles the man he has just attended upon his deathbed. This was the case, and the father saw his son only minutes before he expired and on his way to eternal bliss. The moments that they shared were good ones, and the father was so blessed to have refrained from bringing up the past and the questions he may have had in order to use the sparse time between the two for a better cause. I loved that story. I used a piece of it on my own.

They say there are only about 110 story plots out there, and we all (writers) mix and match until we come up with what we think is original. It's probably true for the most part. This is a good thing, and we are challenged to at least (as writers) mix and match to the point that the 110 become millions of possibilities.

The words we choose, the way we use the words we have chosen, and the purpose we choose to use those particular words should matter. I hope I've done that for each of my chapters and in this one in particular, as the boy in my story has a special meaning to me. I will raise him from a beaten boy to a robust and mighty protector. He will be the man he was told he could never be. He will overcome and he will project what others said was impossible; this is Ewan William Hastings, and he will not soon be forgotten. He will be loved and relatable, and he will be engraved on the hearts of millions forever.

JUDE
STRINGFELLOW
Of Kilted Pleasure

Perfection in a Dish

So, if you know me, you know I cook. You also know I write, and there are times when I compare cooking to having sex - - usually when I'm writing and trying to hold the attention of my readers. Today, joy of joys, I'm just going to talk about cooking and leave all the bedroom innuendoes where they belong - - which is in the bedroom. Today, because I can, I'll talk about making perfected orange chicken over rice. (It's not hard)

First, you make a choice to either buy the orange chicken in a bag at Trader Joe's (they do a great job) or if you're going to make it yourself using the raw ingredients. If you go the T.J. route, the entire thing only takes about 20 minutes once you soak the rice and you're done. I'll start with this method.

- Buy the long or jasmine rice.
- Buy the bag of orange chicken.
- Soak your rice for 10-15 minutes and rinse twice.
- Refill the rice cooker with enough water to only cover the rice that you're cooking. You don't want too much water. Start the rice cooker.
- While the rice is cooking, not soaking, you open the bag of orange chicken, remove the duck sauce packets, and spray a pan so you can load the pan and put it into the oven on 400 for about 20 minutes. (The rice will just about be done when your timer goes off.)
- Once your timer goes off, remove the chicken, put it into a bowl, mix it with the duck sauce, and place it back on the pan/cookie sheet to warm in the oven you just turned off. At the same time, you make sure the rice is actually ready.

- Wash your mixing bowl so you can get that out of the way.
- When the rice is ready, you take the chicken out of the oven, stack the rice on your plate, add the chicken, and if you need more duck sauce, squeeze the little packets you were about to toss into the bin.

OK, now for the real way, the more satisfying way, in my opinion. Preheat your deep fryer and get it ready with new grapeseed or olive oil (extra virgin is best, and you don't need to fill up the fryer; if you're using a smaller fryer, that's better anyway, you only need to use about 2" of oil) You do NOT want your oil to be too hot. You want it to be hot enough to fry but not to burn the meat on the outside. (Check your instructions on the machine you use. If you use an open pot on the stove, be sure not to plop your pieces into the oil. Lower them with a slatted plastic spoon.)

- Buy your rice and chicken.

- Buy flour, eggs, and milk too. (to make a good batter)
- Cut the chicken into small pieces (1" pieces or smaller)
- Soak your rice for 10-15 minutes. Rinse twice, and fill up the rice cooker to the point that your rice is covered, but no more. Start the rice cooker.
- Mix the flour (1/2 cup, 1 egg white, and some milk) into a bowl, and give the egg yolk to your dog, who by this time has realized you're in the kitchen and should be there to help you.
- Dip the chicken pieces into the batter and get them all battered up and ready to be fried.

- Put the chicken CAREFULLY into the deep fryer, a few pieces at a time. When they are floating, let them turn golden brown, remove them, and add more chicken pieces.

- This process takes about 8-10 minutes, so be sure to time it correctly so your rice is not still cooking. You want both the rice and the chicken to finish at about the same time. (I could absolutely have added a sexual comment right there, but I am refraining. Have you noticed how many times I have possibly restrained?)
- When the rice and the chicken are both done, you can start the duck sauce. It's really fun.
- You'll need orange or apricot jam, chili or cayenne sauce, soy sauce, a bit of white vinegar, and garlic. It's 100% up to you as to how much of each you use. I use the following:

1. 1/4 cup of jam
2. 1/4 cup of soy sauce
3. 1 tsp garlic
4. 1 tsp cayenne pepper
5. 3 tablespoons of white vinegar

Mix the ingredients together and pour them over the chicken, or keep them as a dip; it's up to you. Once you top the rice with the chicken, you can say your prayers and enjoy your meal. I hope you have learned something today - - if nothing else, you have learned that I don't always have to mix my fantasies with my recipes. Still, you also know me well enough by now to know I did so in my head. That invisible Scotsman who often likes to join me both in the kitchen and the bedroom made his appearance at least a couple of times during this blog -- he is just too cute for words. Sigh....oh...Craig! Not here, wait...sigh

Beautiful People

I think we all know where I'm going to go with this one. I think, if you know me at all, you'll figure out right away that I believe we are all "*beautiful*" and that we have our own very unique gifts. These gifts are not from our fathers and mothers; that may be the case with literal or blunt beauty, but not with grace, kindness, politeness, servant attitude, or gratefulness; those gifts come from our true Father. When I say we are all beautiful people, I'm not just making up something to make someone feel good about who they are.

I recently finished a novel written in 1816 by Sir Walter Scott. The title is *The Black Dwarf*. In the book (and there is actually a four-book series), the dwarf is a man who is held back due to his deformities. He was repulsed, he was hated, he was lied about, and he was mistreated. Who do you think Scott used to prove to be the hero of the book? You guessed it. The man formerly known as Sir Edward Mauley. He was, yes, a disfigured and grotesque-appearing individual; many feared him because of it. His rude and unsociable attitude and mannerisms only solidified their beliefs that he must be a devil, he must be a warlock, he must be this or that. We do that, don't we? Hey, guess what? Ted Bundy was a handsome man, wasn't he? Do you see where I'm going with this? I thought so.

Many people, both men, and women, seek out self-help sites on Instagram, TikTok, and other social media platforms today, whereas before, they would rush to the nearest drugstore and pick up their copy of Cosmo, Muscle & Fitness, and so on. You understand. They would read the articles, see the precise and pretty poses that the "*beautiful*" people do, and then they'd rush home and try their best to do exactly whatever it was that these beautiful people say works for them. Can they not get it through their heads that the money they spend, the time they spend, and the effort they make are only (and I do mean ONLY) supporting and forwarding the wealth of these paid celebrities or, in today's age, the self-proclaimed gurus and experts who don't actually give a damn about you, they only want your clicks, likes, and Patreon donations. "*Don't forget to pay every month so you can hear how YOU can be like ME!*" Was that snarky? Sorry, not sorry.

I am 100% and all-in for helping others. I am 100% all-in for sharing with others your secrets to success and the beautifying tips that may make you feel a bit more secure and confident about yourself. Yes, by all means, wear makeup if you feel it makes you look, act, and be better. There is nothing wrong with dressing up, dressing down, wearing that particular outfit, going to the gym, and making changes to your physical form to be the better you. I get that. What I can't seem to understand is when "*Life Coaches*," tell people that in order to "*have sex at dawn*" or "*be told yes*," they are doing so in order to bring about a false sense of security or a false sense of self. Get a grip, people. If you're with someone who doesn't want to have sex at dawn, talk about what you want! TALKING is the key; communication is EVERYTHING!! I think the internet has sort of taken that gift from us.

Lately, I've seen an increase in people who have a bit of lower self-esteem either due to being told they are not attractive or because they themselves have never felt worthy. I'm seeing an increase of these friends of mine (mostly men, actually) following social media sites where they are being encouraged to "*be a real man*" by taking control and being that fantasy book-style masculine hulk who swoops in and saves the woman from ultimate loneliness and of course, they end up as lovers and create new memories for themselves. Most lives these days are a bit more complicated than they are in the books. Most novels don't create characters who are working regular jobs, going to community college to get a certificate in I.T., while paying a ridiculous mortgage and beating the system now and again just to put clothes on their children's backs! Forget energy prices, food costs, and other bare necessities. Most novels are escapes....they are not real.

We shouldn't want to be, or even try to be, something we were not made to be. We are the person, the being, the one that God Himself said, *"Hey, I'll make this one now."* We are absolutely unique, and by being absolutely unique, we are, in fact, in all ways *"beautiful."* Can we improve? Sure. Can we strive for a better way of life? I don't think I'm saying otherwise. Life coaches are great when they do their job. They are infectious, callous, and cunning when they tell you what you should do, knowing it will cost you too much, cause issues in your current relationships, and/or pull you from your relationship with God. Don't laugh; a lot of these people think and say (to you) that YOU are the one controlling your life. They tell you that YOU are the savior of your destiny, and what YOU decide will happen will, in fact, be reality. Wow...Satan sort of said the same thing to Eve. Didn't work out that well for any of us.

You are enough. You are like a bowl full of ingredients just waiting to be mixed and baked into the most rewarding and fantastic cake ever created. You have all the right stuff. You are just not there yet. Maybe stop looking online for the answers on those sites with fantabulous photography showing off muscles and mass that could only come from the use of expensive and dangerous steroids. Maybe stop thinking you need someone else to tell you how great you are. Maybe go to the One who made you and decided you were going to be you. Maybe look at what you've done in the past to make others smile. Maybe you can realize that you didn't get this far, far enough to read this blog anyway, without first having been trained to read, and that in itself is a gift. YOU ARE AWESOME. Don't let someone else convince you otherwise if you don't have the right clothes, the right shoes, the right hair, and the right dimples....C'mon. How long have we actually been on this planet?

We are the BEAUTIFUL PEOPLE. We don't need to pose in fancy, sexy poses to prove we're stunning. We are stunning. We don't need $$$$$ sweaters or haircuts that cost more than a car payment. We don't need it because they want us to put our money into their pockets. YOU need your money. YOU need your time. YOU need your face to be YOUR face, and it is. Don't let someone else cheat you out of the life you were created to live. Improve, yes. Learn, yes. Create, yes. KNOW you are the best you and, in fact, the only you. You aren't less than anyone.

You aren't more than anyone because there really is no competition as to who is best or worst. The CROSS is blind to what you look like. When the world tells you you're a mistake, just remember that God doesn't make them. When the world tells you you'll never make it, remember that He has! There's no reason not to believe that ALL THINGS are possible through Christ...not some would-be hack online with a square jaw, precise beard, bulky biceps, and perfect teeth lying to you about what you need or could have. Ask yourself, do you want to spend eternity with that guy or with Jesus?

Speaking of Speaking

You know, I would rather talk than do just about anything else - except maybe writing. I have to write; I don't have any options. You know they say a painter paints, and a thinker thinks. Well, writers write, and there's no escaping it. Talkers talk, and I suppose that's the reason for the millions of blogs - readers read! We talkers, thank you; we really do. Thank you, thank you, and if you didn't hear me the first time - THANK YOU for reading.

I wrote a poem once and even published it in a book, wherein I mention the fact that a writer's pen is cursed. We have to write. We have to express; we don't get out of it. When we dream, we dream in fluid blue or black inkened stains, rubbing and scratching words into thin air. We sometimes see words forming out of clouds on a stormy gray overcast sky, and often, we see words being created in our dreams through the movement of waterworks. It's fascinating!

I didn't have anything to do today. My maternal parental unit asked me what I was going to do with myself, having the entire day without a single obligation -- this doesn't happen often. It scared me just a bit that she somehow knew of my schedule...but she is my mother. I answered that I would be at the university, in my office (commons area of the library, 4th floor), working on working. What that really means is that I would be searching the internet for places to submit my resume and my DVD of me speaking recently at a Victim's Rights Week seminar, and I would be applying for visiting professorships throughout the WORLD - lovely, isn't it? I can actually go all over the world now, not just stay in my own backyard.

If speaking publicly is what I have been doing through amateur mic night, sales, or teaching, then I have over 25 years of experience. I can stand in front of thousands of faces without fear because I ATE MY FEAR in the 80s when I was forced to do improvisational comedy at various clubs in Hollywood to pay for rent! I was always behind in my debts, always spending too much, and since singing for my dinner was out of the question, I simply smiled, added a pause, a little timing to a joke, and I was hot! They kept asking me to come back, and I did. This led to that, and here I am, over 25 years later, standing (sometimes sitting) and speaking and making a living all over the world - hopefully! If England answers my call, my plead, my beg - PLEASE!!

Most of the time, I am asked to speak to groups of people who need inspiration, encouragement, and uplifting. I have spoken at hospitals, military bases, schools, and in public forums such as stadiums full of women who have been victims of domestic abuse. But, to tell you the truth, it would be my honor and privilege to teach through the power of positive speaking on topics of furthering one's education. If we're going to change the world through our immigration policies, foreign market policies, and our short- or long-term goals of reaching each and every kid through public education - we need to be educated about the very system we are working with and through at this time. There are reasons roadblocks and impasses occur!

It is my goal to teach at Hogwarts. If I cannot do this, I wish to speak publicly on the topic of education at Edinburgh University. WOW - lofty doesn't quite cut it at this point. A little time, a little pause, a little prayer, a little application - and a lot of patience waiting for the right person to phone or e-mail me to ask me to do what I love to do. Talking is my thing. I love to talk.

Photo Credit: Canva.com (royalty-free)

Differences (USA vs. UK)

I watch a great many bloggers and vloggers online who are mostly from the UK. Many of them have a standard schtick, if you will, that allows them to showcase the various differences between the areas. I can't say "*countries*" because the UK is a collection of countries, and the USA is a collection of states. There, that in itself is a HUGE difference. If I'm honest, I tend to watch Scottish vloggers. I do watch Laurence Brown, who is from Grimsby, England. He has a channel called "*Lost in the Pond*," where he routinely goes over so many varied differences between the UK and the US. He's been ("*bean*", that's how they say he's been in the UK) living in the U.S. for over 14 years. Currently, he's in Chicago. His idea of the US may or may not be complete. I don't think you can know America until you've lived in the South.

I watch Shaun Alexander; his channel is *Shaun Vlog*, and he's from Edinburgh, Scotland. Shaun moves around a bit. He's lived in Brazil, in London, and just outside of the City Centre of Edinburgh in a beachfront area called Portobello. It's gorgeous! You should go. Shaun and Laurence keep me laughing over their discoveries and their experiences with America and Americans. Shaun has made it to the U.S. a few times, and his favorite hangout is Texas. Shaun gets it. You have to be in the mix, in the trenches, if you want to know who the Americans really are. You don't want to use Northerners as your prime example. Just sayin'.

One of the new favorites is a guy called Tony Broonford. He's the Chief of Clan Broonfood, and you, too, can join and be part of us! We're a highly sought-after Clan, you know. Tony takes us on YouTube journeys not only through and around Edinburgh but all over Scotland, really. His unique and fun traveling experiences have been heralded by a lot of exploring tourists who literally come to Scotland, go to Edinburgh, try to find Tony, and tell him he is the reason they decided to come to Scotland! Wow! That's really cool if you ask me. You can join any of these vloggers through Patreon. Each of their Instagram and/or YouTube sites will have links where you can go and share your good fortune with them so they can continue to share their good lives and experiences with us! It's a win-win.

In all honesty, I love to listen to a Scottish accent far more than I do an English accent. I know I'll have so many people disagree with me on this one, but it's true. I find the rustic and robust sound of a Scotsman to be sexy, while I find the prim and proper elite sounds coming from a Londoner to be rather boring. The UK, just like the US, has so many varied accents, and yes, it is geographical. You'll find hicks there just like you'll find hicks here. What I find hilarious is that when the Brits sing, they tend to lose their accent altogether. I'm surprised and pleased, really, when I listen to my favorite singer-songwriter, Steph Macleod (also of Edinburgh), as he doesn't lose or cover his thick Scottish accent. He'll sound Scottish when he's singing and when he's talking. Yes, I prefer that. Call me crazy!

Today, I discovered a few more differences in etiquette really, and I thought I would share them with you. As you may already know, Americans are blunt, and we say and pretty much do what we're going to say and pretty much do with or without the oversight, approval, or permission of another. Maybe that trait is born into us, but try to remember that more than 30,000,000 of us come from Scottish ancestry. More than 46,000,000 of us (some overlapping) come from British blood, and you guessed it - - we came from those who left Britain to start the New World. We're a bit on the rebel side to start with, you know. We just do it. Nike loves us. Maybe Nike's entire "*Just do it*" campaign was directed at the slower-to-act Brits. (could be)

Americans typically enter a restaurant and wait to be seated. That doesn't happen in the UK. I've waited. I know. I've been stared at. I've been laughed at. I've even been asked to sit down because I was making a fool of myself. OK, the flip side of that is when the Brits come here and just wander into a cafe, they may or may not be seen by the waitstaff. They may or may not be served. It's a trade-off. I was also shocked to the core of my gut when I saw the tiny portions being served and the cost of the experience. I had to keep saying over and over to myself, "*We're not in Kansas anymore*." Some of you will get that.

Once, when I stayed in Scotland for a minute, I stayed in Inverkeithing with a friend. Inverkeithing is in a council called "*Fife*," which is also a Kingdom! It is located just above the city of Edinburgh. You take a bus or a train to ride into the City Centre. You can get there in about 16-18 minutes by train and in about 30 minutes by bus. Buses are cheaper, obviously, but I prefer the train. There were so many things to observe from the point of view of a person who literally drives herself anywhere and everywhere. I don't walk even half a mile in Oklahoma if I want to get from Point A to Point B. I will walk in Scotland. I'll walk an entire mile, even two, if the weather is good. I also overbuy so that I'm not stuck without a passage. That would be embarrassing.

We don't really have passenger trains in Oklahoma. We have a train, just one in the city, and it only goes about 100 miles south, then maybe over to Ft. Worth, but it doesn't take you from too many points to too many Point Bs. There's not a system like there is in the UK. I am only familiar with the trains and buses in Scotland, not the rest of the UK, so my experiences are limited. I did think to myself that it would be really hard to take the dog to the vet if you only had a bus or train to rely on to get you where you needed to go. I mean, sure, there are Ubers, taxis, etc., but that's expensive. You can drive too. Sure, you can drive. LOL...I'm not doing that, but you can if you want to. I like living. (They drive on the other side of the road, and from what I saw, they don't always do that so well.)

In Inverkeithing, and all over Scotland, and more than likely the entire UK, people pay their utilities through their council. They pay a certain amount based on the value of their home in 1991. I find that odd, really odd. What if your house wasn't built at that time? I'm sure they have that covered. You pay XX for energy usage, not by the kilowatt that you personally use in your personal home. That's just weird to me. I've mentioned the no-screen thing before.

They don't have screens on their windows, so if you do open the windows to allow for cooler air, you'll likely have uninvited (or did they consider the opening of the window an invitation) guests in your home. I wonder if they'll laugh too hard if I bring screens with me when I do move there on a more permanent basis. At least you'll know where I live. *"Yeah, she's the American. You can tell; she has screens on her windows, and she's flying her flag off the balcony."* Oh, well, that's not really a flag there, sir; it's a flower pot that has the American flag colors around the base....and yes, I do have one.

My friends from the UK and from other foreign countries (Sweden, Germany, and Spain mostly) will comment on how many American flags they see when they come to the United States. We don't think about it, really; we just fly them. I do have one outside my house. I counted, and 18 neighbors in my complex that has 83 homes have flags flying outside their homes. That's less than I think it should be. I have an American flag decal on my car. I have clothes that have the flag, of course, and even my oven mitt has stars and stripes. If you look in my closet, you'll find six hoodies with the word "*Oklahoma*" or "*Sooners*" too - - we do that. Proud people. Nothing wrong with that. I do think it's more prevalent in the South than it is up North, but I could be wrong. (I'm not wrong, but it has happened a time or two.)

Today is November 18, 2022. It's a Friday evening. In the South, that means it's Friday Night Lights. Our high school teams are playing tonight, and it may be the beginning of the State playoffs. I'm not a teacher, and I don't have any kids in high school, so I don't know, but what I do know is that hundreds of thousands of parents, siblings, grandparents, and friends will fight the cold (and it is freezing). They'll wrap up in the colors of their favorite team(s) and sit out on those stone, brick, or metal bleachers for hours tonight, watching and waiting for their sons and/or daughters to make a splash in the newspapers tomorrow! It's a thang. You don't see that in the UK. You don't and won't see the Brits going to college sporting events to cheer on their families. Here, it's not only expected; it is a matter of family pride and dignity. If you have a kid in sports, you go!

Some of the differences I've seen have been enormous. Some of them are quite small, really, but they are there. We say "*boy*," and they say "*lad*." We say "*dog*," and they say "*dug*," so that's just a sound thing. In all fairness, I probably say "dawg". I've seen the word written out as dug as well. I wasn't about to correct the person who did it. It could be Scots, which is a real language, and I don't want to insult - - look at me being a Brit and not being a forceful and obnoxious American!! Woot!! Slowly, slowly, I will acclimate. (or, as they say in the UK, "*acclimatize*.") Weird.

The Scott Monument in Edinburgh Photo Credit: Tom Isaacs

A Strange and Welcomed Dream

I love it when I have dreams that not only have full stories but also have drama, sorrow, laughter, intricate detailing, and even costumes! I love it when I can wake up from a dream and wonder if I was actually dreaming or if what was taking place inside my brain was real. I'm just coming out of some alternative universe. I'm not being really serious at this point.

I know I'm here, and I know it's now. I realize a dream is a dream, and fantasy is just that; a fantasy. Sometimes, the fantastic happens when I'm sleeping, and boy, oh boy, it's beyond imaginable. It's a FANTABULOUSLY real feeling, and I can even remember the tiny minute details of the conversations I had with people. Sometimes, these conversations are being had by others, so it's not always me doing the talking. I bet you would never have guessed that one!!

I was in another place. I knew I was, and I knew it was another time. I didn't know where I was, when it was, or how I got there, but I did know somehow that my being there was for a larger purpose, and I would be safe. I would not be harmed. I would be fine, and everything was going to be OK. At least, that's what I thought until I was facing several men on a dirt-type road in the forest, and they weren't sure what to do with me. I couldn't understand them; they were speaking a foreign language.

I managed to listen and make a gesture with my finger to sort of say, *"Say that again,"* and one man repeated what another man had said. When he said it again, I made the same gesture but very slowly. The second man repeated the words very slowly, and I understood two things. First, I realized he was speaking Scots Gaelic. Secondly, the only words I could make out were the words *"you"* and *"where."* Ah! OK, they wanted to know who I was and where I came from. Got it!

I told them my name and said I had no idea which direction I had come from because I was sort of lost, not knowing where I was. I also asked what year it was since their wardrobe seemed a bit outdated. After a few minutes of them huddling around and talking, it was decided that I would be their captive, and I decided to disagree. I began walking off, and one of them grabbed me by the arm.

Almost instantaneously, the man was picked up by an invisible force and flung to the ground. This action, of course, led to them all coming to the same conclusion about me; I had to be a witch! Well, as you can imagine, that wasn't going to work out well either. I said out loud to myself, *"Oh yeah, they actually believe I'm a witch. This means I'm stuck somewhere, probably in medieval times, and either in northern Scotland or out really far west on some island."* I hadn't passed or seen anything with any hope of being a landmark. I had no idea.

I thought about just walking away, but these men weren't all that keen for me to leave just yet. I was surrounded by them, and they all began asking me questions. I wondered how they had understood me earlier. Then I realized that they had not understood a single word I said, but they had evidently believed me to be of English descent. One of them had spent some time in the southern part of the country and remembered the words *"believe"* and *"witch."* It was decided I was either a witch or I had some sort of connection to the other worlds, so I was respected, but I was not to be set free. They walked with me, surrounding me, and from time to time, they spoke to me, but again, I had no idea what they were asking or what they were saying.

I wanted to communicate, so I used what little (tiny) knowledge I had of the Scottish Gaelic language, and I made hand gestures as well. Finally, after a couple of hours or so of walking, I saw what looked to be a castle. It was, in fact, a completed castle, and I thought about it long and hard before asking if it was the site of Castle Stuart. The response I received was a mixed bag of surprise, confusion, anger, and excitement.

Pick a man, any man, and he had a different reaction to me knowing that the ruins before me were going to be restored in about 300 years and then be used as a hotel; well, what they would call an inn, but in Scottish Gaelic, the word would be *"taigh-osta."* My Gaelic had a lot to be desired. I really sucked at it, placing words in the wrong order and hacking most of the pronunciations. At least the men figured out I was not from that area but knew something about the castle. When I tried to explain in detail, I was basically forced to shut up. They wanted to wait until they could find someone who could possibly translate what I was saying, mainly because if I was, in fact, a witch, they didn't want me casting spells on them without them being aware of exactly how I was cursing them.

When I made the sign of the cross over my face and heart, they immediately stared at me. I quickly realized that they weren't Catholic; I'm not either, but they weren't happy that I might be. So, it was about that time I decided to shut up and just keep walking with them. I did have to excuse myself to go pee in the woods, and I was fairly adamant about not letting any of them follow me. I made it quite clear that I would not stop talking if they continued to stalk me as I tried to find a few leaves that didn't appear to be poison ivy. I was seriously hoping I was successful with that quest, and I was! Funny how we can't find what we're looking for in a dream. I think I ended up with an actual roll of toilet paper, and I remember laughing about that.

Once back on the road, I noticed my shoes. I didn't know why none of the men had pointed to them and questioned me. I suppose men have really never kept up or been too involved with women's choices of attire. That made me smile. When we reached the edge of town and saw a bit of civility, a woman who was both older and quite English-looking (pointed nose, higher cheekbones, and slightly jacked-up teeth) came out of her house and questioned the men about me. She spoke to them in a broken dialect, but they answered her independently. She turned to me and apologized for the men's behavior. She began speaking to me in what can be described as middle English, but at least I was able to figure out what she was saying! This was good news for me. I told her the situation, not expecting her to understand or believe me. Still, she did say that God works in mysterious ways.

The woman's name was Eula, and she led me to a cabin or cottage in the city's center street; today, it would be called "*High Street*," where a man in his late 40s, perhaps his early 50s, was sitting at a table. He was dusting off his shoes and thinking about getting up to either make his bed or pet the dog when Eula knocked on his door. She rapped four specific times, and he said to himself, "*It must be Eula. I wonder what she wants.*" As it turns out, Eula was married to this man's brother, and her husband of many years had passed away. As the laws and customs were at that time, this man, being a close kinsman who was not married, was expected to marry Eula to keep her protected and to provide for her. The problem is, in reality, neither Eula nor the man really fancied one another. I guess, to be blunt, they didn't like each other at all, and they had both sworn off any sort of arrangement between them. Something had to happen, and Eula began to pray about it.

As the man opened his door, he looked just beyond Eula to see me. He had been with Eula and his brother for years, having lived in or near their household. He grew to learn the English language to a large degree, and he was able to carry on open conversations about their agreement not to unite without the others knowing their plans. *"Woman, you have interrupted me. I was quite busy"*, he lied and protested. *"Liar!"* She exclaimed as she led me into the house before closing the door behind her. Eula then surprised both myself and the man by stating, *"This woman, this new woman, was found in the wood about six miles up Tarmal Rood. She is from the new world and speaks only their English. She's to marry you, old fool, and I will be free from the laws that tie our necks."* Wait...what? I mean, no. I don't think so. He's...well, wait a minute, he's actually kind of cute in a tall, rugged, burly, bearded, brawny, tattooed sort of Scottish sexy Highlander sort of way. I mean, c'mon, it's a dream, right? Go with it.

What happened next was pretty funny, really. I was actually able to stop myself and say, *"OK, this is a dream."* Sometimes, if I see myself doing gymnastics in a dream, I know I'm dreaming. I stop myself if I can, and I go ahead and do more! I actively and purposely fling myself into back handsprings and hang upside down so I can have fun and create for myself a means of entertainment. This time, when I saw the man standing before me in his family tartan, leathered footwear, and hand-stitched shirt, I couldn't help myself; I began grinning and actually giggling because so many of us in this century often wonder what a real Scotsman wears under his kilt. Oh my gosh, did I really think that in my dream? What a loser! I was about to slap myself right there in front of God and everyone, but I said to my dream self, *"Stop being so immature. It's obviously sometime between the 16th and 17th centuries, and yeah, he's not gonna have any briefs on under that magic piece of material you love so much. This could be your chance to snag a Scot who won't fuss and argue with you about wearing his kilt and dirty black boots. OK, the man doesn't actually have to put his shoes back on. I'm good."*

In her best and sweetest hostess sort of way, Eula explained to me that her brother-in-law, Craig Mackenzie, was about 50, but no one really knew. She was a bit older than he was, and her late husband always claimed Craig was a wee bit younger, but again, no one really kept records. Their family book or their Bible was long missing, and he had decided that on the Spring Solstice, he would celebrate his new year.

Whether or not he was born at that time is up for grabs. So, his name is Craig Mackenzie? Ha! I had to laugh at myself again because anyone who follows me knows I have a fictional man, a creation of my own, whom I called Naked Bearded Man for over 30 years. We've been together through thick and thin. This man was, in fact, Naked Bearded Man, but I didn't exactly recognize him because he was actually wearing his clothes rather than being seen in my dreams both unclad, in the buff as it were, and oftentimes, he's literally folding his kilt! Yes, this was, in fact, my Naked Bearded Man!

I suppose I decided to give Naked Bearded Man a real name about a year ago. I wanted it to be something sensual, obviously rough and tumble, as he is quite rugged, and it must be (of course, it must be) a Scottish name. He was named Craig Allan Mackenzie, and here Eula was telling me that this man was, in fact, the same man I had dreamed of for so many years. Well, no wonder I wasn't upset with having been given to him so unceremoniously and without any real explanation. It was

88

at this time that Craig pointed to my shoes and asked what type of footwear was that didn't lace or buckle. Oh...yeah...Velcro. Laughing seemed a bit inappropriate, so I just smiled and took his hand. I looked Craig in his big grey eyes, and I said, "*Well, I'll show you mine if you show me yours.*" He smiled. Eula left the house, and well, I don't really know where the dog went, but Craig and I had a really good time of it - - you know, discussing shoes and things.

I would say that's when I woke up, but it wasn't. I woke up hours later smiling.

Photo Credit: Canva.com (royalty-free)

Oh, the Possibilities

I mentioned to my boss this morning that the company would be better served both politically and in marketability if they hired more women for the trading floor and as sales representatives, especially in the global markets. His look was incredible. I wish I could have bottled his expression and sold it online. Maybe if I could have duplicated his expression, mass-produced it, and then possibly sold it as a commodity or even a security, that would have been even better! He sort of halfway laughed, but you could tell in the middle of the first slight movement of his upper lip he realized how valuable the statement was.

He came back around with an affirmative nod, which was followed by a question. He asked me if I would be interested in setting that up or if I was just spit balling. I smiled right back at him and let him know that Scotland was a point of interest; it may be a great place to start with our eye on global expansion. He walked away slowly, turned, and stated that I may be onto something. I told him I wanted first dibs on Scotland; I wasn't much into London, Dubai, or any other world stage.

To say I'm new at the firm would be a gross understatement. I literally started there less than a month ago. I have, however, been targeted for the sales and trading floor(s) because I showed initial interest when I was first interviewed for a support position. I turned down another position at another firm so that I could grow with the one I am with. I will keep my place for now. I will learn my current role, and I'll take any and all necessary measures to keep up with the growth and progress of the new seed I planted firmly inside the brain of the one person who can make it actually happen.

Our trading floor, and the trading floors of so many investment firms, have an overload of masculine representation, to put it bluntly. There is a lack of female counterparts for a few reasons, the first of which is the tradition of only hiring assertive, often overly confident personalities for the job. Not all sure-footedness comes with a male soul. Some of us stand for what we believe will be best in the way of customer service, sales, and revenue growth, which comes from the sweeter of the sexes. We women can be quite persuasive when we need to be. Our base abilities to garner and nurture relationships are well renowned! Women have been selling, out-selling, and dominating many of the markets out in the big bad world; trading shouldn't be as far in arrears as they have been! Times are changing!

I trade for myself now, and I'll be trained to trade for others later. I'm thinking I will couple that skillset with a business development model that I've used in the past, to not only hone in on a global market (Scotland) as a pilot group but also end up either managing the global outreach program or at least be a part of establishing it. I'm seriously not interested in globe-hopping; I will be satisfied with keeping myself occupied and preoccupied in the land of Heather.

There is/are plenty of fish to be found for what we will need, and it may be that another person may be more interested in continuing the growth abroad. We have offices now in about six or seven American cities; we need Canada, London, and maybe Dublin, too. We need the Virgin Islands for sure, but I think we need Scotland first, even if it is just more or less for personal reasons. We won't go fully global as the trust level of many world markets is/is not what it would need to be in order to both invest in building and sustaining the relationship(s). We can trust Scotland!

It won't happen today or tomorrow, so I don't have to worry too much about finding myself a place to live. When I do move, it will likely be into the City Centre so I can have access to as many vital offices as possible; there are three major banks in Scotland, as well as the Bank of England (a national bank in Scotland). Still, there are over 2000 financial institutions, and many of them would be considered our type of client. I'm sure I could keep myself busy for a year or two on the relations side and trickle in the trades as they come; such possibilities!! I'm in *think mode* at this point. I'll learn what I need to learn, do what I need to do, go where I need to go, and achieve all that I can. Good plan!

OK, speaking of plans, I need to go make dinner! Smothered chicken, or Marry Me Chicken, as it's often called. Woot!

Forex and My Future

It goes without saying that I am in LOVE with trading on the Forex (Foreign Exchange). I am still working on my free demo account through Trading View and Oanda as platforms. It's really wonderful because I don't need to worry about losing actual money. I'm learning the skills I would be doing if I were a pilot using a simulator. You can crash as many times as you wish, and nothing really happens. They just set the game over again, and you mark it down as a lesson learned. I've not yet had to have them reset my account because I'm really overly cautious, even with fake money.

There was a time when I wouldn't even hit the go button on the free account because I didn't want to lose phony money. I'm getting better at it now. I bite the bullet every time still, and I do think about what would have, could have, and should have happened, but I'm learning, and there is NOTHING better in life than learning.

Many, many people trade on the Forex, and because of that fact, there is an enormous amount of money that runs through that market on a daily basis. Literally, every 24 hours (except on Saturdays), more than $6T (with a T) goes through and is dispersed one way or the other! Six TRILLION every day! I can't even imagine that. The other day, someone in Illinois won the Mega Millions for just over $1.2B (with a B). Though I really don't believe they actually won it, I am a conspiracy theorist, thinking it is all a scam; I still can't wrap my mind around a single person winning a huge amount of money because they paid for a random cheap ticket! I know, there are folks out there spending $$$ hoping against hope to win, but dang!

I wouldn't even know what to do with it. I think I'd have to hire a team of financial advisors, traders, and foundation creators so I could distribute the money correctly. Of course, I could also just ask my 3rd born child! She would seemingly have no issues spending $1.2B - her way.

For those who think trading the stocks and/or on the Forex is like gambling, I will say that I suppose it could be if you didn't have a strategy, a bona fide way of tracking and backtracking, a risk management plan. They don't typically have a trading philosophy. Most (and by that, I do mean MOST) traders who just start out with an account (either demo or real) don't do their due diligence, and they end up belly-up within a few weeks or sooner. The secret(s) are to be emotionless, to go through the steps you've agreed to go through in your plan, and to work it rather than to hope for it. If you work it, and you stick to it (providing it's a good plan, to begin with), you're likely to come out on top more than 60% of the time.

Where being successful 60% of the time doesn't sound great, knowing you'll be losing 40% of the time, the other thing to know is when to stop trading and when to leave a deal. It is JUST as important, if not more important, to know when a trade is bad and to have an exit strategy. For me, I use Stop Loss like it's my guardian angel, my guard dog, and my best friend. That Stop Loss and I are connected! We talk on an hourly basis. I am well aware of the power it holds, and it is well aware of my inability to read the market at this time.

Stop Loss is the tool traders use to set a limit on a trade. Say, I'm going to risk 1% of my account on a trade. I can go higher if I want to, but like I said, I am so super conservative in this profession. I am that person you see driving under the speed limit on a rainy day; why would my trading strategy be aggressive? There may be a day when I become more confident and be more like the me who rides barrel horses rather than the me who drives on the freeway. Right now, I'm placing Stop Loss wherever and whenever I find it necessary to do so. You're going to enter a trade; you're going to risk up to 1% of your account. You press the enter button, and you set both the Stop Loss (at about 10 pips below the last swing low or the last swing high, depending on your mode; bullish or bearish trade.) You place your target at a 1.4:1 ratio, meaning if you do end up winning, you'll take 1.4x more than you risk.

The market doesn't care who you are. The market doesn't ask questions. The market is not your friend, your partner, your business colleague, or your sweetheart. The market is market. Price doesn't care, either. Price can do and will do one of two things. It will either go up or it will go down. Staying consistent at the exact same level is not really going to happen. You can find that it goes up and down at tiny intervals, causing the market to become consolidated for a while, but it will eventually go up or down. This isn't gambling if you know this; it's education. You can't control it, but you can become familiar with it using backtesting to see what the market has done over the past several years. Trends are trends for a reason.

I will begin trading for real in November. By putting half of my earned salary into my account each month and trading on it in a relatively aggressive manner, I will earn between 6-8% each month on the account. I will leave it in the account for about 6-8 months, allowing for any and all compounding. After the end of May, I will have a decision to make, and I think I know what I will do. I think I will visit Scotland for three months and live not only off the earnings but continue to trade while I'm there, of course. After I've had about 90 days in Scotland, I'll decide if I want to stay on a more permanent basis. I will have enough to live off of my account for over a year, but I will still be using it to trade as well.

I can write books, promote my books, sell my books, put the money back into the account, and continue the process endlessly or until Jesus comes back. I think I want this. I'm not sure. I'll have to see what the next few months bring in terms of my plans and my strategies. So far, on the demo (which is exactly what I would have been doing if I had the account up and running), I earn 6-8% monthly. I can easily do the Math to know I could sustain my plan if I continue to trade without emotion and stick to the plan. I know me. I'm more disciplined than most. I kick my own butt so no one else has to. This will be a good thing. I just have to make it happen one trade at a time and learn how to do that first. It's like baking cakes over and over again. You do it 1000 times, and you stop relying on the recipe. Sooner or later, there is a slight change, and you realize you need to be careful and do it right every time.

Forex is not new, but it's not very old either. People say, *"If it were that simple, everyone would do it."* Really? Do you play guitar? Do you just pick it up, strum it, and make it do all that you want it to do? You do? Great, was it always that easy? I don't think so. Just like learning to play an instrument, trading on Forex takes a tame mind, a good plan, a philosophy, and a lot of practice. Eventually, you build up those calluses you know you need to keep working - on - and you also get to know yourself pretty well too! I know me. I need my good friend Stop Loss! I'm really glad we met.

Character Flaws (We All Have Some)

As I'm building my novel, the one I call the *"Murder Book,"* I have to be honest and say that I'm not completely sure I want to make some of the characters as cliche as they may already be developing. I mean, I have a *"Plain Jane"* type woman whom I haven't named yet. She's Scottish, possibly from up around Aberdeen, I think I want her to have a Doric accent. She's taller, thinner, and somewhat strong physically, as she's the one who pushes her bi-sexual husband over the edge of Arthur's Seat. She'd have to have some sort of backstory to explain her abilities to do it. Maybe she works on the wharf. Maybe she's in healthcare and handles some of the larger, more dense patients when others can't. Maybe, just maybe, she's boring to look at, boring to speak to, boring to hang with, and her husband found as many excuses as he could to be away from home. Maybe. I haven't decided.

The year is 1931, and the story's locations span the globe from Chicago to Edinburgh. Still, there will be at least a layover in New York City's harbor area. The characters travel by ship rather than an airplane; there has to be some romantic encounter at sea. I don't believe the wife would or could handle a torrid sexual affair, but the man could - - Nah, it will probably end up being my detective Nick Posh who has the love scene(s). Nick is full, chock full, of character flaws, believe me. He himself is suspected of murder in a town just east of Edinburgh called Dunbar. Dunbar is a coastal city, really, with plenty of great hubs and piers to hide a body if one needs to. Remember, it's not the act of murder but the disposal of the body that really matters. Nick is a pro. He tends to business, and he knows his business. His return to

Scotland wasn't accidental; discovering the body of the singer-songwriter was, in fact, accidental.

The murder was just that, a murder. It really isn't the focus of the book. I still haven't decided if I'll keep the singer dead or have him found by Nick's terrier dog "*Hyde*" (for Hyde Park), maybe three days after the fall. Maybe Hyde pisses on the man's face, and we see him twitch? I may just leave him dead. He's not a good guy. He's not a truthful guy anyway. He lied to his wife, their families, the church, the parishioners, and the folks who tuned into their radios to hear him singing live at various times throughout the years. Most Christians would have little to do with the man in 1931. Should I throw in a bit of repentance? Maybe some tolerance? Should he be forgiven or given another chance? How many character flaws can one recovering addict have?

The murder isn't the focus of the book. It's hardly a part of the book at all. It's like the first three minutes of a good cop show where the real or meaningful characters gather for the intel to be shown and seen; the real story is how Nick can find a way to escape returning to the scene of a previous murder and solve the one he found without being caught; without being another tight white curl on the Lord Justice's powdered wig! Nick's ability to weave in and out of trouble is amazing. For years, he's avoided being connected to the gangster life of Glasgow by hiding in and/or around Edinburgh. When the mood hits him, or the timing is right, he books an overseas board on whatever ship is sailing at whatever hour is best to make his exit. Can there be a bribe offered for the Lord Justice this time? We'll have to see.

One thing is for sure, the singer-songwriter has run out of hymns and prayers with me. His best bet now is to cry to God before he gives up that last breath of his. The pen is not the sword, they say, no sir, it is far more brutal and carries with it deeper cuts than any blade. You may have pissed off your Plain Jane and received your rightful judgment; it was my pleasure as the author to see to it that the docket never carries her name within its bounds. Perhaps meaningless is just that, meaningless of no consequence whatsoever. We'll have to see.

Why I'm Not Married

The list of reasons I am not interested in being married is longer than the list of why I'm not married (yet). I say "*yet*" because God isn't finished with me, and I could actually end up being married again if HE, God, were to decide I need to be married. I personally am not seeking a marital relationship at this time. What I am seeking is to do the things God wants to be the person God wants me to be. If that includes being a wife, then by God and all things Holy, they (the Trinity) will need to make that happen by opening every last door necessary; a lady never has to open doors you know. (That's a little added Southern hospitality for those of you who don't know me. I'm absolutely from the South, which is a place where we honor God and expect men to be men.)

It won't make me the least bit popular with the women folk when I say this, but believe it or not, ladies, God made the man be the head of the family; therefore, as a wife, I would understand that. I'm not all that easy to wrangle, manage, control, or handle, so God will need to provide a man who is capable of actually performing that duty before I can submit to him as God would have me to do. First things first, he has to present me without blemish and without blame. Once he can do that, hold his hands up to God and dedicate his life to me both monogamously and show the same love for me that Christ has for the Church, I will have zero reasons not to submit to him the way a wife is intended to submit.

Again, I won't win any friendly smiles or nods from the ladies who have suffered at the hands of the wrong man (me included), but if I were to marry again, that man (my husband) would have the final say over our finances, and that means if I am the one earning those finances, he would be given the last word there as well. That's not something most women in 2022 are willing to consider, let alone do, but if God picked the man for me, I would have no reason to doubt that God would also train that man in the ways and means of how to be the best decision-maker after we had dutifully (as a couple) discussed what we both this is best for our family or union.

He (the husband) would have the last word in all things; that's a hard thing to give up, but if you think about it, he has it so much worse than I ever would. I am only submitting to him, a man, but he (a man) is submitting to God, and he's 100% responsible for the decisions he makes, and guess what, he's (the man) responsible for the decisions I make too! He's the head of the household. It ultimately falls on him to discuss these things with me and to make sure whatever we do is the right thing!

I can't think of a better thing to be than free from having to be responsible for the decisions being made. I have a great mind, and I am a very, very strong-willed woman, so I'm not going to just let any ol' man come along and be the head of my household, take control of my finances, my choices, my desires, and my decisions. No, that's not what will happen. If God, and God alone, decide to make me the EXCEPTIONALLY wonderfully dutiful and respectful wife that I know I would be and could be, He (God) will have to provide the ONE man whom I can be subjected to, who I can submit to, who I can follow, who I can uplift, who I can support emotionally, spiritually, even financially if he needs to work on whatever it is that God wants him to do - - that's a very unique and one-of-a-kind man. There aren't two out there. God knows that.

The list of reasons I'm not married is LONG indeed, but the list can be summed up by saying this; I am not willing to submit until God brings me the one He wants me to submit to. I won't be making a choice if there is another one. Nope! He'll be dropped in my lap, and I've said it before; God will write, *"This one's for you, Jude, you're welcome"* in purple lettering on some random wall. He'll make it so clear that I won't even have to wonder -- don't you kinda feel sorry for that guy right now?

I mean, he's possibly out there minding his own business, just going what he thinks God wants him to do. Maybe he's thinking he can't do it alone, and maybe he could use a really good wife to both help him and support his passion for the ministry God has chosen him for. Don't you think he's gonna be in for the shock of his life if he does ask God for me? LOL...I mean, he may not realize it's me, but yeah, God will know.

To be honest, I think I'd be OK with it. I know I've learned a great deal from life and could be the helpmeet someone needs; love will grow. Honor, respect, communication, all of that will happen -- if it is to happen. The list is short, really; it's because God hasn't said yes yet - - just *"wait,"* and when He says to wait, it's a yes just waiting to manifest -- So yeah, I'm open for a discussion on the matter (as long as the man is right with God and right for me...and has a guitar.

There will be a guitar in this union, or else, I'm not doin' it! I've gone long enough without one! I can't play one, but I sure want to listen to one being played!) Smiles. There will be dogs, too, and chocolate. There will be kilts, there will be coffee, there will be beaches, and there will be beards. There will be great sex, and....did I say that out loud? Well, I should probably stop before I truly say what I want to say - - I do that from time to time, but it's OK; God will tell the man that, too. He'll know. He may already know. Who knows? (God knows.)

Photo Credit: Canva.com (royalty-free)

What's In a Name

What's in a name, you ask? Well, I suppose a name could be an identifier, a way of pointing to someone and saying, *"She's a Stringfellow!"* That statement could mean that I look like my father, or it could mean that I belong to a set of people who go by the last name (surname) of Stringfellow. Both are true. I do, in fact, look more like my dad than I do my mom, and I am, in fact, running with and claiming the Stringfellows I come in contact with, for the most part. I'm going to say Nix on the Englishman Peter Stringfellow, who I have no intention of ever claiming, and hopefully, he was more or less from another branch of the good name.

Names were created and given, and as you (we all) know, they could be associated with the jobs one had (Clarke = clerk) or the area one was from (Robin of Hood). They could be variations of other names such as *"Oh, that's William's son"* later to be known as Williamson in Scotland, but Williams in England. Strange, but true. My name, the name Stringfellow was a variation of the name Strong Fellow and/or even from Arm Strong or Armstrong.

The Scottish remnant of the Stringfellows was not in a clan per se, as we were Lowlanders and Border Reivers. Still, we hung with the Armstrongs and adopted their ways, tartans, people, trades, habits, and bad behavior right up through the Middle Ages. Somewhere around the 15th century, there were those Stringfellow/Stringfellow/Strengefelaw (etc.) who broke from the ranks of doing evil and decided to support the Crown. This led to one of my recorded ancestors, Sir

Robert Stringfellow (1615 Scotland), being knighted. He and his family left Scotland in 1660 when King Charles II took the throne. There was obviously some trouble there.

The earliest recorded spelling of Stringfellow was in the 13th Century in the area of York or Yorkshire, England; again, back in those days, the area went back and forth under English and Scottish rule. Here is what the Surname database has to say about that particular Stringfellow: *"The first recorded spelling of the family name is shown to be that of William Strengfellow, which was dated 1286, a witness in the "Assize Court Rolls of Cheshire," during the reign of King Edward 1, known as "The Hammer of the Scots," 1272 - 1307"*
https://www.surnamedb.com/Surname/Stringfellow

You can see the name(s) go through a lot of history before they become your reality. I knew I was English and Scottish because my dad's side of the family was primarily Scottish, and my mom is an Edwards -- Yeah, English. I fight with myself all the time.

Recently, a Scottish friend of mine got a taste of what it's like to make fun of the *silly Americans* who do DNA tests. He was laughing at me because, as he said, he didn't need to do a DNA test to find out he was 100% Scottish, born and bred for centuries. I called him out on it. He refused at first, but I goaded him into it because his mouth was so much bigger than his brain.

I knew that even most Scots would show Scandinavian blood, Irish blood, Welsh blood, and God-Help-Us-All, English blood. It's just a truth that we really can't get away from. There were simply too many pretty English girls running around, and those rugged Scottish boys just couldn't help themselves. Sure, they married the Anglo-Saxons and gave them proper Scottish surnames, but their babies were born with the stain of English blood for centuries, and they still do!!

My friend's last name was McLaren, or so he thought it was. The funny thing about being an investigator is that sometimes my Bloodhound senses kick in, and that happens. It's senseless to stop me. I go online to such sites as www.scotlandspeople.uk.gov, and I find things. In his case, I found that he was, in fact, born on the day and in the place he thought he was born, which was just outside of Edinburgh; however (and this is huge), his birth certificate had been amended. I guess his mum never told him. It's right there, but people don't look.

The man who raised him didn't sire him. That man, the man McLaren, married John's mum when he was just a wee boy, nearly 5 years of age. She had been married to a Mr. Clarke from the mid-1970s until just before she met the man who would later raise the young lad. Why tell a kid? That was her thought process. Why? Because he doesn't need to be 47 years of age, finding out that not only did he have a dead-beat dad who beat his mum senseless, but he also had a twin brother who was still living and going under yet another name, as he was properly adopted at birth.

The last name Clarke is my best friend's last name now. She married her sweet and loving husband over 30 years ago here in the U.S.A. Her husband's people are more Irish than English, and I wondered if the DNA for my friend would come back green or not; it did. After weeks of testing my hypothesis and knowing what he knew, because I laid the truth right in front of him using the website, he decided to ask his mum the truth. She wasn't pleased.

Not only did his mum not tell him about his father, but she had never told him or anyone really that she had a second baby just minutes after the first. She knew she couldn't afford one baby, but twins were never even mentioned by her doctors. It was the 70's. I get that, but apparently, it was a real surprise, and her mother talked her into shipping the baby off to a distant relative in the western isles of Scotland literally when he was only days old. No mention of it to anyone, not even the father, who had been out of town at the time of the babies' birth.

The thing about birth certificates is they can be amended, but there is a check box that the doctors check for multiple births. I guess she always told folks it was checked by mistake. I don't envy anyone having to find out that they not only have a different father but also have a twin brother they could have been wrestling and playing with and sharing their world with if they only knew. What's in a name? Too much to contain in some cases.

The same site that I used to find out that his parents had married after he was born, of course, told me who his mum had been married to before. That search led to other searches such as arrests, criminal history, rental and real estate history, and occupational history. We searched every nook and cranny for his real father (without having to ask his mum or her family), and we found much more than we expected. The man really never left Edinburgh! Who knows, he and his new family could have been secretly watching the boy grow up. John's mum was seeking divorce when she became pregnant, and it wasn't granted to her until two years after the birth of her sons. The father, Mr. Clarke, was working when the babies were born, so he never knew there were two! WOW! She told him there was just the one. How do you choose one over the other when you decide to send one away?

I'm not saying that research is good or bad. I'm saying that excavating can uncover more than one bargain if they dig where no one has dug in many years. Things had a way of being covered up for privacy, for family, for keeping a good name, etc., oh, the things we do to save face! What is done in the dark will always be brought to light! There is nothing wrong with a woman realizing that she can't keep two babies and giving one to a good family. Where the problem comes into play is not telling the truth in the beginning and some 47+ years later having to have a very uncomfortable conversation about a few issues that could have been dealt with slowly and methodically over the years.

I'm not sorry I had John run his DNA. He knows now that he is not only NOT full Scottish. He shouldn't criticize others for not having the privilege, but he also knows that humans are humans. We act and do human things which can (at times) really screw the world over for ourselves and for others. His mum didn't deserve to be beaten. She didn't deserve to be put into a situation where she couldn't love and give care to both babies.

John's twin brother was found, too! The really crazy (and good) thing is that his parents and family told him the truth as much as they knew. He never knew his mum's actual name, but felt that it was Janice or Janet since every now and then someone referred to her, and he could piece the puzzle of his life together. He lived a good life up in the relatively secluded Orkney Islands after being brought from the Skye or Harris area when his family moved a few years after he arrived.

He was educated, decided to go into the family fishing business, and is co-owner of a fishing boat. He's married and has 2 daughters who are both in college as of 2022. He, too, was sad and upset that he didn't know he had a twin! The funny thing is, they are both tattooed, both play piano, both are Protestant, and both drive Fiat cars!

Fathers

When I think about fathers, I can't help but think about my own daddy. I didn't call him *"Father,"* just *"Daddy,"* and later, as we kids grew up and had kids of our own, we began to call him *"Pop."* Funny how that happens. I know for a fact that he wasn't born with the name *"Daddy"*; he has the same name as my son and his own father, Reuben Stringfellow. My daddy is Reuben Wayne, my son is Reuben Andrew, and my grandpa is Reuben Jefferson. There are quite a few Reu in our lives.

The Bible tells us that children are a blessing from God, and I know that's true. I have been eternally blessed with my three. I suppose I was one of the four blessings my daddy had. I'm absolutely sure all of my siblings agree that he was (and is) one of the best gifts we could ever have received from our Heavenly Father. What I think is really cool is that we can call God *"Father,"* and we can call him *"Abba"* as well, which is the Hebrew way of saying *"Daddy."* I also find it funny how dads claim their baby is saying their name when the child utters something like *"da-da"* or *"Abba,"* we get it; you're awesome! We know this.

I've seen the meme and/or saying that *"Anyone can be a father; it takes a man to be a Daddy,"* and I have to agree with that statement. In my life, I have had two separate men decide on their own to stop being a daddy or a father to their children and to choose women, lust, sex, etc., over the extraordinary blessings sent to them from God Himself. It's heartbreaking, to say the least; crushing, in fact. This is another reason why I think of my Daddy and call him my hero. He didn't have to stay; I mean, he did. Mom would have killed him if he had left her, but yeah, he wanted to stay. He taught all of us lessons far beyond what we could ever learn on our own, from friends, and even from good people who wanted to give us the best of life. God gave us a Daddy. That was and is incredibly wonderful to hold in my heart.

My daddy wasn't the type to play football in the front yard with us. He didn't play around with us, teach us to fight, drink, hunt, or watch sports with us. He took us camping and fishing, talked to us about life, read the Bible to us, and showed us what a husband should be, how a husband should treat his wife, and how a man should treat his children. There's just no replacement for that sort of thing in a child's life. To say I was blessed would be a great understatement. I was impressed, stamped, and dyed in the color of true love, and it will always be that way, even in Heaven.

Daddy decided to go see Jesus on October 5, 2017. He had an appointment he just couldn't reschedule. I know when the trumpet blows, his body will rise before mine if I'm still alive during the Rapture. I know that right now, he's up in Heaven in his spirit, and he's making lots of wonderful plans for my room, house, whatever it is. My Daddy is a carpenter, like Jesus. With his years of experience and love, I'm sure my place will be radiant and unique. I will have that special something that only a Daddy can give a kid, you know, his baby girl.

Reuben Wayne Stringfellow, U.S. Navy (1951)

Legal Action

Let's talk about Legal Action for a minute. People like to throw out threats about pursuing *"legal action"* when they feel threatened, stepped on, or maybe just guilty about whatever it is that they were caught doing and they don't want the world to know. Wouldn't it be best to just have a chat with the person who has upset you and ask them to stop rather than to threaten something you have NO IDEA what you would be getting yourself into? Not to mention cost. The cost of a lawsuit (especially an international lawsuit) would all but devastate a person's savings - - if they had a savings. When people are literally living off the pennies given to them they really need to consider using language less offensive than *"I'll be pursuing legal action"*. It may just be a bit of wholesome and healthy advice, but worthy of taking.

Legal action involves so many things; cause is the main thing necessary. There must be cause or grounds for such movement of the Court. In Johnny Depp's case he had reason to believe he was being defamed by his then longstanding girlfriend, but then again, Depp has deep deep pockets, and the fame that the trial has brought him over the past six weeks is enormous! You can't really buy that type of publicity! It works out for people like Johnny Depp; but that's such an anomaly! We, the average, who don't really have much to gain or lose by moving the Court one way or the other should probably stick to something simply like, oh, I don't know, music, writing, blogging, singing, soaking in the sun with our friends. Let bygones be just that -- gone.

Three of my favorite "*legal*" words are: *Discovery, Deposition, and Interrogatories.* I remember the first time I had to type the word "*interrogatory*" on a pleading. Geez, has it really been nearly 30 years since I've been in the investigatory and/or legal fields of both insurance and corporate law? I guess it has been. Who knew? Years fly by when you're digging up things and learning what you can either for personal knowledge or because you're paid to do it. The word "*Discovery*" is just that; it discovers literally EVERY LITTLE THING about a person, a place, a thing, the nature of, the underlying cause for the bringing of the cause. How do we discover? We use my 2nd and 3rd favorite words "*Deposition*" and "*Interrogatories*".

First, a deposition is something charged with questions and follow up questions, questions that may or may not have something to do with the case in genuine. A lawyer can literally ask anything whatsoever as long as he/she can justify to the Court the reasoning behind the asking, and that reasoning can be as flimsy as paper! It can be something like "*I thought it may lead to discovery*" or it could be *"we think it is relevant to the case"* (even if it may not be so relevant, it can stop a case in its tracks when the right buttons are pushed and the one being deposed chooses not to continue in the mandated discovery.) Interrogatories are questions too, but they are written out, asked and expected to be answered in a certain amount of time.

If they are answered they may trigger the need for a deposition and that/those deposition(s) could be very very interesting in deed. A lawyer may choose to depose the one bringing the case, and he/she may decide to depose one's family members, former spouses, ex-lovers, mothers, fathers, you just never know. At least being married would save a man from having his wife give testimony -- that is, in America. I don't know about the rest of the world.

Legal Action is not something to be taken lightly by either side. Best to settle before attempting the first movement or motion. Best to mediate if possible. Best to get on with one's walk than to trip over the rocks he/she has set out in front of their own path. PUBLIC POSTING is just that, PUBLIC. Anything written or said (or sang) on the internet is for the WORLD WIDE WEB and subject to being seen, heard, used, criticized, speculated about, and shared - - often shared without permission. Oh, and that's another thing; permission isn't as cut and dry as one may think. There are local laws, state laws, national laws, international laws. Geez....best to just play it safe and accept that when you put something out there it is in fact out there. You can't get all huffy about it when it slaps you in the face or if you weren't expecting it to be exposed. That's called *"life"* - - it's not always pretty.

One of the best things about Legal Action is that it is a two-edged sword. The sword cuts both ways, and exposes both ways. If there is a suit, there can be a counter suit in order to pay the fees, but in doing that of course there are in fact more fees. Best to just live your life in such a way that no one can say anything about you that you haven't posted yourself.

That way, if someone REALLY defames you, you have a leg to stand on and you can move the Court through Legal Action. Best you realize that biting off more than you can chew is not always wise - - keep it simple. Maybe take guitar lessons or take a dip in the rustic waters of a foreign country! Live a little, and stop worrying so much about what others think. We're not on this Earth long enough to really form an opinion that matters anyway.

This has been a public service announcement for anyone who is silly enough to think that Legal Action is the equivalent to "*Please stop, thank you*". Civility is king and it can be queen too.

in·ter·rog·a·to·ry

/ˌin(t)əˈrägəˌtôrē/
adjective

- 1.conveying the force of a question; questioning: "*the guard moves away with an interrogatory stare*"

noun

- 1.a written question which is formally put to one party in a case by another party and which must be answered.

Muscle vs. Fat

I can't even begin to tell you how hurt and upset I was when I stood on the scale the other day and saw the number that represents the amount of weight I weigh in pounds! I'm going to start referring to my weight in either Kg or in stones because it really is so much lower than the number I saw; the number that was burned into my brain! AGONY! Oh my goodness, I was upset. I actually sat on the bed crying and I was mostly upset about it because I had been (and have been) both really careful on my intake of calories and the output of energy through walking, dancing, riding my bike, boxing, you name it, I do it - - I jump rope, I climb, hike, ride horses too. About the only thing I can't do is run or jog because of my right knee being so useless, but there I was in absolute disgrace and tears after stepping from the scales. How could that be true? I'll tell you how it's true. Muscle weighs so much more than fat.

I know people say that, they say muscle weighs more than fat, but I thought really they were just saying that to make their friends feel better when they were asking *"Do I look fat in these jeans?"* You know, it was something or is something people say to be nice really, not making a show of the fact that they really wanted to say *"You could stand to put the ice cream bar down and pick up a dumbbell every now and again."* The problem with that would be that I've given up the ice cream and I've been working out so I don't get it!! Now, I get it.

After researching it for real, and then going back over it again, I can tell you with both confidence and authority that muscle really does weigh more than fat! You can't say a pound of muscle is the same as a pound of fat without realizing that the measure you mentioned is the same...it's a POUND. A pound of feathers weighs the same as a pound of lead. A pound is a pound is a pound. A cup of fat however weighs so much less than a cup of dense muscle. I just didn't realize how much more muscle actually weighed until I sat my dermatologist down and asked her to dig out her college manuals to show me! It didn't do her any good to try and convince me with her head knowledge. She's incredibly smart, but I wanted to see it in writing! Something about it being in print made it more real I suppose. There it was!!

Basically, the example given in the textbook was that two people of the same sex could be the same height and weight but one could wear a dress size or jean size much larger than the other due to the fluffy fat content of their body. The more fit person, whose muscles are dense and compact, would and could wear clothes that are much smaller. The example was that of two women both 45 years of age, standing 5'5" and weighing 150 pounds. One woman wore a size 14 dress and the other wore a size 6 dress. WOW...that makes so much more sense now, and I had to pack away the tissue because I'm no longer crying about it. I am also no longer wearing a size 18 dress or jeans. I'm wearing a size 12 and on my way to wearing a size 10. I weigh more now than I did a year ago, a lot more. I weigh 14 pounds more; an entire stone more than I did a year ago. I thought it was supposed to go down to my *goal weight* but it didn't. I'm on my way to my goal size instead.

When all is said and done, maybe in about 3 months or so, I will be in my size 8 jeans if I can find a way to get rid of the belly fat. The hardest part of the entire body transformation is this belly! I'm doing literally everything I can to reduce it. I'm doing aerobic training, I'm taking raspberry ketones, I'm drinking green tea, using all the right methods - - it's coming off but so so so slowly. I may end up resorting to having surgery to get rid of the visceral fat I can't control or shed. I have been battling this for years and it may be time to call in the professionals. I'm doing all I can before that happens, but I won't let it stand in my way of meeting my personal goals. NOPE.

I did notice that I'm lifting weights while I watch YouTube videos. That's something I never did before. I am also walking upward and over 7 miles a day for the most part. I always do 5.5 miles, but I push for the last 1.5 if I can. I used to be really happy with 3 miles a day. Now I think that's slacking off and I get that before noon. When you're working toward a goal you put in the work or you don't. It's either yes or no. To not do it to the fullest is to say no. It's do or don't do for me. You don't have to be this way, it's just me, but that's the way I've always been. Yoda and I see things the same way. Do or don't do, there is no try.

OK that's about it for now, I'm about 30 minutes behind in my walking today but there was a huge rain storm, so there's that. Usually, when that happens I go to the store to walk, but we couldn't get out of the driveway to even do that!! Oh well, it is what it is. There's always another way to get the body moving. I can dance! My poor neighbors. They know when I'm up here working out and punching the bag and they know when I'm dancing. At least I'm smiling when we pass each other in the commons!!

Outlander – My Thoughts

I'm not completely alone, but I think I'm among the minority of those who hadn't really heard of nor watched the Starz series *"Outlander"* several years ago. Nope, I literally just heard of it last summer, that would be 2021; and I think I binge watched every episode from Season 1 through Season 5 in just under two weeks' time. I even went back and watched the entire thing again only because I had paid for a three-month subscription to Starz and besides the more than well-worth-it-ness of it all, I found myself listening to the Scottish accents, drinking in the scenery, and trying my hardest to learn as much authentic history as one can assume is mixed up inside a fictional time traveling wanderlust series as possible. I loved every episode, but no, I didn't love every second of it. I'll explain.

I'm not much of a Jamie Frazer groupie, not in the sense that I think he's the best looking, most attractive, or sexiest male character in the series. I like Jamie because he's a strong and lovely man with a heart for his wife and a good sense of loyalty both to Scotland and to his personal ideals; far be it from me to say whether I agree with his politics or religious views. I appreciate the strong character. Personally, if I was to pick one or the other of the men to fancy it would be Roger MacKenzie or Rupert MacKenzie. Rupert wasn't married, and my morals would have gotten in the way a bit if I had been time-trapped on The Ridge and given a chance to chase Roger. Nope, I would have needed to be transported just before April 16, 1745 near Culloden in the Highlands and maybe found ol' Rupert by the fire. Maybe I would have been able to coax him away from the battle - - tricked him somehow; saved him. Maybe not.

Many people won't say this, but I'm actually glad the series is almost ended. I have great fondness for so many of the characters and going on and on with the plots and seemingly endless twists have almost brought me to the point of boredom! If Claire got raped one more time I think I would have had to throw something at the screen before I fast-forwarded to a better scene! Enough is enough! I think the producers felt the same as I did. Not to be too callous about it, but the last couple of episodes in Season 6 have been equally boring as far as Claire Frazer is concerned. I was pissed, as everyone was perhaps, that Marva was allowed to cut off Claire's hair, but it did shake up the monotony of seeing Claire dose herself over and over again with her homemade ether potion. Nothing could have kept my attention when I saw the ghost or mind-trick of Lionel Brown again and again in the surgery room, the place he was murdered. I will say he deserved it, and sorry, I think Marva got what she deserved as well. The baby didn't need to die; that was sad.

Bree and Roger's mention of Perry Mason and the fact that he could have easily solved Marva's murder was in fact, my favorite moment of the entire series I think. OK...that's not true. Staring at Roger and Rupert was excitable and enjoyable; but I do wish the travelers could have let on a bit more to the audience regarding their origins. I liked every mention of their future selves. I would have really loved it if Ian could have been transported into 1944 to see a dermatologist to possibly remove his facial tats if he wanted to do that; who knows? I know we can't wrap up every loose end, but Jamie's sister Jenny and her husband Ian should have had the opportunity to see their son growing up and even though they would not have quite appreciated his choices they may have understood that they helped him to be the stronger person he eventually became. I like Ian a great deal.

So, my finale thoughts? All in all I'm giving the series a strong and solid 8 out of 10 for entertainment and maybe a 7 out of 10 for authenticity. To be able to think that much of it was true was good enough, and to know there is obviously going to be conflicting stories and creative license(s) used is evident. I loved it. I liked it. I respected it. I admired it, but I am glad it's coming to an end. I can only take so much of the over crudeness and harshness of the ignorant folk. I know it must have been that way, but I don't like to think of my ancestors as being completely brutish. My personal ancestors had been in Virginia about 173 years before the Revolutionary War. I know where their loyalties were; I myself am not in need of a time-machine-rock to know what must have happened to the Stringfellows when it came time to enlist with the Rebels to fight the King's Men. I have history on my side for that.

The books are no doubt as good if not better than the movies could ever be, but I wonder if Roger could be any more handsome in the pages written about him. I doubt it. At least now if I do ever have time to sit and read the innovative and imaginative tales of the people of my people I will be able to put faces with names and images with fanciful visions as I bury myself ever so deeply into the folds of fantastical witness through inkened colloquy! Oh, to be in the Highlands with tartaned kilted men of mind and muscle -- knowing what I know now, I would have to bring a few rolls of toilet paper with me through the rocks. That much I know.

The What If Factor

Here we go. This is a good one. I was dreaming a couple of days ago and my mind really stretched out to the fullest and went for a wee vacation. I dreamed that a particular man at a particular time, from a particular place zapped or teleported from where he was and ended up in my living room, some 4400 miles (as the crow flies) away from where he laid his head in Edinburgh, Scotland. I can't say from his home because he didn't have a home. He wasn't homeless, but he wasn't the leasee on an apartment, flat, house or cottage either. He was somewhere in between homes at the time of his zapping! I'll explain in the next few paragraphs, but for now, I will let you in on the biggest spoiler alert. Sometimes truth really is stranger than fiction - - this was a dream, therefore, fiction.

For security purposes we'll not give the man his real name. Nope. We'll call him Wilson. That's a good Scottish name. Remember, this is a dream, it did not actually happen. I want to make that clear so that no one from NASA comes to my house asking questions and looking over my new smart LED lightbulbs that I've just installed. You know when you do that, when you install *"smart"* anything in your home, you are putting yourself and the world at random risk and peril. Just sayin'.

Wilson, a man in his 40s, recently divorced, recently finding himself released from jail, having served just under a year for something he actually didn't do, but plead guilty to in order to protect his family, was quite upset that having done the gallant and noble thing wasn't necessarily the right thing to do. While in jail he found

122

himself abandoned by the very one he agreed to protect, she divorced him, and she told friends and family that she may have talked the man into admitting to the possession and use of cannabis in order to protect her from a similar fate, but because of Wilson's past (he was documented as being an addict as well as having served at least two stints in rehab for suicide attempts and thoughts) he was not taken to a regular men's prison to serve, but he was regulated to an inbound rehab center that housed him for over 45 weeks and gave him 24/7 "*care*" with homework, expectations of group participation, and the threat of staying longer if he didn't fully confess his wrongdoing and seek genuine recovery. The problem with that is that he really hadn't fallen off the sobriety wagon, so admitting to something he didn't do was both counterproductive and internally hurtful.

After serving 45 long, boring, grinding weeks in the facility, Wilson not only had to sign documents that stated he was guilty and now on the road to recovery, he had to start his real stint of sobriety over from the several years he had accomplished back to Day 1. Down the drain; all because he wanted to give the kids a chance to stay with their mother rather than trying to forge a method of creating an income on his own without her being present were she to be rightfully arrested and not him. He couldn't work, he was disabled in a way, (he was a guitarist, trained classically) and he lacked the credit and had no specific working skills other than regular labor.

Regular labor would not have been keen enough to support the little family; they would have had to move, they would have had to live penny to penny, and without their mother, the kids, about to go into their teens, may have been a bit more rebellious than the man could physically and emotionally handle. The clever wife convinced Wilson to take the wrap - - he did, and she booted his ass right out the second she found the opportunity to do so.

Having left the center, Wilson was accepted rather reluctantly by his father, to share a two-bedroom flat on the lower south end of Edinburgh, where his father had lived for years and had been storing and stashing things (again for years) in the second tiny bedroom. In America we call these rooms larger closets with windows. In Scotland a room measuring over six feet in either direction is considered a "*single*" bedroom.

The room was in fact six and a half feet wide and seven feet deep. The room had a tiny old beaten mattress in the corner, propped up against the wall just so, and a number of boxes, bags, old clothes, piles of useless social worker materials and records which long since could be thrown out. There was a dresser and it was empty of clothes, but full of older papers and things again that could be disposed of, but the day and time really never arrived for his father to "*get around to it*" so it never got done.

Today was that day, and Wilson had started the process necessary to call the place his own room. He may not have much, and what he had may be useless to most, but it was his, and he was going to make it work. His only real possession that mattered, was his guitar -- that was his. It was good. The guitar kept him alive in rehab. Not that he was able to play her, but he knew one day he would do so.

Having managed to forge through the wreckage(s) in the tiny room and built the makings of a real lodging, Wilson decided that a new start would only be enhanced if he were able to have at least a few pair of new trousers, maybe two, and of course tee-shirts, pants (what they call underwear in the UK) and socks. He definitely needed socks. The spring and even early summer in my neck of the woods may be warmer, but not in good old Scotland. The man needed his socks. Calling out to his dad to let him know he would be back, not to wait up for him in case he needed to stop by a take-away restaurant to enjoy real food again; Wilson headed off to the Asda, their version of our Walmart. He was on a mission for a few new things to start this new chapter.

A little over half way to the store Wilson realized he had left his wallet at home and couldn't possibly buy the clothes and other items without his debit card. He had lost his actual bank account while in rehab because when she divorced him the wife took his share of the money of course. His father had loaned him a bit to get back on his feet, and this was his new card in his new wallet that he had left in the other pair of trousers that he had just changed out of in order to be a bit more presentable at the store.

Walking back to the little flat Wilson seemed both preoccupied and a bit depressed, but who could blame him? It's hard to start over. It's even harder to start over when you shouldn't have had to put yourself through what he had put himself through. He was mad. He had the right to be mad, so he rather indulged a bit on those feelings and no, he didn't see the car speeding around the corner just as he stepped off the curb. SPLASH! OMG...water went EVERYWHERE and by everywhere, I mean Wilson's only decent pair of *"pants"* were soaked clean through as were of course his trousers, shirt, socks, and even his light jacket that he hadn't needed to zip up -- there weren't enough words to describe the deep emotional inner voice inside of him that just wanted to scream *"NOOOOOOOOOO"* and be done with it.

Arriving back home more angry, more wet, more or less pissed to the point of kicking anything or anyone that dared to cross his path, Wilson reminded himself over and over again that he was a Christian man, and this was just a fantastic phase, it was a real opportunity to seek a little deeper, to love and praise, to think good things, to send out worshipping whispers, and yes, it took every last ounce of control he had within his body to do just that. He must have missed his dad, not even glancing to see where he may be, Wilson drew a bee-line to the bathroom, undressed and showered. Allowing the hot steaming water to rush and run over his tired and absolutely irritable body and soul. He wanted to lay down and throw a tantrum, that would have actually felt pretty good, but he just leaned his weight against the wall of the shower and let the water cure him.

Dad came to the hall, realizing his son was in the shower, and just opened the door enough to collect his clothes for the washer. I think he may have said something about Wilson being back sooner than he thought, maybe he asked about the purchases, not seeing the bags, and yeah, he took the dirty wet clothes and threw them on top of the half-filled basket already in his collected arms. Upon leaving the shower and wrapping a towel about his waist, Wilson made it to the hallway, looking both ways thinking he thought he heard his dad, but not really making more of an effort than grunting under his breath about this or that.

Once in his little room the towel hit the floor and Wilson began digging through the otherwise tiny pile of his secondhand clothes that were given to him upon his leaving of the center. One or two other men who had been about his size had donated the clothes to him hoping to cheer him up a bit since everything he owned had been thrown out by the more than thoughtless spouse. She couldn't even see fit to let him have his own things.

126

Having not accepted any pants from the men, Wilson continued to dig around the pile of clothes seeking and hoping to find his own underwear but not really seeing them - - his head on a swivel, glancing to the left, glancing to the right, and then it happened. He was literally ZAPPED out of his room, out of his dad's flat, out of his country, out of everything imaginable and there was literally no time between the zapping and the replacement, he was just THERE. Where? Where was he? Good question. He was in my living room, that's where he was, and yes, he was naked.

Keep in mind that Wilson and I have never actually met each other. We know each other. We haven't talked on the phone. We haven't been friends. We haven't really even been communicating in the past year or so since he was in the center. He read my blogs from time to time, and often, to be honest, he was angry about what I had written. He wasn't necessarily a fan, let's put it that way. I had a way of being honest and he had a way of avoiding conflict. He and I didn't have the conflict, no, he had the conflict singularly, absolutely in and with himself about me.

He couldn't understand and he refused to try to understand, that a person (me) could love someone like him without being sexual, and without being possessive. He had a problem understanding that a person like me (actually me) would have a command and/or directive from God (not man) to pray for and to encourage him (Wilson) without the side issues of being in love, infatuated, or otherwise dreamy eyed and upside down with emotion. Well, that would be his cross to bear, not mine.

Glancing around, still glancing, that one, he didn't know where he was. He didn't recognize the wall art. He didn't understand why the sun was still shining when it was clearly setting at the time the car had splashed water all over his body, and that's when he noticed the digital clock on the wall -- it was 3:12 p.m. and when he had climbed into the shower he remember hearing his dad's mantle clock strike the hour of 9:00 p.m. What the hell just happened? It was about this time, maybe what, four seconds post-teleportation, when Wilson realized he was standing wherever he was, butt-naked. Some say buck-naked, but he was thinking more along the lines of *butt-exposed-front-exposed* naked, that and his hair and beard were still wet. What happened?

OK, there was so much more that took place, but the whole gist of this story is this; I saw the man standing in my living room and rather than scream and freak out I realized he needed to be covered. I immediately sat down my green tea that I had just fixed and I moved past him, all the while talking to him, and reassuring him that however he managed to find his naked self into my living room this fine late spring afternoon, I was not only going to accept him into my home, I was going to receive him into my home, and the two things are very different. I managed to find a robe for him that I rarely even use but own, and it did cover him.

Laughingly amused obviously by the story that certainly had to be told, I walked into my bedroom, into the closet, and I pulled out a box labeled "*Wilson*" on the side of it. I had months previously been told of God that I may very well need to prepare for an off-the-wall situation, one that required me to be alert and yes, I had gone to the store and picked up a pair of sweat pants, underwear, a man's XL tee-shirt and a pair of socks. I think I actually bought a 4 pack of underwear and a 6 pack of socks, but in the box was just enough to clothe a man who may or may not just happen to pop into my apartment in need - - and yeah, because God had directed me to do so, I bought the items needed to dress that very

128

man who actually popped into my living room in very much need.

Wilson stared at me with extreme anger and disbelief. Because (BECAUSE) I had presented him with the best gesture of goodwill known, he accused me of teleporting him, or somehow having the ability to do so, and it was literally my doing, my fault, my scheming, and my obsession that forced him to be taken from the safety of his father's house to this, a place he would never have imagined to have come to, and to be with me, a person he would NEVER have accepted or received had the tables been turned. OK....so, what does that tell you? He's an ass and I still love him to the point of praying that God will show him that he's exposed not only physically, but emotionally, and he needs to be protected, prayed over, and given what he needs to function. I was the culprit in his eyes, and he was the one God had asked me to care for in my eyes.

The What If factor comes into play here. What if I had been zapped butt-naked into his father's home? Would I have been received? Possibly by his father who would have been cordial, sweet natured, and curious as to what was happening, but I know I would have been forcefully escorted out of the nearest door by Wilson. The police would have been called. I would have been labeled an exhibitionist even though in reality I had been teleported without my knowledge, and into a place where I had no control.

The WHAT IF factor comes into play here in that what if Wilson's daughter had been zapped into my house instead of himself? I would have been accused of being a kidnapper, a pedophile, and somehow I would have been labeled a stalker - - even though she was zapped into my place without my consent, and without my blessing. Now, flip that. He was zapped into my apartment. He was standing in my living room naked. I didn't call the police. I didn't scream. I didn't accuse him of misconduct. He was the one blaming me. Even as I handed him the clothes, and was trying to explain to him that months before God had directed me to not only buy the articles, but to write the event in my journal. I was still being blamed for the actual teleportation.

My saving grace in this entire matter was that I don't even remotely understand quantum physics and I wouldn't have a clue how to draw up a scheme to somehow transfer a person's body from one spot to the other. Here's another WHAT IF. What if he had been zapped to another house instead of mine? What if he had been taken to his music producer's house where there is a wife, kids, and possibly neighbors having a block party? Would he have been accepted? Would he have been received? Cared for? Protected? What if he had been zapped into the London Heathrow airport? Maybe Asda? Maybe a nursery school? No!

There was ONLY ONE PLACE that man could have been teleported to and have received the care and necessary compassion where he received it -- and that's with me. Even his own cousins would have betrayed him, taken photos of him, posted these photos and made dreadful fun of him. Given his situation with the recent stay at the center, he could have been rearrested, given 5-10 years for exposing himself and more - - even though it wasn't his choice and he had no control. God knew exactly where to send the man.

I convinced Wilson to take a seat, have some dinner, and drink some tea. I think I even offered him a bit of Melatonin (10 mg) to calm his mind and take the edge off the twitching and the tightening of his shoulders and arms. He was scared and with good reason. His phone was back in Scotland, and he didn't know his dad's phone number, but using Facebook he was able to reach his dad and get through to him. His dad called my phone and the two talked for a while about what had just happened. It was decided NOT to tell anyone because he could face legal ramifications for having "*flown*" to the U.S. without a passport. His father put a box together with a few things including his wallet, passport, and new clothes, clothes his father purchased for the box before sending it through Amazon to my place.

Wilson, after three days of being heard, listened to, pampered, fed, understood, and we'll go ahead and say being befriended, decided that I wasn't the complete and utter enemy he may have believed me to be. He once had mentioned to me that he knew I wasn't an enemy, but he didn't feel comfortable talking to me about personal issues. I get that. What if? What if I was the only one to really understand?

So many of our friends fall off the "*friends*" lists and the "*follows*" when or if they get wind of hearing that you've done time for petty felonies and/or harder misdemeanors. Not wanting to give you the benefit of the doubt or even listen to your explanation, an employer will let you go, fire you, terminate you, even ask you to never contact anyone from the company again, just because you screwed up and had to spend a little time incarcerated or maybe on the community services list.

You tell your employer you need off to do community service and guess what, you're no longer employed. Friends and family find reasons to not communicate. Hell, even church members shun you, ignore you, or they put that pious face on and say they'll pray for you, but ask them to hold your hand and pray, and yeah, that's not happening. What if you were zapped away and taken to the ONE place you would never have imagined being at on your own, and with the one person you've put blame on for so long (because others told you to) that you began to listen to the lies?

Well...here's the thing; it was a dream. I know it was a dream, it wasn't real, but I would like to think that Wilson (if only in real life) would begin to understand that I'm there to help, not to hinder. Since the whole thing was so realistic and strangely rational, I decided to do what I think would be best. I went to Walmart and bought a pack of underwear (XL boxer briefs) a pair of sweats (also XL) and a man's tee-shirt with short sleeves. I figure if it's cold outside and he may need another shirt I can find a sweatshirt hanging in the closet that my son left behind. I bought socks too. I have them in the box, and yes, I even wrote the man's name on the box - - sort of a joke really, but not really, because if anyone is going to be teleported into my house and cosplay as Naked Bearded Man, I really wouldn't mind it being - - well, we'll call him Wilson.

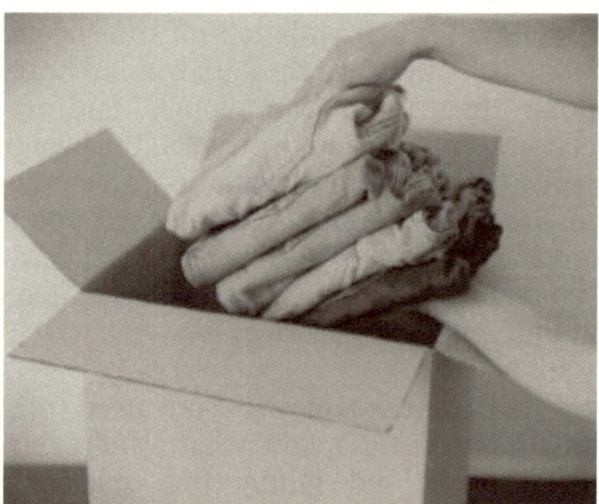

Photo Credit: Canva.com (royalty free)

Homelessness for Children

I could bore you with all the gory details, the stats on how many kids today are either homeless or without a bed to sleep in at night. I could tell you the numbers, draw your attention to the data, and cause your brain to dull out from overload, but I would rather just get your attention another way. I've been teaching in one capacity or the other since the beginning of the 21st Century. Though it doesn't seem like it. Sometimes, it seems like it's been 100 years, while other times, I barely know I've learned anything at all about the profession. If I'm not learning on a daily basis, I feel that I'm falling far behind my peers. One thing for certain that I do know without having to look it up in a book, online, or use a lifeline is that children who are homeless do not thrive in educational environments due to the fundamental facts that they are displaced physically, mentally, emotionally, financially, and spiritually. These kids have a greater chance of self-harm than any other demographic. Look it up. It's real.

By nature (and perfect design), a child is brought into the world in the same old-fashioned way that every last one of us arrived here. We were either conceived in love or happenstance, but we were conceived, and if we're living and breathing, we were born. We weren't hatched, and we weren't made in a baby factory, found under a cabbage, or brought to the doorstep by a big gangly stork. We were born. We may have been born to good parents, as being homeless does not mean that the people who find themselves in this situation are innately bad, but many are born into homelessness, abandonment, and a general state of playing catch up from the day they arrived. It's not uncommon in my particular school district where I live, to run across kids who have lived on the streets for more than two years running. Some of the more grounded homeless kids are those who, in fact, have adapted to their living arrangements, be that as they may be. Some of the more challenging homeless students are the ones whose parents have only recently found themselves under more exigency times. Now they must face unbearable decision-making regarding whether or not they can even find a way to get their child to school to the place where he or she will at least be warm for eight hours, be fed breakfast and lunch, and at least have a roof over their heads for now. No wonder these kids show up early and leave later in the day.

A kid without a bed is a drastic thing. Sure, there are families living with other families, too, and crowding too many faces into a house, I get that. We see that as often as we see kids living in cars, under bridges, and literally inside the bus stops. Driving to work each morning, I pass the same woman and her two young daughters who have made rest at the back of a church; the church can't allow her to come into the building when it's closed, but at least I feel that when it is open, they may allow her to wash up, use the restroom and maybe do something for her.

I have stopped to talk with her, but she doesn't speak English, and she's not willing to get too close to someone she fears could turn her over to authorities. It must be gut-wrenching for some of these immigrants who expose their souls to give their families a new way of life only to find themselves begging for bread and a place to wash their hands each day. Dealing with issues I've never had to deal with and have really only read about and watched on television, these parents and children walk it, talk it, breathe it, move it, manage it, and when they can't manage it, they lose it. I feel so helpless when I realize I can't do much more than pray.

One of the statistics that just goes right through me is the fact that a homeless child is nine times more likely to fail a grade than any housed child. A homeless child is usually displaced more than three times during a school year. Each time he or she is displaced or moved around, he or she loses nearly all of the educational study he or she may have begun to retain. The new school may not be teaching the same things, or it could be teaching exactly what the child has already gone over, so yeah, they may get that lesson down, but not the one before it which wasn't taught at the older school, but now maybe forever lost and you know there isn't time to go back over the who, what, when, where, why, and how of the *"Tell-Tale Heart"* or *"The Giver"* when the real questions sound more like *"Where am I going to sleep, what am I going to eat, who is going to try to hurt me, when will this be over, and how do I even cope with all of this?"*

Interestingly, one of my homeless students told me she was homeless. I think she did this because she understands that under Oklahoma law, I must report it to the Department of Human Services, and maybe they can find her a shelter or a better way to cope. She wanted me to know that even though she wasn't living in a home, more like a tent in the woods (her words), she would read every word of every story because it gave her an escape from her reality. I couldn't hold back my emotions. I couldn't restrain my tears. We're not supposed to hug the kids, really. Those days have passed, but I couldn't stop myself from reaching for her and just squeezing her. I let her know that if she ever needs more books, she can take them. If she ever wanted more paper, pens, or just anything I could provide, let me know. You know I'm that teacher who finds a way to sneak an extra bit of string cheese, apple, Pop-Tarts, or something to the ones I know are struggling.

When you think about the school year starting, and all you can think about is COVID-19 or if the school's teachers or students are wearing masks on their faces, change your thoughts every now and again to the harder, colder reality that there are students who slept outside last night without blankets. There are students who eat once a day if they are lucky and can only really get food at the schools.

Think of the kids who fight for everything they have, which may include the one pair of jeans they wear every day because they just don't have anything else. It is never, and I mean NEVER, the kid's fault that they are homeless -- as a society, we need to do so much more, and I'm not talking about just building shelters. We need to build relationships. We need to understand that one terminated father or mother could lead to four starving children who lose it all -- over what? The father or mother may have used their cell phone during work hours to call home? We have too many issues in this country to deal with to have to be so petty as to release parents from their jobs for lesser reasons. The consequences are dramatic in most cases.

The Bethany Christian Trust, a homeless shelter and social refuge for people in crisis, is a great place (in Scotland) helping more than 7,000 homeless people, many of them students, on a daily, weekly, monthly, and annual basis. We need more places like BCT here so kids can go into a safe place to talk to adults, get to know people who care, and understand that there are ways to survive drastic circumstances. Through God, through Jesus, and through the Spirit, there are ways to share our love and our resources. Until we come to these conclusions, we are destined to repeat the strangely routine methods we've used for too long, and that has caused so much damage. A homeless child is five times more likely to succeed with a suicide attempt because they truly want out of their current pressures. We need to stop that before it becomes six times, seven times, and more. We need to know the signs and be willing to reach out when our hearts are pricked - - will you help?

Some of the signs that a child is homeless are:

- They pull away from crowds.
- Lay their heads down to rest more.
- Hoard food, steal money and food.
- Show up to school really early, and stay really late.
- They often wear the same things, but they aren't clean most of the time.
- They talk about the days they had a place to live.
- They speak in the past tense about being OK.

We should all be a part, or willing to be a part, to end this horrific reality for others. We are blessed. We are given the responsibility to do more with that blessing. There, but by the grace of God, go each and every last one of us, literally.

Major First-World Issues

Talk about being spoiled. Let me tell you, I am the Queen of it. I'm not rude, and I don't huff and puff like a little brat if things don't go my way. I'm actually more likely to just make a face and curl up the side of my lip at the culprit, whatever is causing me to be inconvenienced. I will usually walk away, scratch whatever plan or scheme I was working on at the time, and regroup. My tantrum days are long gone. I will, however, let people know they inconvenienced me. I figure they need to be held responsible if that is at all possible. Today, the issue was not one where I could really lay any blame, so I just sighed....three times.

I work at an amazing office. Let's get that out of the way first. I mean, these people are way above and beyond excellent, and I am just all too happy to let each and every one of them know this when I see them throughout the day. Yes, we have some gosh-darn work warriors at the company I work for and with. That being said, not one of the men (and there are plenty) knows how to make a pot of coffee, fill up a coffee filter so it can be used to make coffee, nor do any of them know how to look for, find, or resupply any of the sweeteners, creamers, or flavors for said coffee. Nope. Not one. So, in order for this grave and immensely debilitating problem to actually remedy itself, I decided to hold an impromptu staff training session! At first, no one wanted to attend. When I asked the Human Resource Manager's assistance in the matter, I suddenly had 11 volunteers! Good job, men!

The coffee issue may seem small, but it's not. We have over 50 people in the office, and we have two pots of coffee brewing at a time. We also have a Keurig, so that's the reason I only had 11 volunteers to attend my little Do-It-Yourself class this morning. Many of the employees, including myself, use Keurig. Trust me when I say that the clean up after yourself portion of my little speech was both animated and I had visual. I even asked for a volunteer to assist me; I'm telling you; these people are awesome!! I had no trouble assuring the others who chose not to attend that the 12 knowledgeable people in the building who now know how to brew will do so, but if we catch any of these others who did not attend the meeting, finishing off the last cup, there will be another session!

Another First World issue we addressed today, because it actually came up during the first session of our coffee-making lesson, was the fact that both of our (HUGE) refrigerators and the independent water dispenser standing next to the refrigerators were not dispensing water. The refrigerators weren't dispensing ice, for that matter, either. Our ice maker (yes, we have a separate one) was on the mend from a power outage we experienced. Hence, the backup plan was to use the two fridges and the very handy-dandy and always-accessible water cooler. Now what? We literally had no automated filtered water to make the coffee. We were going to have to resort to using TAP WATER! Are you serious?

It was decided that the Keurig, which is connected to the same mechanism that sends water to the two refrigerators, may not be dispensing water either? We were lucky; it was actually working, but it was incredibly slow, and here we stood, all masters of our own personal crafts, but not one of us knew a dang thing about plumbing. You really don't want me messing with the plumbing. I can tell you that. We used props and talked in hypotheticals. We couldn't really make the coffee, and that was, in fact, a big First World issue for a bunch of Market traders and their support staff. This is a company that will spend $$$ to house any of us in the three-star hotel next to our office if the weather is going to be too bad and there's a chance we won't make it back to the office. The Market does not care who you are; the Market does not stop or wait for anyone. We know this. We need our coffee.

Just about the time I was wrapping up the DIY demonstration on all things percolating, the boss stepped in to let us know that while we were being educated she was making calls to repair people, and within a few minutes, we had water! Money talks. That's the bottom line to this story, folks, money talks. Some of us, myself included, took our Keurig coffee mugs into the breakroom and watched as the plumber explained what our issues and problems were. I know I listened. If this happens again, I want to at least explain it to the next plumber. I can't really say I learned a great deal, but I did take notes. I can read the notes back to the next plumber if I need to. I trade money for money, and I help others (support) when they sell bonds. I'm not into tubes, lines, faucets, panels, and drains. The plumber did ask me if we were having problems with our ballcocks, but hey, I don't have any of those either. I smiled.

So, apparently, I did learn something today. A ballcock is a device that helps the water flow evenly and stop when it needs to. They're usually on toilets, and that's where they found the plumber. He had been called up from another floor where he had been working on a lavatory issue. Our building is about 40 years old, so it does have its contentions. We made it through the entire morning thinking about our coffee, our water, our ice, and, yes, our ballcocks. I couldn't resist asking the ladies in my office if any of them had any personal experience(s) with a ballcock. This sent the one man (a younger man) in our office, right through the roof with laughter. He was the only one of us who knew what it was, and he even told us that he had two! I guess now that I know what it is, I can admit to having two myself. Not lying when I tell you I have ballcocks made of brass! Who knew?

Photo Credit: Grainger.com

Story Time!

Everyone loves a good story, right? I am no exception, but what I am (as far as exceptions go) is someone who will openly (and honestly, thank you) admit to being that person you know who talks to themselves. I do. I am the one who will not shy from it. I will not make excuses, and I will not deny it. I am forever and constantly talking to myself, telling myself sometimes the best stories out in this big green world. I can come up with some real doosies. Dang...I can entertain myself from the moment my eyes open to the second I fall asleep praying. I don't mind being blunt about this because I am just so darn good at it. George used to love it when I'd pretend with him being the hero. Dachshunds are like that, you know. They are superheroes in disguise.

Most of the time, when I reach outside someone else's comfort zone, I'll quickly stir the pot by asking them if they talk to themselves and, if they do, if they answer themselves as well. It's not something the average bear asks, and it's not something the other average bear admits to (readily) anyway. Nine times out of 9.5 times, they say no. I think I see them shift just a little, and they either cross their arms across their chest in an attempt to somehow protect themselves should I pursue the matter (I generally do), and they may sort of walk away from me. That's when I know the truth. That's when I know I have them....on the hook!

Everyone loves to hear a story, and most of us have one to tell. I just like to make up new ones as often as possible and let the day's events add to the fiction. I pretend (mostly silently in my head), and I create reasons to open my eyes a bit wider; my ears may prick a bit, and I could see something inside of something that wasn't there, to begin with, but if it had been there it would sure add a bit of welcomed flavor to the overall tale of the day! I might start off with pretending I found a baby in the dumpster; cute little thing, and then start trying to sort out where he came from, who dropped him off rather than taking him to the hospital, it's just right there! I live about 1000 feet from a very large hospital complex. Was the baby born there? Was the mom OK, was the baby stolen? Too many questions. I need answers. The day begins, and as it unfolds, I create something really awesome with at least six or seven villains and superhero types along the way. If a speeding car goes down the street I imagine the person who stole the baby is driving that car, where are they going?

Anyway, that's the truth of it. The fact that I can keep myself fully occupied is really a good thing because it adds to the events of what could have been a mundane Monday or a weak little Wednesday afternoon without a single breeze to carry my imagination into the stratosphere. I need the lift. I need the air! I want to fly, and my brain has no limits with either how that happens or where I can end up after a few minutes of pondering. To be honest, I think I take creative license a bit far at times but who's to say if that's illegal or not; I'm the one footin' the bill on this one. I make it, or I burn it. I don't have to keep the wheels turning I can stop them at most anytime if I wanted to....but do I want to? Why would I want to? Oh, I remember...I have to pay my bills! LOL, I can't always be a writer. Sometimes, I have to spin straw into gold.

Anyway, that's my thing today. I thought I would answer that one burning question that you may or may not be wondering about me. Am I nutters? Nope. Just creative and fancy-free. I don't have to be grounded in reality for too long. I can pop off into a really great fantasy at any moment. If I feel like I need someone to go along with me, you know I'm asking my husband and lover, Naked Bearded Man, to join me. Sometimes, I even wonder if he'll put that kilt on or just continue to swing it around while laughing and saying something in his deep and ever so breathtakingly sexy Gaelic; that man can bring me to my knees - - he's just so wonderfully Scottish. I mean, he's so absolute Scottish the Scottish wish they could be him - - he's both rough and tumble as well as sensitive and protective. I'd love to take him to more places, but without a stitch of clothes, he could end up thrilling someone! He'd just bust a gut laughing if he did. There are moments I wish I could understand him, but he speaks so quickly and uses words I know aren't really even supposed to sound as if they are part of the Queen's English; rebel that one.

What about you? Can you admit you keep yourself company? Will you allow your inner speak to come out and play? I bet you could wield a pretty interesting story if you thought about it. Most can. I hope you'll not be like so many and shy from the challenge -- whenever I'm caught talking to myself, I don't play it off as some do. I don't pretend to be singing under my breath; nope, I just look the asker in the eyes and continue my conversation as if I were never interrupted -- why lie? I giggle, and I move forward - - always forward. Always smiling.

PTSD – We Don't Always Talk About it

I decided to write this blog in such a way as not to harm anyone who may be innocent, someone who doesn't deserve to be hurt. I'm not talking about the man that raped me, no, he probably hasn't changed much, but he may be married or have children - - even grandchildren. They don't need to be stigmatized or feel the need to question the man after nearly four decades. I won't say his last name, but I won't change his first; his name is Dale. Dale raped me on July 2, 1981, in Norman, Oklahoma. I was 19 years old. I was a virgin. He had no right, and I don't regret my actions - - just maybe their result. He should be dead.

In the summer of '81, I was dating a sweet and loving soul named David, and we were about at that stage where I may have thought about being intimate with him. We had known each other for a few months; he had dated a schoolmate of mine and was no longer on her arm, so I questioned her about it. With her permission and approval, I asked David for a date; he accepted. This may have been in March or early April of the same year. Just after finishing a 5K run/walk with David at a park near his home, he brought me to his place to meet his mom and dad; again, very traditional, very sweet, very normal.

During the evening, David mentioned that he had a good friend at the University of Oklahoma (where he was attending) who needed help with his English project before he graduated. This being late June, I wondered how it was even possible that the friend was in school, but of course, universities have summer classes. Apparently, this guy needed to make up a credit to fulfill the end of his graduation packet, and yeah, I guess English professors can hold up the process if you owe them work. I told David I'd help his friend. I mean, in 1981, I wasn't a professor of English (not yet), but I certainly knew my way around an essay!

I remember so many things about that day, things that shouldn't really stick in my head this long after the fact. I remember I didn't have a car, it was in the shop, so I literally walked over two miles to a friend's house to borrow her car! It was a red 1977 Oldsmobile 442; wow, what a dreamboat, and powerful, too. It blew the doors off my little Volkswagen Beetle bug. Cops didn't really pull people over for speeding down I-35 from OKC to Norman, not then, I could have simply dropped my foot and hit over 80 or 90 miles per hour easily in that machine, but no; I drove like I do now, slow and smart! I've been driving since I was 17, and I don't have a speeding ticket - - knock on wood! It was truly an experience to be in this magnificent car of hers. I made it to Norman in about 30 minutes, average time.

I knew then, exactly where the man was living because David had lived with him for about a minute at the beginning of our new relationship and I'd visited him a couple of times in his dorm; an outside sort of cottage really, not the typical high-rise unit on the proper campus. It was more outback, you'd say, more on its own with a small group of other units. I think they've been removed since then, and an entirely new academic building has been built in its place. That's the one thing in my mind that I can't pin down; where exactly did this happen. I just knew how to get there, but I couldn't tell you the address now to save my life. I let that slip out of my memory, and I don't know why. Too much, maybe?

I remember knocking on the door, I remember Dale answering. I remember him being polite. I remember him asking me to sit down at the desk and go over his notes. I remember doing just that. I remember the way he grabbed me, the way I fought. I remember the screaming; I remember him laughing. I remember him being naked. I couldn't for the life of me remember when he took off his clothes. I didn't see that; I didn't hear him. I didn't realize this was even a ploy - - there were notes. I was reading notes. I was sitting at the desk, reading, when I was abruptly grabbed from behind and lifted off the ground.

I think on that day, I may have weighed 120 pounds if I was wet and carrying my dog; in other words, I was not the robust woman I am today. I think I earned the nickname *"Stringbean"* from my high school years. I stood 5'7" tall, but had absolutely no defense against this man; he was not that tall really, only 5'10" I think, but he was buff, and he was strong, and believe me, he had the advantage of both surprise and force. He hit me. He hit me squarely in the face, and he landed that one punch perfectly. I was out.

When I came to, I was not completely naked. I still had my purple and white striped Polo buttoned-down dress shirt draped around me, but my bra was undone, my jeans and panties missing, and I had one shoe on my foot, the other I think was just under my thigh, I could feel it. Maybe he tried to take them both off; I will never know. I know that I woke up; I know that I was feeling pressure both on my body and inside my body. It was not just painful. It was confusing as I had never been sexually active; I'd never even been intimate at this point; what was happening felt foreign and combative. I know that I knew I was being attacked. I immediately resisted until I felt a calm come over my soul telling me to think, not push, not scream, not react, but think. I put my greatest strength to work - - my brain.

Deciding to pretend I was interested in what was happening was my weapon of choice until such time I could find another more physical and tangible weapon. It wasn't long before the brutish base asshat on top of me, inside of me, decided to relax a bit, thinking the sounds I was making and the moves I was showing were both submissive and engaging - - his folly. My left eye caught a glimpse of a whiskey bottle, perhaps a Jack Daniels bottle, I don't know. I wasn't a drinker, I wasn't into bottles, but I saw it. It was half full, but it wasn't half full of liquid. I saw pennies and dimes; I think I saw quarters, but maybe not; maybe they were nickels. I saw the change. I saw an opportunity. He didn't see anything. He didn't see it coming - - he felt it. I'm absolutely certain that he felt it. I was free - - I was still pinned under his now more impossible weight, but I was, in fact, free.

Because I was nervous because I was scared and no longer using my inner strengths, maybe just a whole lot of fear-driven adrenaline, I picked up his jeans and my other shoe, my keys, and my little purse, and I left as fast as possible. I don't even remember putting on his jeans, but I had them on when I arrived at my friend's house to return her car. We didn't have cell phones in 1981. I could have, if I had thought about it, stopped at a gas station and used a payphone. I'm also sure there were about six different police stations between the OU campus and Bethany, Oklahoma. I didn't stop at one of them either. I made it to Carol's house in under 20 minutes - - I wasn't driving my usual slow and easy steady pace, I suppose.

I don't even remember if I remember the route, but it must have been one that I had taken in the past, and it was probably the same one I took going down to Norman, but I just remember pulling into Carol's driveway and

148

running up to her door with Dale's blue jeans falling off my waistline and hitting the porch! Carol wasn't home - - we didn't have cell phones in 1981. I walked over two miles to my house - - again, not stopping to call my mom, not stopping to call the police, not stopping to call an ambulance for Dale. However, I was absolutely sure he needed one.

When I did arrive home I was met by my friend who had been called by another friend of his at a gas station who said he saw me walking home, that I was about a mile away and I was not looking too good. The guy thought maybe I was drunk. It was in the middle of the afternoon -- and I didn't drink, but this man didn't know that. I call my friend my brother; he and I were raised together.

My brother knew that I didn't drink. He knew something was wrong. My brother walked up the hill from our houses just as I was making my way to the same hill to walk down it. It didn't take me very long to explain to my brother what happened; the bruise on my face, the fact that I wasn't wearing my own jeans, both were enough for him to use his greater strengths - - he didn't use his brains, he used his fists. Maybe it was wrong of me to do so, but I told my brother exactly where to find Dale.

Years have passed, obviously, and though I never sought medical treatment or anything remotely close to psychological assistance to overcome any post-traumatic stress disorder due to the attack, I have come to grips with two solid facts about myself; I am a survivor, and I will kill if I have to do so. I wasn't trying to hurt Dale that day; I was trying to kill him. I wanted him dead - - I was hoping when my brother found Dale, he would be lying in his own blood and not breathing, but that's not what he found. He found Dale sitting up at the desk, holding my jeans, but he was dressed. He found blood on the sheets of the bed but it wasn't Dale's it was mine. My brother found himself facing a man about the same size as himself, but the advantage went to the man whose friend and sister was abused - Dale spent the next few days at Norman Regional Hospital fighting for his life. At the time, I wished he had lost it. I checked the papers every day to see if he had in fact died.

Jesus is the great physician. He healed my soul, He healed my body, He healed my spirit, and He healed my heart to the point that I eventually, years later, was able to pray for Dale and hope that whatever it is that he's doing, he would do it with repentance and without hurting another woman. I'll not ever know the truth about what happened to him.

A day or so after the attack, because he had reported a completely different story to the medical staff at Norman Regional, I was questioned. The fact that I had Dale's jeans in my possession and my brother found my jeans at the dorm was enough for the detectives to start an investigation. I just wanted to talk to David to let him know what happened - - his mother refused to let me speak to him after she was told what happened. She told me to my face that I went there, to the dorm, knowing what was going to happen and that just because I changed my mind didn't make it rape! Are you kidding me? David didn't argue with his mom. Imagine. Just imagine.

The pain of the event is still very chilling. I remember as much as I remember, but my mind and my heart are always settled when I think about what took place. I know I wasn't asking for trouble. I know I was trying to be helpful and was taken advantage of. I also know I was right to fight back and to get as far away as I could. You'll have to forgive me if I don't apologize for my actions - - today I would have hit him three or four times and stood over his bloody corpse to be really sure he was dead. I wouldn't need my brother, but I may still explain myself to him. He would understand. Today, I pray Dale has accepted Christ, but that doesn't excuse his actions from before he did; I am a survivor, and I will kill. These two things I know about myself. I hope to God that I never have to prove it.

To anyone who has been attacked, who has been violated, I commend every effort on your part to survive and to cope with the aftermath of what is left in our thoughts, our dreams, our lives after having experienced such hardness; it should never happen, but it does. I pray for peace, and I look for peace. I believe through the years; I've found it many times over. I know I raised my girls to think before they act, to be strong and forceful when necessary, and to be mindful of their surroundings. It's the least we can do to create a better tomorrow.

IF YOU or anyone you know is suffering from PTSD, remember, it's not a *"military thing"*; it's a life thing. It happens to many. Ignoring it can be fatal - - at the very least, it can deprive you of the joy you deserve. Seek help. It's out there. Here is a link that may help.

https://www.ptsd.va.gov/gethelp/crisis_help.asp

I'm Good. No, Really. Thank You

I feel like posting or pinning a statement on my Instagram that reads, *"Yeah, no, I'm fine. I don't need or want to date you. I realize you're just phishing for someone out there who will listen to your bullsh*t, but that someone isn't me! Have a great and blessed day. I'm not only out of the market; I never stepped into it. Not shopping for a man! THANKS!"* Lately, maybe the past 2 years, really, almost on a daily basis, I receive a request to chat from some lonely man online (Instagram). First, they're asking me to move over to WhatsApp so we can chat. I typically block or ignore the man, but it makes me question their abilities to read and comprehend what part of "*NO*" was so confusing.

I'm good. Thank you. I don't need or want to date. I have my own place and my own car, and my bank account is positive. I have a dog that loves me. If I want to go out and celebrate or just hang out, I have three really adorable children, and two of them have plus-ones who can join in on the whole fun thing. I have friends I chill with. Since I don't drink, I don't go to bars. Since I don't want to hang out with anyone who may have future plans with me, I don't respond. I'm really not being rude, mean, nasty, or purposely aloof. I've stated it a number of times, and if anyone who REALLY wanted to "*get to know me*" could be so kind as to read the 3000+ Instagram posts, they may realize pretty soon that I'm probably (most likely anyway) not the type of gal they want to call their own. I'm absolutely stubborn, opinionated, strong-willed, thick-skulled, and independent. I'm an intelligent and educated woman, and sometimes I speak (no, wait, I always speak) my mind. I'm not even going to apologize for it. It was what I thought. Why lie?

Recently, a man with whom I have been speaking because we're friends in real life told me that he can see why I'm not married. He had advice for me. I thought about blocking him, but he was sitting in front of me. I thought about walking away, but I drove, and that would leave him stranded. I don't do that. I thought about simply saying, "*No, really, I'm good. Thank you. I don't care why you think I'm single. I'm single because I don't want to be otherwise.*" He ignored my silence and my stare. He went on to tell me, as if I was interested or would be interested, that he believed I was single because I am one of the most hard-headed, obstinate, blunt women who seemingly doesn't need a man for anything other than to open a jar now and again. OK, he may actually be onto something, so I listened. *"Go on,"* I urged him. *"I'm listening"*. You see, it's not that I think I'm all that or so great that all these single dads (usually military or surgeons on Instagram) would want me. I just know it's a scam when I see it.

He said I was a good woman. I was both a Christian and had my head in the game when it came to knowing what I needed financially. These are things that attract people, he told me. He told me that because I was trying to stay in shape and eating correctly, taking the right supplements, talking about better health online, and showing photos of my food intake, I was literally begging men to write to me so I would, in fact, feed them as well, and maybe work out with them, go for a jog, or a walk on that long stretch of beach that people are so apt to talk about when they describe their perfect dating scenarios. I gushed..."*Oh, OK, thanks...I guess*", was my answer. Note to self: men want a woman who can bend over without falling, and they want her to cook. Check.

I asked him why he was still hanging out with me since he knew I wasn't ever going to take him up on going out on a *"real date"* or allow him to buy my dinner. He said I was an interesting subject to observe and to watch and listen to. He said he could absolutely count on me to tell the truth, not to sugar-coat anything, and if I wanted to pay for his dinner, he knew all he had to do was ask. Such a guy! I let him know I needed to get back to my studying of the Series 66, so we should probably head back to the parking lot where he left his car. He smiled.

It's not that I'm anti-men, no, not at all. I love men. Some men are so amazingly brilliant and captivating that I could literally stare and watch them all day. I read about men, research them, study them, observe them, I even dream and fantasize about them, but I just don't want one at this time. Maybe that will change, but there's no chance in Hell or Hades that I'll change the title of my personality or who I am, so that guy better darn well be the ONE, and I'll know he is if and when God says so, not me. I won't make that mistake again. I learn from my past. I don't make the same mistake twice. I'll remain happily and forever single before I settle, compromise, put up with, or deal with someone who just isn't the ONE. Tall order? Well, maybe six feet or so is fine. LOL...sorry, I couldn't resist.

When do we know there's a ONE? We don't. We hope we think, we plan, we imagine, but we can't know. That's where God comes in and makes the choice. If God doesn't tell him and me that he's the ONE...he's not the ONE. If God tells him and not me, you can bet your ass that man is being blocked, ignored, shunned, and never addressed again as long as there is a Sunday on the calendar. If he is the ONE, God will let him know, and God will let me know. The same goes for God telling me. If God tells me that this guy is the ONE, then He will also tell the guy -- I won't approach. I won't tell him what I think. I won't tell him what I think I think. I won't even hint at it because if he's the ONE, he'll tell me, and I will have already been told. I will follow him. WHY? Why would I just do that? Because a woman is supposed to do that for the ONE, but only the ONE.

I'm good. Thank you. I don't need one right now, but if there is ONE, God will dress him all up and present him in such a way that I will have no doubt, and when or if he approaches me, let me know he's the ONE...I will have already been told. That hasn't happened, but my heart and soul are open to God should HE decide I need to respond. Don't hold your breath. I'm likely to be single a bit longer, and really, that's OK. I can keep myself busy with all the plans, dreams, schemes, and decisions I make. In some ways, I feel sorry for the guy whom God pulls aside and says, *"There's your wife; you're welcome."* He's either really screwed up to the point that God is cursing him, or he's been really deeply in need of a loving, kind-hearted, gentle-natured woman who loves unconditionally and whole-heartedly. We'll see. For now, I'm good.

Pyrates Love Their Coffee & Cigars

OK...in true Pyrate style, I have stolen a picture of the two things that make Pyrate Nyte active and worthy. I could have thrown in a picture of a bottle of rum as well, but the point is that I stole the picture - in honor of the Pyrates. We (the Red-headed, Scorpio, Celtic women of the area) are hosting our little party again this weekend. I think...no, I know, it will be fun. I have not, repeat, NOT mastered the technique of hanging upside down on the pole outside while smoking a cigar...I have therefore offered to buy all the necessary coffee, rum, and cigars.

You gotta pay one way or the other, right? I'd rather do it with money rather than embarrass myself again in front of my dogs. Last night was one of those practice nights. 11 bruises to my shins and inner thighs later; well, let's just say I could try out for a cop show as a victim. I'm beat up.

The fact of the matter is I found Rum Runner cigars. This picture isn't of Rum Runner, the only shots I could find of them were smaller, too small to show off the little pyrate on the band. Cute little pyrate, too, I might add. I'll have to have my good friend JD make a little character and draw it up for me so I can frame it. I love framing real art - anytime one of my former students makes me something pretty, I try to keep it. You can KICK the teacher out of the classroom, but you can't take the classroom out of the heart of anyone who loves their kids. Teachers teach... Administrators need to know that. Pyrates rule. Once a Pyrate, always a Pyrate, huh, kids?

This Friday as the cars turn their head lights on I'll be starting it up back at the ranch as they say - this time the ranch being the condo. I'll have the fire brewing, the brew fired, and the whipped cream by the case. We're throwing a little wicked twist to this one...we're allowing men. Someone has to judge the dancing. Someone has to light our cigars; someone has to prepare the feast, and since men don't rightfully believe that a woman knows how to handle a grill - we'll indulge one of that species to do the honors.

Since the pool will be opening, we'll hold off on the rum until after closing that portion of the party down, and let me add this...if you think you've seen sexy, you haven't seen sexy until you see a strong woman smile when she takes exactly what she wants. (Darci will be asking Jason to marry her, and that's the stuff Pyrate Nytes are made for.) He can't say no; if he does, he has to face the gauntlet of women standing before him with crop whips, chains, and toothy smiles.

Fly the flag! Light the fires! Memorial Day should be...remembered. It's too bad we can't all take what we want that night. Smiles and puffs, puffs and smiles....someday. It's the stuff patience is made for. Port Royale wasn't taken in a day. Edinburgh needs a few pyrates to make it saucy.

Sausage Hashbrown Casserole

OK, so I made an amazing casserole, and now everyone wants the recipe. Can you say no when they ask? I can't. Here you go, but you have to follow it, OK, and don't complain to me if you don't do it the same way I did. Here we go. By the way, Happy 120th birthday to my Granny Edwards.

First, start the oven at 375. You have to spray the 9" x 9" glass pan with spray oil so the hash browns don't stick. I use olive oil and try to find it cholesterol-free because I don't like adding cholesterol (she says that but uses pure butter). Then you dump 1/2 a bag of frozen hash browns into it. Don't buy the small bag and then tell me there weren't enough. Get a good-sized bag, something like 20 ounces. I didn't look when I bought it. It's a store brand, nothing fancy.

After the hash browns, you add sprinkle (generously) about 1/3 cup of Parmesan cheese. I'd tell you exactly how much, but I don't usually measure anything. You can grate it if you like. Add about 3 tablespoons or so of Ranch dressing. Again, I don't measure it, so I just squirt it out and drizzle it all over the entire mess. Then add 2 whisked or beaten eggs with 1/4 cup of melted butter. I don't measure the butter, but I know a 1/2 a stick is 1/4 a cup if you buy the type that has 4 sticks in a box. I microwave the butter by itself for about 40 seconds.

After the egg/butter thing, grate or add shredded cheddar. This time, I used white cheddar. You can do whatever your heart desires. I grate enough to cover the top lightly. Then I add the sausage. Sometimes, I tear it up, and other times, I don't. The one in the picture only has 8 patties, so if I was serving 9 people, that would be a problem, but this only served four since we like to eat it, and 8 can be divided by 4 pretty well.

Pop that puppy into the oven (no, you don't get to email me and say I was being cruel to animals; I'm from the South. We say that sort of thing. It's not going to change just because you're offended. You're allowed to be offended.) You cook it for 45 minutes at 375, and depending on your oven, it will be ready around that time. I think I cooked mine for 47-48 minutes today. Then I took it out and let it set for 10 minutes before I dug into it.

The recipe is one I've used for a long time. Some people add half and half, and some people use sour cream instead of Ranch dressing. You can do it with ham, chicken, or turkey, too. You can do it with fish, but I don't think I'd eat it if you did. I'm not going to do that to myself. The famously wonderful Southern restaurant Cracker Barrel has a hash brown casserole, and they do it well; this one is sort of like that one, probably. There's just so much you can do with certain food items. No one holds the patent on how to cook this sort of thing, and if they did, our grannies wouldn't give them the time of day they were asking for. Then again, my granny didn't use frozen hash browns.

There you go, that's it. That's the big ol' secret to what I had for breakfast today. I started posting what I was eating, and so many wanted to talk about it. I'm sure they can do the same thing(s) I'm doing. Some folks just need a nudge, and others need a push. Pinterest is a great place to get recipes and ideas if you're thinking you want to do something special for someone or for yourself, but you just can't figure out what it is that you want to do. Try that!

Hope you have a good one! I have been thinking of ways to revamp my pulled pork, too; thinking of adding peppers and green onion and serving it on a big fat 1/2 a bagel.

Well, Fudge

This is the last blog of 2023! OMG....I can't believe it. Tomorrow, if I do blog, it will be considered my first blog of the new year!! So crazy!! If you're in America, the date is 123123, but that isn't for anyone else; we do write out dates differently here.

Anyway, the day was very lazy, just so beautiful in so many ways. I don't have plans to go overseas. I don't have plans to ring in the new year at some over-crowded venue such as Times Square, Princes Street, or even downtown OKC...nope, I'm just going to probably go to bed around 12:05 a.m. after I write to my three kids and say *"Happy New Year, I love you"* in text messages. To say I'm rather boring is probably rather accurate, but then again, I'm not with anyone special today, no reason to *"ring in"* anything other than just be happy with me! Just me and Jesus! (and my dog)

I decided to make fudge, which, if you've never done it, will make you think twice about making it from scratch. Is it worth it? I don't know. It's cheaper, but it's not an easy thing to do, really, not when you read all the things you have to do in order to make it set up correctly and then behave itself. Mine didn't. I'll go into it, but it's funny how I even decided to do it.

I went shopping the other day with the thought of maybe doing it, but I thought to myself, I won't need condensed milk. I think I saw three or four cans in the cupboard; I only need one. I remembered I only use condensed milk around the holidays when I make things such as fudge - - but I couldn't remember having done that in a few...wait...had it been a few years? Were those cans that old? Yep!! The youngest one was in 2016.

I threw out the six cans, not four, and I laughed myself silly over it. I found a recipe online that used actual milk and sugar, and even though I knew there would be an added step because of it, I thought I could handle it. I laugh now because I didn't really handle it. I fudged it. (LOL) No, really, I made the worst fudge, and you could even call it sludge!! I will not let that fact stop me from eating it - - nope, I am on a quest now.

I had dark chocolate chips, butter, sugar, half and half, vanilla, bourbon whiskey, cayenne pepper powder, and honey. Let me just tell you - - it's some hot mess. Yes, yes, it is, but I enjoy every bit of it. I'll be eating on this thing for two weeks I'm sure, but that's OK too. I'll make the sacrifice. I'll make it happen, and when I do, I'll think of all those poor folks who have to share their fudge with others. No one is stepping up to the plate to share mine. No one.

I melted the chips in the butter, added the half and half, brought it to a boil, added vanilla, bourbon (the liquor is cooked out), and then the sugar, and finally, the honey, bourbon, and pepper. I stirred. I stirred a lot. I let it boil again, but apparently, I didn't let it stir long enough. I poured it into a lightly greased 9x9 glass pan and put it in the fridge. When it hadn't set in 3 hours, I poured it all back into the pot, brought it to a boil again, and this time, I stirred it for 18-20 full minutes, just like the recipe said...at a boil.

I did the whole "*soft ball*" test, where you drop a tidbit into a bit of water to see if it balls up. To my surprise, it did. There we go. I let it set for 2 minutes, poured it back into the cleaned, re-greased 9x9 pan, and put it back into the fridge to set - - but it just sort of thickened. It really never did what everyone else's fudge does. I had to use a fork to pry it out of the pan because using a knife only made the sticky mess you can imagine that it made. Yes, the fork is the choice utensil at this point.

After a few bites, I decided that even if no one else was brave enough to join me, I'll be happy as a clam just digging into it, pulling it out, sucking the sludgy goo sediment all the way to the silver prongs of my handy-dandy fork. I'm 100% OK not sharing it; no really, it's not that difficult of a task to just be the only person willing or present to indulge. I'm pretty sure it pairs well with just about anything I decide to eat with it. I may try to ice my popped corn chips with it. I may try to spread it on toast. I may just spoon it out if I think a fork isn't sufficient for my needs. I am not above trying new methods.

Trust me when I say that fudge is not the easiest thing to make. I've been having "*kitchen*" issues lately with my oven not baking evenly, and some of my cookies coming out browner on the bottom than they do on the top! Not a happy camper! I gave the oven a rest and took it to the stove today, and this happened. I believe it is a fitting way to leave the year 2023 behind and to look forward to making things happen in 2024. I don't care what the world dishes out to me; I'm going to take it, make it mine, and turn it around doing what I need to do until it suits my fancy!

Bring it 2024...I'll put a fork in you! You're done!

Experimenting in the Kitchen

If you know me, you know the characters in my novels often "*experiment*" with different feelings, actions, emotions, or whatever so they can feel and experience life on a new level. I can honestly tell you that I often have one or more of my books. People actually do or attempt to do what I really have done, or maybe what I think I want to do. That sort of experimenting is not limited to the kitchen; not for them, and not for me. The only limitation I have (and have had for 25 years) is that I don't have a partner to play with - - but I do in my head, so I'm good. (He's really cute too. His name is Craig Allan Mackenzie, and he's about 500 years old. He's from up around Oban, Scotland, and he's...really...yeah, he's great.)

Anyway, so here I am today, in reality, in my kitchen, thinking I want to do something in a very different way for the Christmas dinner table. I say that, but Laura and I haven't even set up our tree. We haven't hung garlands or any lights either. I did find a door hanger with bells and put that out for the cats, but they really don't care at this point. They probably never really cared, to be honest with you.

I decided to try a "*dump*" cake, using 1/2 package of a basic white or yellow cake mix, poured over canned fruit, with added butter and cinnamon, but this time, I went with 1/2 can of pumpkin with 1/2 bar of cream cheese and an egg. We'll see if it works. I have no idea. It may or may not, but what the heck? It's fun to try something new. It could be really cool. It could be a huge mess, but what do you want to bet I'll end up eating it anyway? I will.

Craig absolutely loves it when I experiment. He heard from the ethereal grapevine that I was about to experiment, and always the keen and quick man for the job, he presented himself as he usually does, which is in the process of unwrapping his kilt before removing it, folding it, and setting it to the side so we can experiment together. He wasn't upset that I had chosen the kitchen for my foreplay, but he was wondering if we would have room on the floor itself or if up against the wall would be a better location for us to...stir and cream the mix before putting it into the oven.

What I did was, (without Craig's assistance) was to empty the large can of pumpkin, 1/2 of it into my mixing bowl, and the other 1/2 into a container for refrigeration. There was no sense in using the entire can if my fantasy - - I mean, thoughts, weren't going to pan out the way I had hoped. Sometimes my mind can be really enthusiastic, and I become so blinded by my pleasurable activities in my mind that I forget that some things need to be put back to chill for a minute. No use in wasting anything - - waste not, want not.

I added an egg to the bowl and 1/2 a bar of cream cheese. I blended it together and placed it into a loaf pan. Loaf pans are about nine inches long. Some are glass, some are metal, and some are made of rubber or silicone. It's a preference thing; I like glass myself. (Easier to clean) After the mix is in the pan, you cut up slices of butter, maybe 8 pieces. You want to be sure and add enough butter to really slick things up and cover the entire surface of your...area.

When you do that, you spice it up a bit!! Make sure it's level, spread out nicely, and then sprinkle sugar and cinnamon for that leather and lace effect. I don't know if you know about leather and lace effects in the kitchen, but they work the same there as they do in any room where you're "*cooking*" or otherwise pretending to. I may light a lilac and a lavender candle at the same time. I may add mango to my tomato salsa; you just need to play around with your options and find out what works best for you. When it comes to baking anything with pumpkin, I will add sugar and spice - - usually cinnamon, but I am not above defaulting to nutmeg - - I will go there.

Finally, for the top, you dump the cake mix. You just dump it right there, right in front of God and everyone. You don't have to dress it, but I will add more sugar and cinnamon and even a bit more butter if I think I may need to make it a bit more moist; that can be nice, too. Again, preferences. It's all about preferences.

Heating it up is important, of course. If you preheat - - you know, "*fore*" the oven temp up to the degree you want it, or where it should be; in this case, 375 or 400, you'll find that working with the whole kit and kaboodle becomes easier to do. You're introducing your loaf into a very receptive range, one where all the bakers can be pleased. Time passes, things settle into place, and after about 30 minutes of it, a smile is brought to your face - - the deed is done. It may take longer. You decide.

Of course, it could be that it may need some time to cool before you plunge into it again - - think about it; don't burn yourself. That's never fun, and it would or possibly could mean bringing on an entirely different fantasy - - thought process; playing doctor can be fun, too.

Enjoy your pumpkin dump cake. Oh, and Craig had a great idea; he suggested you throw in some nuts...just maybe a couple or so.

The Gourmet In Me

I always say I'm not a gourmet cook because I have never been properly trained to be one. I can take a recipe, follow it, and tweak it, and I can make really good food. I know this, but there's just something about saying (out loud anyway) that I'm a gourmet that makes me feel really arrogant. I was, however, thinking it in my head just the other day when I went out to dinner with friends and spent far too much for far too little food, and the quality was good but not brilliant. I was saying in my head and to myself, "*You could have done that so much better* ."The thing is, I could, but is that the point? I mean, it could be the point if you're trying to compete, but I don't compete. I don't do the whole chef thing or the *beat-them-at-their-own-game* thing. I just cook really good food.

Today, I was interested in doing something a bit different, and I found a recipe for something that I hadn't tried before. It seemed extreme, and in the end, it has a bit of a kick to it, but not in a bad way. It's more of a zest than a hot, so I'm OK with it. I will survive. One thing I don't do is hot, spicy food; sorry, it's just not gonna happen. I'll make it for someone else, but I can't taste it to see if it turned out or not. My belly says no, my bowels agree with my belly, and then I'm on the floor dying. It's not pretty, and no, it's just not gonna happen. Today's event was intriguing enough for me.

I made what Pinterest referred to as Italian Slow-cooked Chicken. It called for a full cup of zesty Italian dressing; I think I could have been OK with only 1/2 a cup. It called for a full bar of cream cheese. Again, I think I could have been OK with using only 1/2 of the bar for the four pieces of chicken breasts that I ended up cooking. I let them all heat and simmer together with another 1/2 cup of parmesan cheese and onion spices before I added the celery and basil. It's really good, I'm not going to lie, but next time (and there will be a next time) I will cut the ingredients in half. I did use some of the drippings in the rice cooker to make the rice, so we'll see how that turns out. I'm thinking it will be pretty great.

One thing about the slow cooker is that you can literally turn it on and leave it. You can simmer a brisket for 10-12 hours in the hickory and smoke sauce. You can cook your stews for 4-6 hours (don't forget a little baking soda to tenderize the meat). The chicken doesn't need any extra assistance; the heat and the vinegar in the dressing are enough to break it up sufficiently for your meal. After I eat this meal, I'll take the leftover chicken, shred it, and use it in a chicken salad panini sandwich tomorrow. If that's not on Pinterest, it should be. I may add it. I can you know, I'm not above that.

One of the reasons, in fact, the #1 reason why I tend to cook at home rather than go out to restaurants to get fine dining is, of course, the cost. The chicken dinner I had with friends was over $27 for my meal, and when I say I was upset about it, you haven't seen me upset until you get me to pay $27 for 1/2 a breast of chicken and less than a 1/2 cup of rice with a few green and yellow vegetables adding up to maybe a 1/3 of a cup if stacked on top of each other. They didn't even include bread with the meal; it was an appetizer.

They did drizzle the sauce on the plate and add little dots to make it appear chic and edgy. Yeah, I'm not interested. The atmosphere was louder than it should have been; I may as well have stayed home and listened to the dogs play or kept the television on in the background. (For those of you who don't know me, I don't watch TV I may watch a show online, but the TV stays off most of the time unless the weatherman is really excited about something.)

Yeah, I'm not an official gourmet. I just have really good spices and good timing, I guess. I was trained by the kids who were learning at Pratt's Culinary College back in 2003. I was their Gen. Ed teacher. I can say that! They trained the heck out of me for all the extra credit they could get. I know how to use the system!! I learned a great deal, they learned a great deal, and we all ate well. It's a win-win. I will say this: I won't go out with friends and spend $$$$ again. I'll invite them over and let them eat my food, and we can spend the money going to the Oklahoma City Zoo and walking it off. That's a much better plan!!

Grammarly is a Thing

After not doing such a great job of editing my works from the past three or four (OK, nine) books, I decided to bite the bullet and buy a monthly subscription to Grammarly. Remember, I'm only doing this for the month, and then I'll likely buy a year's subscription because it is so worth the money. (They can pay me to say that so that I get it for free if they want to.) Grammarly is kicking my butt, but I am loving it.

So, there I was, here I am, thinking I know what the heck I'm doing when it comes to writing and applying the correct punctuation, but no, I suck. I suck so badly that even when I'm typing this, there are red lines under the words. You can't see them; they are there. I'm making corrections, and you'll never even realize I did. This is the power and the magic of Grammarly.

I told myself over the past 9 books I wrote that I don't need it; I can do my own editing. I lied to myself. I didn't lie to the audience; I lied to myself. If and when I have the money and time, I'll pull all the other books and run each chapter at a time through Grammarly's AI and make changes before uploading them again. It should have been done before, but to be honest with you, when I uploaded the chapters in the past, I didn't realize that Grammarly was a paid subscription. I thought it only lets you make 100 corrections, and then you make your own. It was a tutor of sorts. (It's not; it's a flat fixer, and you should buy it.)

I'm doing the one-month thing now as it is $30 a month, which, for me, is expensive. I'll do the yearly subscription soon. It's only $12 a month, but you do have to pay for it one year at a time, so $144. But...and this is huge, it is worth it. It is worth every penny of it. I'm finding so many tiny and more significant mistakes. I'm correcting about 87% of them because I want some of the things I said to remain as they are to reflect a character's voice or attitude. I intentionally misspelled some things when I wrote.

For example, I'll say "*gonna*" or "*hangin' around*." Those are not really supposed to be written out that way, and they would not be used in a white paper, but they can be used in an informal novel. I'm seriously going to write a white paper, though, just to add the genre to the mix of things I've written. I'm that way. Getting back to the Grammarly thing, I'm on Chapter 4 of "1211" right now, pushing it through the AI, and it shows a potential 122 mistakes! WHAT? In one chapter? Well, let's be fair; much of it was spacing because I do the two spaces after a sentence, and apparently, you don't have to do that now. I do that.

I overuse the semi-colon, and the AI tells me so. I underuse the comma, and the AI tells me so. I have run-on sentences, which I KNOW I do, so the AI helps me write to clarify. I appreciate that. I also drop letters off of words because I'm typing and not thinking. I'll say "*his*" for "*this*" or "*as*" for "*has*" or "*was*," and the AI will find my errors. I love this thing. I really do love it. Feel free to get it or to use it. It has been so enjoyable to find out exactly how wrong I have been and am currently. I don't mind changing my ways; it's hard sometimes.

I've got to get back to it. Have a great Valentine's DAY!! I hope you have the best of times and get as much chocolate as you expected.

Mentally Speaking

I am about to write a book (I will not reveal the title until it is produced) wherein I will discuss mentality, mental illness, mental awareness, and the invisible wounds, scars, and disabilities that rise up and hold people hostage from life. Whether it is because they don't or can't see their worth, or because others can't see or refuse to see their worth, the fact is some are in fact essentially invisible, ignored, overlooked, and even (sadly) dismissed.

The book will reveal industries, entire industries that choose to ignore people, and even those people they have sworn oaths to assist and protect. The book will shed light, shine exposure, and peel back the corners to blatantly put the blame where it should be put and, in some cases, surprise the world with what I can show so boldly.

Some have told me not to write the book. I've been told I'll be threatened if I do. I'm writing it as a fiction novel; there will be no real names, real corporations, or real attachments to what I suppose or suggest. I'm holding out a light and lifting it up so that you, the reader, can see for yourself what is literally all around you. You're in your car; you're next to them. You're shopping at the store, you're next to them? Who? Who are you next to, you ask. You're next to the invisible people, and you're next to those who purposely don't see them. My desire for my audience is that they LOOK.

When you look, when you see, when you hear, when you listen, and when you understand, you'll be in a better position, hopefully, to either lend a hand, say a prayer, or make small changes that can affect everyone. We're here at this time for a reason; not one of us knows how long we're allowed to remain here. There will be a judgment for all of us, not for punishment necessity, but for blessings poured upon us for having made the right choices to be there for someone else without expecting anything in return. We are to love, and this book is about that about love.

I think it was Albert Einstein who said that if we "... *judge fish by their abilities to climb a tree, it will believe its entire life that it is stupid.*" Take me, a woman with a Ph.D. and the ability to write a 390-page book in under two weeks, and you put me in a room with an orchestra on the stage. You can't compare my worth or my experiences. I would be lost. I have no talents that could compare or be useful in that room. I am only as worthy as I see or know myself to be, and if I allowed myself to think I was worthless because I couldn't play an instrument, read music, or make extraordinary sounds, I would be depressed and anxious, wondering why I was so damaged.

We, all of us, are wonderful. We are all genuinely genuine and creatively creative. We are bountiful with our own us-ness, we are unique and singular. This book, I pray, will allow someone (even if it's only one person) to know that you are not alone, you are not unseen, you are not worthless, you are not invisible. You are not less; you are not reduced or void. You have everything you need to be the one thing you were created to be, and that is YOU. I'm the only me that I could ever be, and that's a good thing - - there should not be two of me out there.

Stay tuned. I'll keep you posted.

Waxing a Bit Nostalgic

I just watched a YouTube video showcasing the differences between the kids born and raised in the 60s and 70s and those born in the mid-2000s (Gen Z). The whole video had me laughing, shaking my head, agreeing with the guy narrating the thing, and saying *"Yes!"* or *"You're damn right"* on most of it.

Times were different. We went to church. We walked to school with or without our friends (my first-grade teacher lived across the street, so yeah, I made it to class on time. She walked me from Kindergarten to fifth grade every single day! She carried a Winchester rifle, too, and yes, we shot game hens and rabbits on the way to and from school. Not lying.) Mrs. Earp's husband was related to THE Earps. She was rough and tough, to boot.

As kids, we didn't try to get in trouble. We were quite aware that if we got in trouble at school, we would get in more trouble at home. At the parent-teacher conference, the kids sat out in the hall, and we were told to stay quiet. If my parents had come out of the room and I wasn't sitting right where they left me, I would not be able to sit down for two Sundays in a row. It was that way. My teachers never lied. They didn't give me any grade I didn't deserve, and they never made excuses for me either. Ethics were a thing in our day.

Some of the more dangerous things we did as kids have been talked about and demonstrated in so many YouTube and TikTok videos. We slid down hot galvanized steel slides that were banked on concrete and had rivets sticking out where the rails were connected. We scalded ourselves, fell off, and scraped our knees, hands, heads,

174

and elbows. We got over it. We used the water from a garden hose to wash off, and if we were thirsty, we drank from it. We rode in cars without seat belts, with our parents smoking in the car, and maybe - - just maybe one of them would roll the window down an inch or so to let the smoke out, but not in the summer; they couldn't afford to let the cool air out.

We became spit-friends and blood-brothers, even if we were girls. We cut our hands or fingers and mushed them together, swearing our oaths to remain besties forever. I think I am still keeping that promise with Jeannie -- so they did actually work. We were given pocket knives around the age of six or seven and guns around the age of nine or ten. We were taught to use both. I think my dad taught me that I could kill, gut, and skin a fish or a squirrel with my knife - - and he may have mentioned that if a boy tried to kiss me, I could do the same to him.

We tried out for sports and for cheerleading. We weren't accepted just because we showed up. We had to keep our grades above a B, not a C...and if we dared to show our faces with a C on our report cards, we had to do the dishes and take out the trash all the way through the next nine weeks until the subsequent reports came back with better grades. It just was the way that it was.

We played "*Pin the Tail on the Donkey*" with a stick pin that was run through a ribbon. We were spun around in circles a dozen times and set loose to try and find the paper with the donkey on it, and we were blindfolded. There is no end to what could have happened and most likely did. We snuck drinks from our dad's beers and finished off mom's coffee at tender ages. We were swimming in lakes, ponds, and creeks with the fish, turtles, gars, and whatever else decided to show up. I remember tossing a snake at my sister when it swam in front of me.

There were trees to climb, and I'm not talking about lower branches. If you were caught sitting on a lower branch, you better have a book in your hands; otherwise, you called a chicken. We threw dirt clods that were hard as rocks at each other from greater heights and chased the culprits down the streets on our bikes without caring if a car was in front of us or behind us. We knew the drivers had eyes and could see us. I don't remember having a set of lawn darts, but we played it when we went to my cousins' houses. Yes, we tried to spike each other; it's what you did.

Another thing we did was ring doorbells and run away, or we'd ring them and stand there waiting for friends to come out and play. We rang doorbells to hear them chime. We usually got a look from the father or mother of the kid we just said goodbye to, but sometimes, other people's doorbells were cooler than mine were. We prank-called people, too. You know we did. We didn't do all the mean, nasty, sinister stuff like telling people they had three days to live. No, we just said things like, "*Hey, is your fridge running? Better catch it!!*" We were dorks. We were really cool, though.

Our skates strapped right onto our tennis shoes, and we had to tighten them with a key. They were metal, and the wheels were metal, too. The tire swings we affixed to our trees hadn't been cleaned, and if it rained, it rained, and we dealt with the water sloshing all over us. We nibbled on the tar that the city crews laid down on our streets, but not before we popped all the bubbles. What? It didn't get hot enough where you live to have your street tar bubble up? Well, sometimes you had to use a stick so you didn't get burned. Do you know what else we had back then? We had horny toads. (Brown Texas Horned Toads) They were everywhere.

I miss those kids. I miss that my kids were probably the last age of kids to have spit fights, impromptu mud-wrestling, or sleepovers. Times have changed, but not for the better. I can't wait to get to heaven and do these things again -- maybe not the door-knocking thing, but yeah...the door-knocking thing, too. I'll do it.

Judy (nearly 6), Melissa (Missy) Parker (4), and Robin Hatt (nearly 6) I'm babysitting Missy and Robin now   Oct 1967

POEMS

Kaleidoscope

His grey eyes fixed on mine
Not understanding my heart
Not comprehending my reason

He asked, and I listened
"How can you love me?
How could you even?"

Words were there but lost
Between my gaze and soul
Words were not enough

"I'm broken, he said.
Completely without anything
I'm not who you think I am"

"You are broken," I answered
"Not like an umbrella
One would cast away if so,

"You are broken like stained glass
Which after it is gathered
Becomes a Kaleidoscope"

Raku

Choosing to love him was not my choice
The fire broke everything I believed I controlled
The air that surrounded me disappeared
I was left to smolder in the coals

Formed, I was. Treated as mere thick clay
Never giving my consent, only shown the end
Told, more than asked. I was led, I was worked
Milled and shaped, pounded even, hardened

Why me God? I beg to know Your mind
Why should I continue rolling in searing flame
To become the pot, the vase, the urn?
Will You use me then? Will I hold? Embrace?

You are the Potter. I am your clay. I know this
You choose, I listen. You will, I bow
The prayers, the time, the years, the faith
I understand You've planned, I follow

Until the last pyre I remain incomplete
Knowing there will be blessings, I agree
Knowing he needs me to continue
To lift his soul through the pain of my own firing

You are the Potter. I am your clay.
My destined colors will forge with time
Your strength is given in my making
I am who You have decided to create

If my mission is to pray, I bow my head
Your command is well within my power
Power given by the One and accepted in whole
Raku me. To be the vessel You desire

Entreated

What colors do I see?
When I think of you?
Could there be a shade
Sweet enough to be expressed?

Am I bound by a veil so lovely
At the very sight of you?
Are you captured by my
Heart's eyes – unimaginable?

What sound is it that I hear
As your voice dances on air?
As your presence leans upon
My soul to rest.

How I am lured by the melody
By the symphony, by the lyrics
By the chords played evenly
By our hands.

What anchors my very being
To the thought of you each time?
Each time I am drawn without force
Held captive by music, by love.

Him

I could tell you that I love you
Or maybe write it in a poem
I could wrap my arms around you
Or whisper a sweet hymn

Will you ever truly be mine
Is my soul to ever rest
My joy is the hope
My happiness – your bliss

Could I mention you in passing
Would it be of any use
I'm not sure if you could love me
So why go through the hurt

I could tell you that I love you
Or let the days pass on
I could be there when you need me
If that is all you want.

I wear the mask completely
No one would ever know
I must be like a sidekick
I may even be a joke

I could tell you that I love you
Would you even hear
Could you ever understand
My heart is not my friend

Amethyst Sky

I lay beneath Heaven at her dusk
Hues too vast to hold
Lifts of pale blue, turning mauve
Eventide sings his song

Grace, for an hour, accompany me
Teach me to be still
Patient evening bear with me
Let conscience guide your will

Share all manner of meditation
Finesse and poise my thought
Ease your gentle-mannered ways
Through my senses, giving hope

Ornate vault of heaven, gloss
Your hours of colors pass
Amethyst blankets hold each star
In place, in time, en masse

Sleep begins her soft barrage
Inviting me to dance
Invasion of the sweetest sort
Two steps and I am gone

You

How can I sleep when
Fairies are dancing
When the keys of your piano float
        into the sky?

How will I dream when
Your touch lingers in my soul
Your fingers tickle my very breath
        Each stroke new

Where will my slumber take me
"Dancing on the Light?"
"I'm Missing You Now"

Touch is deeper than your kiss
Air becomes my song
Music, coursing through my veins
        I want you.

Slowly drifting, slink into one
Our bodies feeling every note
No words, soft saxophones cry
        We are one

My Jesus

Grace, grace, God's grace
Grace, I don't deserve
I peer upon the King's face
And to know I'm heard

I come to God's throne
With bended knee so low
I can know He'll always
Welcome me back Home.

Faith, faith, God's faith
Faith abundant, free
Held within my heart's heart
I know that He loves me

Never will I understand
The price He paid that day
Why a King would leave His throne
To end up in the grave.

Erupting from the grips of death
To put it all to rest
No other name lives on and on
The King, my King, Jesus.

Praise, praise, God's praise
Blessings I will sing
Endless days of singing
Endless love He gave

Me Mutter

Well, there she goes
Just 'a walkin' down the street
Singing this and that and
Whatever else she wants - - BECAUSE
She is me Mutter.

Some may know her
Some know her smile
Some don't give a damn but
It's OK because she don't either
She is me Mutter

There's another poem out there
One about a mom
This is one about mine and
No one else's, except my sibs
She is OUR Mutter

I love the stuffin' out of her
Think she's pretty daft
Think she's smart as hell too
At the same time, she's all that
She is me Mutter

Not one to mess or fart around
Maybe just a toot or two
She can paint and laugh and sing
But mostly she just smiles and loves
She is, and will always be...Me Mutter.

Ruled By Heart

I couldn't ever start to know
The cravings of my heart
Her drum in me beats on its own
She lays out her own desires
I am forced to do her bidding
By fear that she may stop
If left alone she'd harden
Her need for me is soft

We fit together - harmonized
True, she rules us both
If she decides to fall again
If she desires to love
I won't fall, but have to wait
Wait until she frees me
I won't fall, but have to hope
Hope that she releases

I have but one heart to serve
She has but me to rule
Strange, our timing always off
Her silent beat abuses
Clinching to the next dreamt scheme
Silent beats - such thunder
Serve I will, devoted warrior
Pray she does not wander

Terra Cotta Man

Branded in my stony soul
His lamps – his eyes – so green
A terra cotta man
          The best I've ever seen

Through strength is nowhere near me
I feel his presence clear
Even in his absence
          The silence often jeers

What passion could persuade me
To fall so fast within
My dreaming – full of visions
          Every glance is him

Eyes that linger haunting
Stare brazen emerald rays
A terra cotta man
          What beauty – perfect grace

Waiting, waiting, yearning
Reasons burning white
Coals of wonder hearting
          My heart – both day and night

Waiting, wanting, fever
Fading, rise, and rage
Terra cotta man
          How then – can I wait

Green glowing beams stare through me
Their hold is so unknown
This terra cotta man
More love for him unfolds

Grandpa

He's old, his eyes were ninety-one
Before he closed them tight
His laughing smile told me tales
I promised to keep quiet

The fishing pole he'd always hold
Remained the best at catch
He seemed to call fish to his hook
No matter where he sat

And with one leg to prop himself
The man would scoot and climb
He'd tend his garden every years
The work took all his might

The loving man would watch me grown
And sit me on his knee
He'd kiss me once, and laugh out loud
Then kiss me two, then three

So many stories of the past
He held within his heart
He'd seen the pulling of the plow
The making of the car

I'm sure like all, he had to sin
I know he had his faults,
But never once in front of me,
I love you still - Grandpa

Embraced Darkness

Sounds of whispered blackened ruins
Your voice – soft – in sketches
Tracing once the rim of light
Now leers – empty darkness
Full aces hazed by dreaming eyes
Catch glimpses – only shadows
My enemy must be the Night
I wait – she brings her gallows

Embracing me by fear and strength
Her hours hold and tease me
The way I feel I fall in dreams
Circling, spinning, catch me!
Visions only stay a while
The morning sun erasing
Rescuring my betrayed soul
Slow tears – remembering

Remembering the things that were
The Night – she will be back
Torturing me again until
I run from her attack
But when she dances with her skirt
Twirling, gracefully spinning
I fall to her - - I lose my heart
Love forever winning

Jude Stringfellow

Tangible Shadows

Gone are the valleys of dreaming
Run away with the visions so clear
Daisies and roses once dancing
Surrender their grace when you're near

Not a flower could stand in your shadow
Your beauty would put them to shame
Your colors, your wonders – so many
Not a field, or a meadow could claim

Green leaves fall at your footsteps
Birds quiet their song
They know one whisper from you
Would prove all their lyrics were wrong

Love, it's so easily mistaken
Time, it was ours for a while
Memories, all for the keeping
Tears edge the lines of my smile

Gone are the touches you offered
Run away with the fears you would go
Daisies and roses weep fragrance
What I feel – somehow – they know

Little Poems

Little poems and power plays
Words that cut and dance
Haiku wit – immortalized
Papered ink enhanced

Whispered wills and twisted fate
A few more puns won't hurt
A smile for now, a wink or two
Dare I say – a flirt

This world is mine, I claim it well
I write a nightly journal
With peevish joy I steal the boy
But leave him for the real world

It's just a play thing that I do
I make up worlds for scheming
Nothing real, just a thrill
My writings are just dreaming

A quick thought here, I jot it down
A little poem or prose
Perhaps I'll tell you what I think
I may -- but I will choose

Little poems and power plays
Rewards I think so charming
Hardened hearts are not allowed
Into my world so cunning

PART 2

Murder in the Blue Room

I decided to watch a couple of older movies that deal with murder so I can get a few ideas for my new novel "*1211*". It's going to be to research this way; I love old cheesy movies anyway, and those that have murder as a theme make me smile. I'm not smiling because there's a murder, per se, but you know what I mean. There are always detectives wearing Fedora hats, and women with stupid expressions! I love it.

Universal Pictures put out a film in 1944 with June Preisser and others. The movie is "*Murder in the Blue Room*", and it didn't disappoint. It was cheesy, it was lame, it was one of the worst films out there in terms of actual acting, but let me just say I loved it. I'll recommend it to anyone who wants to spend an hour of their day watching dance routines, listening to old tunes, and trying to figure out the plot.

I'll admit, I knew who the killer was almost right away, but I didn't see some of the twists that were thrown at me. I didn't particularly like the "*ghost*" as he was not only faker than fake, he was just too - - well, lame. I can't find another word, even though I have already used it. The ghost was lame for sure. He's not needed or necessary, but he's there, and it does make you shake your head and giggle - - so maybe he did his part.

June Pressier is the smaller of the three "*actors*" who come and perform for the guests in the house. She is an amazing acrobat and performer. She used to dance in the streets to get money for her family back in the late '20s. Just such an amazing soul - - look her up on

Wikipedia and learn something fun. Here's the link: https://en.wikipedia.org/wiki/June_Preisser

When you have nothing else to do - - and you're not even writing a sequel to a murder book, you too can watch the movie on YouTube and just laugh a little. I'd suggest grabbing some popcorn and making a thing of it. Don't expect too much, OK? Don't think it's gritty, gutsy, or even glamorous. It's pretty...well, I shouldn't use the word "*lame*" again, but there it is. It's lame, but it's amazingly so. I loved it.

Now, I can come up with a few cheesy things for my characters in "*1211*" to do or say. I like having real inspiration and being able to credit it. I will too!! I'll write something in the book about the movie, even though the movie doesn't take place until 1944 and my book is placed around 1931...I can figure it out. I can make it happen. If nothing else, I'll leave a link in the back of the book - - and I guess I can leave it here too. Enjoy! ("*Murder in the Blue Room*")

https://www.youtube.com/watch?v=CsHnvXj22FU

Making Clotted Cream

This could be the single most important thing I do all week. I am about to make clotted cream. I will start it at 7:45 a.m. tomorrow morning, and by 7:45 p.m. tomorrow evening it will be done, but I will have to let it set out until it cools to room temperature, and just before going to bed tomorrow night, I'll pop it in the fridge and it will be ready for me on Friday morning. Can't wait.

HOW you may ask, does one make clotted cream? I can't believe you're asking me that when the real question is, WHAT is clotted cream? Well, clotted cream is the best thing ever and it goes on anything you can think of that you may add butter too; and more things than that even. Clotted cream is literally just heavy whipping cream baked, cooled, and scooped. There is ONE ingredient in clotted cream, and that's...well, cream. It's heavy whipping cream in the United States and in the UK they call it "*Double Cream*". They have it pasteurized and extra or ultra-pasteurized, but to do the clotted cream correctly you'll just need the regular heavy whipping cream or double cream, nothing too fancy.

Using a glass rectangular or square glass pan (glass works best) you'll pour the cream into the pan without spraying any oil into it. You just pour it straight in and you pour it about 1.5 inches thick before popping it into the oven at 175 degrees F or 80 degrees C. You bake it for literally 12 hours, but I check it around the 10-hour mark to see if it's about done. I've been known to take it out at 10, not lying. Then, after you take it out, and it has the light golden colored (tiny bit) thicker top, you can use a spoon to take a bit off the top to see if it's nice and creamy (thick and spreadable) underneath. You'll set it on the cabinet or table where the cat can't get to it, you may have to put it inside the microwave until it cools to about room temperature. I find that it takes 2 hours to do that. Then just send it to the fridge to cool off completely.

SUCH a good thing. In grocery stores in the U.S., if you can find it, it is about $9 for a very small amount. Whole Foods is the only place I know that has it, and yes, it was $8.99. In the U.K. I bought it for about $3.50 (USD) and it was a bit larger, maybe 15-18 ounces vs the 6 oz jar I got at Whole Foods. A good quart-size carton of heavy cream is about $4.00 USD and will make about 15-18 ozs or so, you will need a container to put it in. Maybe save an old butter tub. WORTH IT.

NOW...here's the deal. You have a top or a shelf of clotted cream at the top, and the underneath liquid is there to use to make biscuits or scones. Yep, you don't throw it out, you use it. The skimmed topper is the clotted cream you've been waiting for. Lift it, scoop it out, and put it in a container to use. Be sure to have a lid or a way to cover it.

If you've never had clotted cream, you are absolutely missing out. If you just won't try it because the name *"clotted cream"* sounds bad, think of it as roasted heavy cream; that may help you out a bit. Just tell people you're British and need this to keep you going. They may understand. It really, no really, is really very good...really. You can add jam, jelly, and cheese, you don't have to add anything. I top my bagels, biscuits, cookies, pies, just anything - - but it does add calories; you should know that.

OK there you go, one more thing off my list of things to make on Pinterest that has been super great and wonderful. I will likely update the photo when I make mine, but for now, you get the one I found online. Enjoy!!

UPDATE: So, I baked it for 12 hours at 175 but think it needs to stay in another hour or so. I raised the temperature to 200 as my oven may be a bit less heated than others, but there is a nice soft golden crust. I think it will be great.

My Opinion. Not Necessarily Yours.

I have friends and family, sometimes just people I meet, who say things like, "*You shouldn't think that way*" or maybe they'll phrase it differently, they'll say, "*Well, that's not right, you can't possibly believe that.*" I know they mean well, I do. I think they want me to have the best the world has to offer, etc., but the thing is, I am the only me I can be, and no matter how long we are left on this planet, my opinions will always be MINE and I don't mind sharing them, but you can't force them out of me just because we disagree.

I try really really hard not to sound the same as they do, not to commit the very folly I find them distributing so freely. I try to be open, and I try to be understanding. If it goes against GOD then we may have an issue; but the issue is I won't agree ever and we'll just have to agree to disagree. God is always right.

Let me give you a few examples so you'll know exactly how very crazy I am. There are gifted people in this world who are either musicians, artists, writers, singers, etc., and in their very essence they are incapable of being clerks, doctors, lawyers, engineers, or anything resembling anything other than who and what they are. There may be a talented engineer who also plays piano, but he or she is capable of making a living as an engineer, whereas the artist may or may not be.

He or she is true to his or her own craft and if they make a living they make a living, but if they don't we need to help them. OK, there is it...I just said WE need to help them. Most, if not all of my friends and family, and yes, those randoms on the street, will say to me, "*No, we don't have to help them, they can get off their ass and get a job.*" This is where we differ. I don't believe these souls can actually function in those other capacities other than who and what they are. They are rare. They are few. We can help them, so we can continue to benefit from their God-given talents.

I'm not talking about the people who are both talented and capable of taking on other jobs. I'm ONLY talking about those who are ONLY capable of performing and working within the confines of their mental and spiritual genius. It could be one reason someone created Patreon and other platforms. You've all seen these types and several have shunned them for not "pulling their weight", to which I question, *"Can you, the hater, also play as wonderfully? Can you bring peace through your vocals? Can you paint to the point that we see visions on canvas and not just color?"*

When a man or a woman meets, falls in love with, and then subsequently marries one of these/those people, it doesn't take too long before the bread gets thinner and the spouse begins squashing the dreams and means of the artist to get them to subject themselves to physical and/or intense mental stress for the purpose of bringing a buck into the house to pay a bill. Here's a thought: YOU KNEW they were a musician. You KNEW they were a writer. YOU KNEW before you married them that you may or may not see $$$ coming into the bank account, stop pretending that a swan can be a goose or a duck! Love the one you loved the way you are supposed to love them. FREELY.

If the musician, artist, writer, etc., can make money for themselves or the family, that's great, but if they are one of these rare and unique beings who absolutely can't be subjected to forced labor without killing their spirit, STOP forcing them to do so, and just support them. YOU

DID PROMISE to do that. You did make that oath. You did give your word. YOU DID SWEAR TO THE ALMIGHTY through your vows that you would CHERISH and you're not cherishing anyone when you force them to be what they are not, or cannot become. Let them strum. Let them think. Let them play the keyboards, ENJOY!! You have a gift and a present like very few others have. That person can probably keep the house clean for you, he or she can watch the kids. They probably have no issues shopping for groceries, or perhaps making dinner. Talk about it before you sign the dotted line, that's all I'm saying.

If there were millions of these types it may be different. They are like the golden eggs being laid by that one magical goose that came by now and again, but we can't capture it either, and we can't force it to lay another egg just like the last one. They are all so very different. They are all so very precious. If someone in this position abuses his or her position, then he or she is NOT actually that soul.

I believe, and again, it is my opinion, that the true artist is on loan from Heaven to fulfill a purpose and we have an obligation to assist them so they can be in line with what God has in store, and we will be blessed not only for helping but because we are probably going to hear them, see them, admire their work, etc. If we squash their energy we cut off our noses to spite our faces! We lose, they lose, and the world loses. LET THEM PLAY! Money is not the end-all.

I'm not capable at this time to host someone like this really. I will be someday maybe soon, but not today. I thank God every day for the talent and the gifts He gives to others who both entertain me and bless me. I see it, I hear it, I feel it, I am moved by it. To think that others would purposely shut that down so the person can work at a grocery store as a clerk, or as a crossing guard for minimum wage; thrusting their talents into the sewer as well as creating mental angst...it's repulsive. YOU KNEW IT when you met them; you had to.

They were probably holding a guitar, a pen, or a paintbrush, and they were no doubt showcasing their latest discovery or project. YOU KNEW. The problem isn't money really, it's love. If I read my Bible correctly, it says if I delight myself in God HE will give me the desires of my heart. If that's correct, and I have a musician or an artist in my arms, I'm going to let them seek and do exactly what God wants them to do, this both allows them and me to please God. God will provide the rest.

The problem that come up in these sorts of relationships, and in many relationships, is that one or the other person tries to live outside of their means. Then they expect and force the other person to keep up with their idiot decisions; forcing the couple into fights and upheaval. Don't live outside your means. Don't have a champagne style on a beer budget. Be frugal, save, think, and if you can't do that with the gifted person, give up the gifted person to someone who will love them and keep them, care for them, help them, and watch them please God.

If the person is NOT pleasing God, not doing what he or she is supposed to do with their talents, that's not what I'm talking about. I am talking ONLY about those people who have been called by God, and given the talent by God to please Him. Let them. Be their wind so they can fly. Watch them. It's amazing. It's simply amazing.

Yes, I may be crazy, but I'm a very happy crazy.

ENTJ - - Runs in the Family!

My son! My precious, wonderful, ultimately best-looking-man-ever-made, son is an ENTJ! That's right, he's one helluva chip off the ol' ENTJ blockhead of a mom. He's a true Son-of-a-Bitch, that one. He is, and I'm not ashamed to say it. I am so very proud that he's "*that way*". If I had to guess I bet Caity Baby is "*that way*" as well. Really, though, just as soon as I had typed those last words I thought about it. Reuben and I have the single trait that separates ENTJs from ENTP which is the overt and innate trait of needing to debate or argue. We do argue, but we know we're right, whereas ENTPs will never back away even when they realize they are dead wrong. Reuben and I (especially me, Oh My Gosh), hate to be wrong, and there's never a need to chide either of us, we will kick our own ass(es) when we're wrong due to the simple fact that somehow (dang it) we're wrong. We do not like to be wrong. It's just so....well, wrong!

Laura has to have a personality that begins with the capital letter "*I*" for Introvert. She's the strong silent type. You can hear Caity and Reuben (and me) coming from a mile away, but Laura will be right next to you for hours and you may never realize it. She doesn't like to bother or interrupt. She isn't one to make a stand or noise publicly. She really prefers to be the one blending into the woodwork whereas Reuben and I set the stage, start the trend, make things happen, make the way, make the wedge, forge forward, and neither of us can understand or comprehend when we turn around and there's no one following us. We have the answers and the answers will always, most always, be the correct one. We're willing to bet our own lives on it, and certainly yours. Caity, quite probably an ENTP, would only bet your life. There is, in fact, another difference between she and her oldest sib. *(Laura would remove you from the situation and place her own life in front of you before she allowed you to be harmed. Reuben and I will allow you to be harmed if you're stupid enough to put yourself in the middle of our protective shield and the enemy.)*

When Reuben posted this week that he had taken the extended 16-Personality Myers Briggs test, and that his results were a firm ENTJ, I was all but in tears with rapture. My baby! My son! My joy! Could it be that growing up he was actually paying attention? Was I molding this kid into the Commander that he has obviously turned out to be? Oh, if I only let myself dream that I had some small part in making him as grand and outstanding as he is, I would be able to die a happy woman. I've been so busy trying to make sure that I didn't influence the girls to the point that they screwed up as badly as I did. I thought all along that Reuben would be a survivor. *(Now, after saying that, and typing that out, I realize that if any of us will ultimately survive a Zombie Apocalypse it will be Caity. We will all be sacrificed first before she takes one for the team. There is no team with Caity - - she will take the prize. Laura will die first.)*

I lament the fact that I am a Ravenclaw in a house full of Gryffindors. Truth. I am the ONLY Ravenclaw Stringfellow that I know. Reuben, Laura, Caity, Caity's husband (best SIL ever) Brandon, even my two grandchildren are Gryffindors. I don't know how that happened. I was clearly careful about what I taught them and how I trained them. They obviously had thoughts of their own, and without thinking these thoughts through appropriately, they decided to act (action) upon them. Action! Action! That's what I had to put up with for years upon years. Even before J.K. Rowling had us separating ourselves into distinct "*Houses*" I was quite clear about training, lecturing, and mentoring my little minions. To my chagrin each and every last child has not only outplayed me, they have outlasted me. They have not however outwitted me. That is my weapon. Wit and the fact that I kill at Chess. Reuben, to his credit, has beat me ONE time. ONE time.

So there it is. I have the opportunity now to breathe, to rest, to know that I have raised and successfully raised three amazing and incredibly humans. I am an influencing factor. I am and I was useful in their upbringing. I can't be blamed, but I can be credited. I won't take blame, and I won't take anyone saying I didn't do it right, because I KNOW I did this correctly. I have the evidence in front of my face -- thank you, Jesus. We couldn't have done it without Him. To think. To sit back and just think, that my son takes after me in more ways than just saying what's on his mind whenever he feels the need; but to know he will forever speak his mind bluntly and directly, expecting any and all who hear him to understand that he is doing so for their benefit more so than his own - - makes me weep just a wee tear out the corner of my eye - - my heart is pounding. So proud.

Reuben with Evie

Mom Mode.

Once a mom, always a mom. I guess you can say the same about a dad, but there are just so many more cases when a child is made fatherless by the choice of a parent than the other way around. At least that is the experience I have both as a person who has been through a extreme divorce, and a person who taught many hundreds of children who have been through the divorce and separation of family as well. When I was divorced and going through a child custody Battle Royale, my ex was able to convince the judge that I was a maniac and that I had mental illness.

I think he used my raging hate and distain for him as a backdrop for his evidence. Could have been the fact that I not only threatened him with the business end of my Remington, but I learned to box as a younger sister and I let the man have it to the point of finding himself face down a few times either on the carpet or the concrete. You just don't piss off a Southern mama. (FYI, I still box, and I'm just as good with my left as I am my right.)

Whatever the reason, the stupid and inexperienced judge took my custodial rights away from me, claiming I was a potential hazard to my kids. Asshat! The thing is, as a Southern mama, I was protecting my kids to the point of death, and that's something that the Yankee-born judge wasn't familiar with. I suppose there are more subtle and gentle ways for a woman to show her methods of protection, but for me it was *"come near here again, and you'll face Jesus!"* Looking back, I don't regret a thing I said, nor a thing I did. The kids ended up with me in due time, and having suffered at the hands of a truly mentally ill parent, they were grateful to be in the capable hands of a mad old wet hen!

The judge decided that day, the day she took away my rights, to have both myself and my ex tested on a very professional clinical level so she could make a permanent decision for the custody of said children. She had us both subjected to a $1500.00 (fifteen hundred dollar) test, that took over four (4) hours to complete. By the time I got to through 10 minutes I was already bitching about the fact that the test seemed to be asking me the same questions over and over again and they weren't even clever enough to dress up the way they asked the question. It was quite literally the same question verbatim! I think it was designed to see how we would react after the 11th time to be asked. Bottom line, the results of the test proved that I am an E.N.T.J. (Myers Briggs) and he is something else, I can't remember, and I really don't care. My E.N.T.J. attitude and personality was all she needed to see to make a determination that I wasn't necessarily crazy, but I was blunt, forceful, honest, truthful, determined, dedicated, committed, and commanding. I was argumentative, I was demanding, I was insistent and I was expectant! She gave me the kids with an official apology from the Court.

Today, my 33-year-old daughter was at the local Tag Agency getting her license renewed. Mind you it was to expire on Tuesday and this is the Friday before that. She had to be wrangled to go, and I had to literally driver her there to be sure she did it. That one can procrastinate and it ends up costing her fees and penalties. I didn't want her to have to go to the DMV to wait in line and prove she is an American if she didn't get the dang thing renewed today!

We get to the agency and she's being questioned by two men who were fighting to speak to her. (She's cute, and she' looks 18.) Both men were in their early to late 20's and they were going over her application and checking out her address and noticing that she didn't have an apartment number but the records show she did. She confirmed she did, and one wanted to know if she lived alone! WHAT THE HELL? She was about to answer, Laura's like that, she just answers, but before she could get a word out of her mouth Mama clicked! I click. I use my tongue and I make a clicking noise. It's how I train horses, and for over 36 years now, it's how I get the attention of my kids.

When Laura looked back I ran my hand across my throat to gesture not to answer the question. She smiled and said "*I live with my brother. He's in the Army.*" What an answer! I would have said, "*I live with Mr. Smith and Mr. Wesson*", but OK, that works. The next guy wanted to know if she had horses since she had a horse on her phone case. She answered. He wanted to know more. She answered. He asked if he could come ride with her. I laughed. She laughed. We both just laughed. Why do people think it's OK to ride someone else's horse? NO...you cannot ride my horse; he'll throw your ass before you sit down on him. He's a bit of a brat! She smiled politely and asked him if he had ever ridden. The answer is always the same. They rode in camp when they were 10.

Anyway, the flirting went on and on, with Laura being far too sweet to stop either of them, but I could tell she wanted to be saved. I looked up and said something like "*Are you almost finished sweetheart we need to get you back to the center for treatment.*" She turned and looked them in the eyes and in her best A.I. (Artificial Intelligence) voice began her goodbyes. Laura is a talented voice actor as well as a gifted horse trainer. It was just hilarious to see them back away from the counter at the same time as she took her new license (papers, they don't really give you a license now, they mail that.) She looked at me as we walked away and said *"Thanks, Mom. I don't like to be rude."* Well, I have never really had a problem with it.

Laura with Valor

Southern Women Rule (You May Need to Know That)

I am an American. I say that proudly, and I will never give up my American citizenry. I may end up moving to Scotland, but I will go back and forth as long as I can, and I will always be a Southern American woman when someone inevitably asks me where I'm from. They can't not ask; (double negative) it's in my voice, it's in my actions, it's in my demeanor - - making me a bit demeaner than some I suppose.

Having fallen in love with Scotland, and all things connected to the great country, I can't help but want to visit it as often and for as long as I can each time I go. I can't tell you the heartbreak that happens when I have to leave it. I implode to a degree. My daughter has a VR set and she'll look up videos and 360s of Scotland and I'll just sit there for 15-20 minutes and stare - - wish, dream, think.

Today, because I'm so very connected to all of my roots, I decided to make a great Southern breakfast for myself and think of all the Scots who would pay me good money to bring this particular meal to their neck of the woods. I made myself biscuits and sausage gravy. Now, in the US when you say *"biscuits and gravy"* it's always (almost always) assumed that the gravy will have pork sausage in it. Mine is a bit different. I put a little gravy in the sausage. I'm going to pile that sausage pretty dern high up on top of my biscuits and you'll see the gravy of course, but you'll know the main characters for sure. For me, and maybe it's because I'm not only a Southern woman but also an Oklahoman, I will pile that sausage right up there.

I tried a dozen times to make scones, I promise you I did, but it just never worked for me. I wanted to do it - - I did. I followed YouTube videos and I watched so carefully. I read up on it, I Pinterested the subject, but no matter what, my Southern oven just wouldn't do it. The ingredients just felt too close to those of a good old-fashioned biscuit, so that's what comes out of my oven each and every time I tried to scone it up for good measure. I have come to grips with it; I may be 48% Scottish, and even another 47% English, but I am 100% Okie, and there's just not going to be a high-topped floured treat in my life...unless I buy it.

So, today, and other days, I decided to make biscuits and sausage gravy for breakfast. I have the cutest little tiny food processor that processes the one cup of flour and 4 tablespoons of butter that I need to make 8 good round biscuits. I added the other ingredients as well, but of course, the milk comes last. I really do prefer the food processor to me trying to fight the slicing and the blending. It's more even, and though my Granny and my Aunt Wilma may give me a stare or two from above, I'm satisfied that some things are better in 2024 than they were in say...1924.

I will say that I remember my Granny being able to make taller biscuits than me, but I was quite a bit younger at the time, so maybe it's just a visual perception. I don't know. What I do know, is that I can't scone for anything. I just can't. I have given it my last go - - until I decide to try again and become just as disappointed as I usually do. The thing is, I wanted to make scones so I could say I did it - - and to be able to split one in half without it falling apart. You can't do that with a biscuit, not a good biscuit.

They crumble when you try. That's the basic difference I suppose. Caity's always turn out better than mine, but I'm OK with that. I made her, so it's a win for me, too.

Maybe my biscuits have more flour. I could play around with that, but in the end, it's the same. I like thinking of scones with clotted cream and jam, and I end up doing the clotted cream and jam, but only with biscuits, and it's not as "*regal*" or pretty. It's flatter and more crumbly - - broken up and pathetic really. They do taste good. I will say that, the biscuits with the clotted cream and jam do taste good -- they just won't win any awards for aesthetics. My biscuits and sausage gravy may not win any beauty contests either, but I will say that mine are better looking than those that have only bits of sausage in the mix - - yeah buddy!

So, there you go - - ask me -- I'll tell you, I was born in the United States of America, right in the middle of Oklahoma City. I was raised in a good old-fashioned Baptist home (we eat a lot) that believes in being able to make food for the congregation from an early age. I was under the age of 10 I know, when Aunt Wilma dragged me into the basement kitchen of the 40th Street Baptist Church to peel potatoes and boil them. She would have tanned my hide if I had cut myself too; just telling you the truth. No blood in the water! She would have spanked me good if I had bled without permission!

Growing up in the South (Southwest) meant that we ate a lot of biscuits. We ate them with gravy, with butter, with jam, with bacon, with meals, with eggs, and just all by themselves. There are few ingredients, and they're cheap to make. A good biscuit can last a week if the weather isn't too hot outside; but you do have to sort of heat them up now and again - - please don't tell my Aunt or my Granny that I use the microwave and a wet paper towel to make that happen. I think Granny put a damp cloth over the pan and let it steam the biscuits on lower heat.

There you go - - Scones will be purchased or eaten if someone else can make them. They will be gloriously appreciated as well. I don't have to worry if anyone likes my biscuits. I never have a single one to heat up again unless I'm making them for myself. I can't seem to use less than a cup of flour, which makes about seven or eight. I've been on the other end of that where we used over 10 pounds of flour to cook enough for all the people at the church who were counting on the kitchen ladies to feed them on any particular Wednesday night. I miss those days. I really do. At least I raised my kids correctly. They know the truth.

Gramma Becky. A True Southern Belle

Let's Talk About Love

I mean to tell you what, (Southern drawl) when I was in my earlies I was not only a fan of Van Halen, I actually dated Alex for a minute. I swear, it was only a minute. You can't hang onto firecrackers very long folks; you get burned! I was young!! It was a moment. In 1981 I had just been hired by Gulf Oil, a major energy company. This was before I was licensed as an insurance agent, and during the time I was going back and forth to Hollywood to work with and for James Garner...yes, THE James Garner. He was and still is, my most handsomest employer ever.

There's a blog about that actually. https://judestringfellow.blogspot.com/2007/04/mr-handsome-my-2nd-favorite-boss.html Working for Jim I was able to go on and off of numerous studios, and I did. I met Alex and we went out. He came in concert that year and we went out again. I worked for the concert promoter when in Oklahoma, when not working for Gulf, when not working for Jim. You see, I've always been a good multi-tasker.

Love takes on so many faces and it has within it so many angles and depths. I think the Hebrew language has something like 16 words for the word "*love*", whereas in English we have a few. We'll say *"puppy love"* or "*sweetheart*", but what about the love a man has for his father, his mother, his children his sibling, or his friend? What about the love a woman has for those people? What about the love we have for mankind, for community? We need more words to describe an immediate knowledge of

215

what we're talking about when we say *"Oh my gosh, I love that!"* We're probably not saying we want to marry it, or spend the rest of the day with it, let alone our entire lives. We need more words like "*agape*" which is the word the Hebrews use for the love that God has for us, unconditional love.

I wasn't in love with Alex; and in fact, I'm really happy we didn't continue to go out because there's absolutely no way I could have expected him to remain faithful to me or even expect that he would ever consider it. Why on Earth would he? He was young, in a major band, he was touring, he was hot, rich, and all the things the world says and sees as being successful and in control. He was magnificent to hang around with, and I will add that (surprisingly enough as it may be) he was an amazing gentleman the entire time we "*dated*", which is even too strong of a label to attach. We went out a few times. It was what I'd call now, a moment in time. Certainly not love.

I sat in my chair today, the chair I sit in to read and write in my journal or to pray in when I'm not in the closet praying. I sat there with the dog, covered in a wee soft blanket while holding the Kindle. I was just about to turn it on to read the book that was queued up to read, but my eye caught something directly in front of me which couldn't be ignored. I saw the hope chest that Daddy made for my daughter Laura. He made one for Caity as well. I think he made one for all of his granddaughters in fact. My daddy was a cabinet maker before and after he retired as Regional Chief Wire Tech at Western Union. (Wow, just saying that makes me cry as I remember the love I had for the offices and backspace where Daddy worked at that low-profile building downtown with its amazing capabilities.) My daddy worked the night shift, and he was the one they called to fix circuits during storms - - he was a hero.

The hope chest is a wooden box with a little relief heart attached in the middle. If you look at the "*feet*" you'll see that one has broken off, and when we put it back under the box we didn't do it correctly. I think that actually adds to the character really; Daddy would have made us take it off and do it again. He was like that, but he'd be shaking his head and grinning the entire time. He did that too. I think of the love I have for that box. It's deep and it is solid. It's a love that reflects and transfers the love I have for its maker. He is my father; he is my dad. He is now a guardian as he watches from Heaven, no doubt applying the same wisdom and guidance he instilled in me while he was allowed to be with us. I don't miss him in the way others may. I am glad he's where he is because he wasn't happy here; not in the end. I love the memories I have of him when I was a kid. I love the memories I have of him when I was a teen and needed advice. I love the memories I have of him when he would take my kids for rides on the lawnmower or let them *"help"* him with cabinet building. (They sanded pieces of wood on the porch while he worked in the workshop)

Love is a very splendid and complex thing. I can love a person without knowing him. I can love a poem without having written it. I can love a dream I will have tomorrow or the one I had last night. I can love and I will love, and if I had anything to say about it, I would wish and pour love onto everything I see, hear, touch, taste, smell, or feel (or think). I would wrap myself in love if it were possible and I would never let Love leave without taking me with it. I like the verse Corinthians 13:13 *"And now abideth three things, faith, hope, and love, and the greatest of these is love."* The King James renders the word *"charity"* but it is translated properly into the general word for love. Love really is the answer. Love really is the key. Love really is the evidence, and love really is all we really need. It never ends and it never quits and it never dies, not if it is real love.

Oil Pulling. (Yeah, I Do)

If you were like me, and you had never heard of oil pulling, you wouldn't know, as I didn't know, that this very basic and simple (ancient) ritual, is pretty cool.

I still don't pretend to know all about it, after all, I've just learned it even existed. I'm studying it, researching it, finding it to be both inexpensive and doable, and I'm asking myself, *"Why not?"*. That's basically the stage I am in right now. In fact, I am actually oil-pulling while I write this blog so that I can do it longer than I have done in the past three days.

This is my fourth day to oil pull, and the first three days were around 5-6 minutes. Today, because I'm writing, blogging, and basically not thinking about it, I'm able to keep the oil in my mouth much longer. According to the gurus online, you're supposed to do it about 20 minutes a day. I don't know if I'll do it that long, but maybe 15. We'll see.

So, what is it? Simply put, oil pulling is using oil (coconut oil specifically) to pull the toxins out of your mouth, and by doing so you'll help your body rid itself of bad bacteria that can cause bad breath, tooth decay, and all the other things that bad bacteria does to you; you know, bad stuff. Does it work? I don't know. It can't hurt! I mean, think about it, you're swishing coconut oil in your mouth for 15-20 minutes a day. It's not like you're swishing something around in there that isn't 100% organic and natural to begin with.

Unlike swishing water, the oils pull from the sides of your mouth and get in between your teeth to get to the gritty ugly stuff in there as well. Some people say it's helped them break up plaque. OK. I'm OK with that too if it works. I'm just not seeing a downside to all this. I only see good. It's not as easy as it seems either because your mouth does become sore if you're not used to doing it, but you do get better at it.

You don't swallow the oil, that's important because if you do, you're swallowing the bacteria right along with it. You spit out the oil into the trashcan, not the sink or toilet. It is oil after all, and you don't want to start the makings of a clogged-up sink since you're doing this every single day. I looked it up, you can do it every single day. The oil appears white and foamy when you're finished and it's good. You can almost feel that you did the right thing just by looking at the discolored oil - - I use 100% organically cold-pressed coconut oil. I think I paid $7 for the jar. Super cheap.

You can use coconut oil in your coffee or tea to help you lose belly fat. You can work it into your skin after a bath. You can soak the tips of your fingers in it (heat it for a few seconds) and then after a few minutes of soaking you can massage your fingers, and file them, keeping the cuticles clean and your hands softer. There's just a lot of things you can do with coconut oil. I also use it to make soaps. It's the main ingredient I think, or one of the first two.

Lots of fun, lots of uses. Go look it up for yourself, and even if the dental industry is trying to say there isn't enough evidence to say whether it works or not, consider who's saying it -- someone who doesn't want us to stop paying them for dental care. I think it has to have some benefits. I'll give it a good 30-day try and if I like it, I'll keep it as a daily thing.

Who knew? (about 8,000,000,000,000 people from the yesterdays)

Photo Credit: Canva.com (Royalty Free)

Galashiels. (Possibility)

Where I very well love Edinburgh, and in fact, it is my favorite city, there is no way I would want to live there on a permanent day-to-day basis. First of all, if I did, the poor man I pray for would be torn between pulling his beard out or diving off of Arthur's Seat, and I really don't want him feeling stressed; nope, only blessed. I think it's best, for his sake if nothing else, that I make my plans to reside about an hour's distance by train, to the city of Galashiels, in the Scottish Borders. I'll tell you why.

Galashiels, like Avon, Indiana, is really an amazing little place that is both affordable and beautiful in its own right. Galashiels is not very big, but it's the same size as Avon, maybe a bit smaller, but it has all the shops I'd need, and it's smack dab in the middle of the moors, streams, dwellings, estates, and historical places that I would have so much fun visiting. There's even a museum of sorts for a $7,000,000, 143-panel tapestry of the history of Scotland, which of course, I would have to see. If I had to go to Edinburgh (she says with a giggle), which I would be going, it's only about 54-60 minutes by train, as mentioned, and the train is a great way to travel! I would simply love it. I wouldn't need a car, but I may rent one after learning to drive in the UK. I wouldn't drive the said car to Edinburgh or Glasgow, but I would drive around the moors and backways. I would do that. I would visit the sheep and coo.

Galashiels' prices are amazing compared to Edinburgh and, really, compared to a lot of places. The same two-bedroom and one-bath apartment I could buy for (I have to use USD since I don't have a symbol for the British Pound on my keyboard) $90,000 would cost me 3x that in Edinburgh. No, thank you. Yes, I would be closer to the castle, but I can see it on my trips once or twice a month. Yes, I would be closer to the Royal Mile, the Surgeon's Hall, etc., but again, I can visit those. They aren't going anywhere. $11.00 train ride (times two, as I would be returning) would be worth the price of not driving myself, not paying for insurance, and not paying for a car payment if I chose to not get a car and not pay for gasoline or maintenance. Why in the hell do I have a car? I'm really thinking this through now, aren't I?

I would most likely (very likely) live in a flat downtown and rent for $650 a month for a two-bedroom, one-bath flat. Not kidding. It's unfurnished, but it has the "*whites*" or the appliances, and it has a bathtub. I'm not going to rent anything that doesn't have an actual tub. That's just silly talk right there. The same apartment in Edinburgh would be $1100+, and it would not necessarily have a bathtub as they have closets for bathrooms, and sometimes, no, I am not kidding, the sink and toilet are in one closet while the shower is in another. In Galashiels, I would have a regular flat, no crazy tourist noises, no crazy nightlife noises, and I could lease a horse. Yes, I could lease a freakin' horse! But, I would have to find someone who wouldn't mind me riding said horse western style. That may be harder than I think. I may have to buy my own horse now that I put my brain to it.

Galashiels has been a burgh since 1599 and has a "*Braw Lads' Gathering*" with riders on horseback running through town, and they're not all boys now. There are quite a lot of horse enthusiasts there. I like that. Sir Walter Scott built his enormous estate just outside of

Galashiels; it's too amazing. There's one university there, the Heriot-Watt University, a school for textiles and design. I could ask if they need a general ed professor, one who visits and teaches Philosophy, Logic, Humanities, Composition, and/or Romance Novel writing. I could do that. The thing is, I'm going to be a claims adjuster, work really hard throughout the summer and early autumn, then take off and rent in Galashiels this coming year or early next, and when I do, I'll have the withal to figure out if I want to stay or just have extended visits.

I can write, I can trade, I can lecture. I don't have to be paid. I can volunteer as long as I'm, again, not being paid, and I can research my books. I can stay up to six months without needing a visa, and with the claims adjuster gig, I can find sponsorships. I could stay! I don't know if I want to yet, but I could; the thing is, I could IF I wanted to. I think what I'll do is take it one pass at a time. I'll go, I'll hang out, maybe stay 5-6 months this time, and see what I think I could handle. I passed on Fife because I really think I want the moors over the sea. I know that sounds incredibly silly to some, but I'm a land lover, a woodsy kind of girl - - I like castles, trees, creeks, and streams over larger bodies of water. I like the architecture of the Scottish Borders over what I've seen in Fife. (Don't get me wrong, I love the Kingdom!)

This is my plan. It's something I can hang onto and dream about. I could wake up, walk the town, get my coffee, get my steps in, research, talk to people, and hang with the horses and the dogs. You really can't get better - - unless you take the train to Edinburgh and stare at musicians in the park; not all of them, just you know...interesting men with guitars and stories to tell through their music.

The Great William Ginn

Among us, mere mortals (humans) walks a man who is by far, by so very far, greater and more radiant than any of us has a right to consider him or herself. His name is William Ginn. No, this is not a Billy, Bill, or Willie, this man is the real McCoy - - or Ginn. He's a real Ginn. He's apt to be titled really, maybe deserving to be called "*Sir William Ginn*", which now that I think about it, he very well could have been. His mother may have actually called him that as a child, which would explain at least a little of his behavior.

I worked with the man, the legend, for only a few short months between May 2015 and March 2016. We were officed in the same space and we worked for the same agency through our state's government. I'll protect him further now, by not telling you what agency it is, but he is a full-blown Director. He's that important; we'll just leave it at that.

When I worked there, he was a director as well, but I didn't work for him, only with him. I would have given anything to have worked for him because then I would have given him the title of my favorite boss. He does hold the title of my favorite co-worker, and that's saying something considering how many jobs I've had and how many co-workers I've worked with. To be #1 takes a lot of conning and let me tell you, this man is that man.

The director I worked for, and subsequently, the same man that Ginn worked with (not necessarily for) was a con artist in my humble opinion, and I couldn't stand him. I couldn't stand to look at him. I couldn't stand to hear him. I couldn't stand to say I was his admin - - he repulsed me. The ONLY thing that kept me at the office every day was the bright and sunny smile of the man whom I give homage to; Mr. William *"Sassy Pants"* Ginn.

Ginn would show up and we'd have a bit of a ritual every day, several times a day. We'd say certain things to make each other laugh. He had a particular chair in his office that he would fantasize that a certain someone (I won't give his secrets away too easily) would one day sit in. I would pretend to be that woman, and make him giggle. Ginn could giggle. He was a master of the craft. When I say I only stayed to be near him I mean it. I wasn't in love with him, (sorry William) but I was in love with his heart, his mind, his intellect, his being, his attitude, his moxie.

If we never meet again this side of Heaven, we will be linked arm and arm up on Glory Street, skipping and laughing, I know it. He has traveled the entire world by himself, and on his own, taking with him his can-do attitude; sometimes scaring the living tar out of me when he would travel about because he couldn't text or use a smartphone to save his life. Here he would go into the depths of the forests and wildlands of Bolivia, Mexico, Brazil, and other places....Peru, I think, and he would do it without a means to communicate!!

When I met the man he was OLD...we'll just let that one sit right there. He knows it, I know it, we all know it. He started working for the state when he was just out of high school I think, right around the time Teddy Roosevelt signed Oklahoma into statehood in 1907. Don't quote me, but Ginn is over the hill, OK. He's old. The thing is, I'm about to go into semi-retirement and he's working every day. He told me today that he's working to pay for his traveling; he's got more to do apparently.

Well, just so you know, and you should know, I wish the best for my buddy, my pal, my tea-drinking friend of yesteryear. I can't wait to skip the golden streets with him and make silly faces at those we never believed could have made it to the pearly gates!! I'm that type, and thankfully, so is he!

Blessings my friend. Enjoy your next 178 years!!! You Rock!

Ferguson / Fergy

So, there we were, Laura and I just minding our own business in PetSmart because you know, we do that; we mind our own business. There we were thinking we needed to buy a few crickets for her Leopard geckos, when out of the blue, completely unrehearsed, and without any real plan whatsoever (except we generally ask when we go into the store) Laura asked the store associate if the store had any geckos for adoption. You see, the adopted pets are free; not the cats, and yeah, not the dogs, if they have them there through an organization, but if you find an adoptable lizard, snake, bird, or rodent at the store, you can actually take them home with you for free!

We do that from time to time because we enjoy rehabbing and rehoming. We never charge anyone for the animal, just for the tank and supplies if we sell that with the animal. This time, however, I'm keeping the little Fancy Leopard gecko that I've chosen to call *"Ferguson"* until I find out if he is a he or she is a she. Then, it will still be named Ferguson, but I'll call it *"Fergy"* or *"Fergus"* probably. For simple and probably biased reasoning, I am referring to the little reptile as a she currently. I have every intention of making my apologies to him/her if I need to later.

You do feed live crickets and mealworms to geckos, but it's not the same feeding those live creatures as it is (for me) when you have to feed live rodents to snakes. In the past, I've rescued snakes, but I didn't like having to feed live. I had one and only one that ate frozen pinkies, but even those are sad because they're all fuzzy-ish or about to become so, and they're dead in your refrigerator;

not a good look when friends and family go snooping...it does raise the eyebrows.

Ferguson is what is called a Fancy Leopard, and I really haven't seen much of a difference in the various types. My daughter Laura knows a great deal more than myself. I have had them, and I have loved them. I have also had bearded dragons and love the stuffings out of them as well. To be honest, I'm sort of waiting for one of them to become available through adoption. I need to set it up first, so I'm ready when they get one. I wasn't ready this time, but Laura had a spare tank.

What I think I'll do is get a couple of smaller tanks on Craigslist or Marketplace. I'll clean them really well, make sure they have lids and such, and then I'll start collecting hides, plants, bowls, and a lamp or two. That way when a dragon comes along, or another sweet Leopard gecko, I can do that...you know me, or maybe you don't, but if you did, you'd know I love to rescue. I don't like to spend a lot of money doing it, but I do love to rescue and care for animals that others have either thrown out or given away.

In the past, I was all about rehabbing and rehoming. I thought I was going to keep my last dragon but she was very shy and didn't want to interact whatsoever after having her for six months. She was abused I suppose. She was gifted to a classroom where she can have plenty of things to at least look at and watch. I'm told she comes out of her hide and watches the kids. She doesn't like them getting too close, but she's intrigued, so that's good. I hate that people abuse anyone or anything, but they do.

I don't know PetCo's policy, they may or may not have adoptable animals for free, but check out your local PetSmart if you're into reptiles, spiders, and such. This will give you the chance to be kind to a life, and if you decide to keep it, it will give you the joy of being a friend to someone who could use a good face to stare at now and again. We play with our animals. We take them out, hold them, love them, talk to them, and even let them watch TV with us. (We don't do that with the cats or dogs in the same room...just need to clarify that for anyone who may know I have furry things too.)

So, Ferguson is about 3 inches long because she's lost her tail. She's about 2 months old, so I'll give her September 1 as her birthday, and she's sort of Ball Python looking, to be honest. I think the term is: Tug or Tug Snow if she is apt to remain light with darker spotting. She's pretty. I like her. She's really fast too, by the way. Laura transferred her from the little box thing to the cage and lost her! Zip! Bam! Gone!! That was fun, and yeah, a little scary too. For now, she seems content, and I'll keep you posted.

Ferguson / Fergy

Ginger Loves me...and My Chicken Wraps

One of the problems with cooking for one or even two is that you have so much left over if you buy in bulk. When I go to WinCo to get my chicken breasts I know I'm going to come out with 10 breasts for just over $12.00, which is amazing! It's an amazing price, and yes, that's why I go. It takes a minute to cook it all, but it will be cooked. I cook for two right now, myself and my daughter Laura who I can't seem to convince it's time to fly the coop. She's one of those daughters. She's almost 34, but she knows a good thing when she has it, so yeah, she's still clinging to the apron strings and this Mama bear is about to take off the apron; let me tell you.

LOVE YOU, but you gotta go, and if you don't go girl, I'm leaving. It's just a matter of time before that actually happens, but until it does we can talk about food. Over the weekend I made an awesome chicken dinner in the slow cooker. It was something like an Italian Marsala dish, but I didn't add the mushrooms. I should have; I had them. I don't know what I was thinking. It was just simply fantastic, and since there were several pieces left over (I only used two large breasts and cut them in half) I decided to let them sit in the pot (in the fridge) and soak up all the sauce and cream cheese. That happened and then I did something really cool.

I shred the chicken into very thin pulls, making the mix really soft and gooey. Chicken, cheese, cream cheese, and veggies kind of gooey, and after another hour in the fridge, I had a perfect blend to make toasted chicken wraps, adding a bit more cheese (hope you like cheese) and toasted it on the George Foreman (panini) grill. It really does make an excellent sandwich. I only eat 1/2 of the larger-sized tortilla wrap, so you guessed it, I had to call in Laura to do the cleanup. She had no problem doing that. I added grapes, olives, and pretzels to mine. She wasn't nearly as snazzy, preferring just to eat the wrap as is. I hardly ever eat any meal without fruit these days.

The point is if you're going to make something, and you know you'll have leftovers, get yourself an artisan loaf of several-grains bread or a package of good large tortillas and make wraps and panini for the next couple of days. We've had the same thing for about four meals now, to be honest. I had NO idea the chicken breasts were that big, but they were...are, I have 6 more. This week I'll have to throw in a few beef, pork, and even shrimp dinners, but I have to wait until I can get the rest of the chicken eaten. I could give it to the dogs I suppose; that's always an option, and they don't mind helping. My dogs love me.

Pinterest hit a home run on this one. I think I spent less than $12.00 total on the chicken, cream cheese, regular cheese, Italian dressing, celery, and diced tomatoes and we're talking a full dinner for two, then three more meals of sandwiches! Yes, this is a good family-type meal maker that can be easily made, easily devoured, and easily cleaned, and it won't break the budget. You can't say that about the same thing you would buy at the fancy schmancy restaurant. The same meal I made over the weekend for one would have been $14-22 depending on where you go and what sides you have with your meal. I'm not going to open up any cafes or restaurants any time soon, but if I did, the Italian Chicken wrap would be on the menu. It's cheap to make and I could make BANK on it.

I just handed the last bite or two of the wrap to Ginger; she was patiently waiting by my side. She knows me. One of the ways I stay so fit is to feed some of (if not 1/2) of my food to the dogs. I tend to think about it first, wondering if they'll be able to eat it without having digestive issues. Then I remember that I'm really old and have owned dogs my entire life. I've been "*abusing*" them I suppose, for about 60 years if you think about it. Shoot darn-it. So far, not one single dog has ever complained or died from my table-scrap supplements to their diet. Sorry fancy schmancy vets out there claiming otherwise. I'm gonna have to go with good old-fashioned good sense and a track record to beat the band. My dogs love me. (unlike my kid, I won't kick the dogs out of the house.)

Ginger Girl

Yuuki.

After just over the threshold of sixteen years, it has become apparent that our sweet little once-solid-black Chiweenie dog Yuuki be taken to the vet to be escorted over the Rainbow Bridge in just a few days. We decided to wait the weekend so we could spoil him, have a few more good days with him, and let him know that we truly appreciate him. He realizes too, that it's been a good and long life on this planet, and that it's time now, to step into his newness and the gifts that Jesus can give him.

Laura, my daughter, had just come off of her one-off tour with Ozzfest 2007 when she decided to get herself a little dog. She had just moved out of my place and was on her own (well, with her little sister) and she thought it would be great to have a little dog to spoil. We're rescuers, so buying a dog never enters our mind; however, that being said, there was a woman in our city claiming to have full-blood Chihuahuas for just $150 and though they didn't have papers, she knew who both parents were...yada yada...you know where this is going, right?

I told Laura she was about to pay her hard-earned money for a mutt, but if she wanted to do it, that was her choice. As it turns out we actually did rescue Yuuki. The conditions of the place he was in were dismal at best. Though we knew the second we looked at him that he wasn't a purebred dog, we didn't care. He needed to be out of that place, and we were on our way to the nearest law enforcement facility! The puppy mill that woman was running was nasty to say the very least.

We still have no idea what the police or the city council did for the puppy mill or its owner, but we felt pretty good about bringing at least one sweet face home with us to be loved and cared for until his last breath. That was literally 16 years ago. Since the day we brought him home with us, Yuuki has seen three or four of our other animals face the same situation he's facing now. Why animals can't outlive all of us is beyond me. They give so much, love so much, maybe that's it. Maybe they burn both sides of the candle of life trying to be the best they can be. Just sitting there and smiling is really all they have to do. They were made perfect.

Yuuki went with Laura while she sang, while she performed on stage, and while she worked he sat beside her, while she did anything, he was her dog. He held that position until right at one year ago when he began distancing himself from her and becoming less and less interested in being picked up, cuddled, or nuzzled. He wanted to be in the room maybe, but not held. Over the course of this past year, his health has really declined. He was hard of hearing about two or three years ago, but it's nearly complete now. He can still see and smell quite well, and he still likes to bark at what he perceives to be strangers.

This past month has been the hardest for him. We can tell he's not in good spirits most of the time, and he has finally begun to lose control of his bowels. He has never been this way, so we know it's something that he can't reverse. The doctor (such a very very sweet man) has told us that it's time, and we suspected it before we took him in to see him. We decided not to do it today. We decided to take him back on Monday so we could spend a little time with him at the pond, a place he truly enjoyed as a young puppy, and of course whenever we can take him. We lived in the same complex when we got him, moved out, moved back, and he remembers it.

He'll be cremated at the clinic, and the doctor told us his ashes will be scattered over the flowerbeds and tree bases outside the office; the ones that are so pretty, and so lushly wonderful. They have greeted patients and clients for years. The thought that he'll be part of that family of friends means a great deal to me, but the most important thing is that he'll not be in pain, he'll not be depressed. He'll be happy and healthy, and whole again, and he'll find our other pets (and millions of others) who will likely show him the ropes until Laura can come to Heaven to claim him all over again.

Please pray for us, but think a second or two longer in your prayers for Laura. She was only 18 when she picked him up that brisk September afternoon. Our lucky boy was literally born on 07-07-07. We brought him home on September 14, 2007. He's been both a nuisance and a miracle for us all. Aren't they all? Where we know that death is a part of the whole cycle of life, it's still chilling and hard to let it happen. We'll mourn, and we'll cry, but I'll also laugh when I walk over to OUR chair and he's not there to chase away from it. It's been a morning ritual for well over four years now. Sweet boy. Thank you for your prayers and good thoughts. (If you're wondering why I have to chase him from my chair it's because he refuses to share it with me...stinker.)

Yuuki (he passed in Dec. 2023)

Dance – Dance – Dane-ccc

The good news is I don't care if I sweat, stink, or make other noises when I'm dancing because it is just me, my CD player, my dog Ginger, and sometimes my cat Bilbo. I say sometimes Bilbo because he's not always to be counted on; he leaves when he gets bored which is usually after the 3rd or 4th song. Ginger, on the other hand, is waiting for me to drop down into the doggie-downward stance so she can feel as if she's doing the same thing I am doing. She loves doga!!

When I dance, as opposed to when I walk, box, or stretch, I throw it all to the wind. I move. I have zero inhibitions and I let my mind race back to my senior year in high school when I was something like 120 pounds at my current height of nearly 5'7" and I was flat as a 12-year-old boy! Dagnabit, I miss that girl! If I could, I would sell these big boobies and donate any extra fat a good licensed surgeon could use for his/her next patient. I'm ready...I'll trade it in a heartbeat.

Speaking of heartbeats...I need to get one of those gizmos to tell me what my heart rate is while I'm dancing. I tend to slow it down when I think it's too high, but you just never know. I may have to get something to remind me; maybe something with a buzzer on it that screams at me when it gets to the thrashing point. I could do that, or I could stop playing Head East and Boston, and put something a bit tamer on the CD player - - maybe Steph Macleod. (Talk about heart racing! LOL Maybe I shouldn't do that.) Maybe I should think about my 17-year-old self with a bit of precaution - - but gee-golly...she was fun.

From 1980-1984 (off and on) I worked for a music production company as well as being an indie writer in Hollywood. The company *"Concerts West"* through Quicksilver and 96X radio, worked hand-in-hand with over 200 venues to bring or produce great names. My role was that of a gopher really - - go here, go there, do this do that. I drove, I cooked, I found food, found this, found that, and worked security during the shows. I met and hung with some of the greatest names in music - - and the reason(s) I was allowed to stay on was because I didn't take photos, I didn't get starry-eyed, I didn't date them (except Alex Van Halen) and I managed to keep a steady-mind and an even keel when they threw their (very often) tantrums; as you can imagine many of them did...David Lee Roth, Steve Perry, and The Pointer Sisters come to mind. Talk about dancing!! Talk about constant movement.

In 1979 we weren't really headbangers as much as we were just spinners, and twisters. We did a lot of dropping and popping, and we did a lot of shoulder movements. I remember that. There's another thing I do in my wee little space that I've cut out for myself in my bedroom for the particular excitement. I do cheer leading moves - - think 1979 again, nothing like they do now. I couldn't compete even if my 17-year-old self was standing in front of me. Nope, the girls today blow me, and memories clear out of the water!! I see Simone Biles and I just lose my breath! Such an inspiration! (I know, she's not a cheerleader, don't email me.)

I'm about forty pounds over what I want to be. I'll never ever get back to 120, and to be honest, I don't want to be. I don't mind my hips. I like my hips...they're cool. I can see myself at about 140-145 and I'll be happy. It can happen. If I don't force it by exercising, I know I can pay for it to happen, but let's see how close I can get with this regiment. I don't mind putting myself through it. I know my discipline. I can set my goals and meet them - - by myself, I don't need anyone else kicking or nudging me.

I may move my boxing apparatus into the bedroom and store it in the corner so I can pull it out nightly and pound away for two songs; that's a good 7 minutes, maybe 8. I can do that. I can continue to walk 3 miles a day, dance, box, stretch, and think really fun exciting thoughts. Believe me when I say my exercising is not just a physical experience. NOOOOOO, I go places. I do things. I'm flying, I'm swimming the Firth of Forth. I'm chasing men in kilts up the moors - - sometimes I catch one! (Music lulls, I take a few breaths...and start over again.)

This will be a good program - - I have a doctor helping me this time. She's only known me for a few weeks. She'll be pretty excited when I see her this week and let her know what's up; she may even provide me a gizmo to keep up with my heart rate. We're going to both be pretty excited when I see the pounds drop because I know that my higher (not that high) cholesterol was connected to the extra weight. I can set a number and try to go for it, but I've not ever had a higher-than-normal number, so I don't know the needed metrics to get it below what it is supposed to be. I can't remember the exact numbers; I have a blog out there about it. But that was a month ago - - I'm sure it's lower.

OK, I think I'll call it a day for today so I'm not overdoing it, but when I was 18 - - of majority age, I would dance literally 4 or 5 nights a week at the Quicksilver club here in OKC from about 7:30 to about 10:00. I never drank. I was the designated driver. I got my orange juice or water for free - - good times.

Be Careful, You Could End up in my Next Novel.

As a writer, I really do have full and complete control over who I write about, what I write about when I write it, and how I decide to write it. No one (and yes, that does include sweet songwriters who try their hardest to blend into the woodwork) can tell me otherwise. I will write because I write. I will literally change what I've planned to write to include something either really fun, scary, nasty, obnoxiously wild, or careless just because someone decided to tell me no when I asked permission to add them to my book. I am so not above that. I am not above changing the entire plot of what should have happened to what now happens if I decide it needs to be done in order to make some trivial or trifle point. Yes, that is incredibly petty - - and being petty is a form of ugliness, but I will (and have) do it.

When I wrote *"Of Kilted Pleasure"* it was my intention to write that sweet songwriter I was discussing earlier, in the book. He was going to be a hero type, someone who saves the day, or at least part of a day - - but then things changed, and the man I wanted to showcase as being one of Scotland's most prolific and talented artists decided he didn't want me to grace my book with his image, name, or likeness and I think I offended him by saying I didn't need his permission. Well, it's true, I don't need anyone's permission to add them to my book, not even if I wanted to use his actual name; but I was being polite. He wasn't thrilled.

Rather than seeing things from his point of view, my short-sightedness decided to please my own spirit (the spirit of creative writing that lives within my veins) and I wrote him into the book anyway. He wasn't the gallant hero I had intended, but instead, a meek and mild minstrel who happens to be kidnapped off the docks of Leith by pirates, and he's captive on their vessel for about a year, and then before releasing him, they tattoo his ass. True story - - oh, no, it's not a true story that it actually happened, no. It is a true story that he told me I couldn't use him in my book so I used him in my book, but had him kidnapped, abused, and tattooed.

Was I mean to do that? No, I don't think so. I didn't use his name; just his general description, which if you say it out loud could be about a million other men in the area. I mean, I know it's him, and he's not doubt probably figured it out by now, but he can't get all legal beagle on me and make threats because I don't defame him in any way, I just let him know that he can't tell me no and get away with it - - which is again, obnoxious and rude on my part, and I accept that. I will possibly even work on it, but I don't think I'll actually change. The character is much loved, and in the end, the man's grandmother ends up leaving him a lot of money, land, and a house. C'mon, I wasn't that mean.

Another woman I had decided to put in my book was treated completely differently. She was purposely left out of the book; and then, when I did add her likeness, image, personality, and part of her name to my next book, she loved it. She thanked me a hundred times because it's cool to pick up a book and show your friends that you (or your likeness) was written into a novel!! I put myself in my books all the time. I don't put all of me, just parts and pieces, stories, and things that have happened. It makes it more relatable.

Twice now, no wait -- several times, I've asked someone if they wanted to be in my book and they agreed but said they wanted to be murdered or they wanted to be the bad guy! I said OK, and Nathan Fuentes of San Antonio, Texas ended up being murdered in my book "*Murder Book*". Laci B. became a very intelligent student. Another guy named Matt Wittie became a twelve-year-old boy who sold my hero character a pair of horses. Tony Broonford of Edinburgh (YouTube sensation https://www.youtube.com/@ClanBroonford) agreed, and he became the hero instead of the songwriter! Michael Givens and his lovely wife Jedelle are memorialized also in "*Of Kilted Pleasure*" as a fabulously famous play director and actress on the stage! Famous composer Alan Williams is also himself in the book - - although it is the 1740s...but still.

It's not a bad thing to be in a book. It's a good thing to be a book. It's a really good thing to be remembered as being really cool, or really talented, or really awesome. The problems crop up with an author (or maybe a songwriter) if and when they have a great and sensationally awesome and awe-inspiring idea, but you say you don't want to be a part of it - - oh...well, OK...but you're still probably going to be a part of it. You may end up kidnapped by pirates, but you will be a part of it. You may end up being the side-kick to the hero, who then forces you to strip naked and join him in a hot steaming Turkish bath to avoid being arrested for stealing something from the police's storage closet, but you will be in the book! (That's what happens to the man in "*Murder Book*".)

Why do you suppose we who have these penchants to be so direct, aggressively creative, and unashamed when it comes to sharing our thoughts with the world, can be so...direct, creative, unashamed, and aggressive? Some write songs, some write books, song play guitar, some walk dogs, some teach, some preach, some make soap while others make sand castles, but we are all very gifted in some way. Some like to share, while others prefer not to be shared. At least I didn't use real names when they preferred not to be named. I should have used my ex-employer's real name, but I didn't. I simply had him murdered, his fat body fileted, and then his organs and tissues, head, hands, and feet fed to pigs while his skin was tanned for other purposes. (Was that too much? Maybe, but he did piss me off.)

I can say this...I have never murdered anyone in reality. I keep all my violence and any violent tenancy I may have contained within the written and very fictitious world of novel writing. I think it's best; don't you? When I ran across a t-shirt that literally read *"Be careful, you could end up in my next novel"* I did have to buy it - - it's so me....oh, and my horse's chiropractor Dr. Lacey Hoel told me I can use her real name, likeness, image, and everything!! She's in *"Bay Sorrel Ranch"*, which is the drama novel I'm writing now, and get this, she's my equine chiropractor in that book!! Woot! (She doesn't kill anyone, I promise, and she's certainly not going to be killed.)

Homeowners Associations – My Thoughts

Everyone has their own point of view about this or that, and I am no different. I have a very distinct opinion on homeowner associations because I've been on both sides of that issue. I've owned a home in one, and I've owned homes that are not in them. Let me just say, I prefer them. It's a matter of neatness, not necessarily uniformity. Can they go too far? Yes, absolutely, and that's when the homeowners form an alliance to either sue the HOA to force them to change or move and find one that better suits their needs.

I understand that not everyone can adjust to the often-stringent requirements set out by some of the HOAs that exist. To be honest, there are some that step way over the proverbial lines, and they do impose their way onto the people who spent their personal hard-earned cash on a home that happens to be inside that particular HOA. BUT...and this is a HUGE one; the homeowner, or would-be owner, knew the rules before deciding to live in that HOA. I don't ever remember hearing of an HOA that cropped up after a neighborhood was established. I could be wrong.

The most annoying rule that I ever ran across was that no flag could be flown on or around the outside of the house, and that included the American flag. We got away with it by forcing them to recognize the First Amendment, but it wasn't easy to do. Their reasoning was to keep down banners for rivaling teams, states, and countries, and to not cause an issue. I understand that, but no one will ever tell me I can't fly Old Glory. That won't happen. They allowed it as long as it was attached to the house or gate and was no bigger than 15" or something like that. I'm OK with a compromise. I kept my OU flag inside the house and hung my "*Blue Star Mom*" flag in a window.

Most of the time, HOAs are there to keep the lawns straightened, cut, and cleaned. They are not there to lord over people, or to make them feel uncomfortable. Often times the units will have a similar look, so they want to maintain that for aesthetics as well as for maintaining the valuation of a home. Property values will decrease if a wayward neighbor has painted their garage a bright pink and their house trim a mustard yellow; or if they have 6 cars in the drive, two that are jacked up on concrete blocks, uncut grass, and vines that look like the Amazon rainforest in their front and back yards. Face it, when someone next door to you has a broken panel in their window, a few slats of wood missing from their fence, and plays their music 24/7 from a loud boom box, it's good to know there are rules and guidelines you could have imposed if you were in an HOA.

Another reason, and perhaps the #1 reason I like living in an HOA is the fact that my fees literally pay for the insurance of my home from the studs out to the air. All contents and even the drywall are my responsibility, and they do have insurance for condos for that reason, but they have to pay for any hail, wind, fire, water, or vandalism damage that takes place outside the house and the roof. That alone is usually 70% of the fee. The rest (in most cases) pay for things like water, sewer, garbage pickup, and lawn maintenance. If there is a pool it pays for that. If there is security patrol or cameras being monitored, it pays for that. I'm good.

If I had to pay $2100 a year for insurance but could save 70% that's a $14,700 savings, and the rest is about what I would end up paying for renters or condo insurance. Now, why would I say I save 70% of the $2100 if I pay the HOA fee? Why not the whole thing? Because it's only from the studs out - - I'm still responsible for the contents, the drywall, any specialty tile, carpet, etc. I may have to pay $600 a year for that. My water/sewer bill would have been $60, my garbage would have been about the same, and to have someone maintain the lawns, pool, security, and cameras for that little money...yeah, I'm good. I know I've said that, but I am...I am OK with paying $220-250 a month knowing my exterior insurance is paid, my lawn will be cut, my house is watched, my water and garbage are paid, and I have a nice pool to use in the summer.

Some HOAs do not have pools, security, or cameras, and some don't pay for water. You'll need to know your association to see what they cover. If it's too much, don't live there. If they raise it, it's likely because it happens...inflation happens. Why people continue to complain about inflation is beyond me. We're not going to change it, it is going to happen. We need to just move forward; if at all possible. I know it's a hassle, it's terrible, but it really is JUST a first-world issue, and thank God, you live in the first-world right now. It could be so much worse. Look, I'm writing about the woes and cons of homeowner associations, not about bombs, insurgency, or war. There's a reason we are called blessed.

Since I'm being so kind and sweet to the HOAs, I'll go ahead and talk a bit about the two times (besides the flag thing) that I had to complain about and felt that I had a right to do so. When I moved into a condo as a renter, not a buyer, I was told I could have my two dogs and my two cats. The owner of the unit paid the fees and he never mentioned my animals to the HOA. I got a letter asking me to find homes for two of my pets, and I declined to do so. They fined the owner, and then he asked me to do the same, and I told him no. I had them when I went under lease. I was not renewed for the lease, as you can imagine, but it was a problem. I wouldn't have moved there in the first place if I had been told the rules.

The 2nd time was when my son had returned from Iraq and needed to blow off a lot of steam! He had a big tractor tire that he bought and then brought to my place because it had a bit of a slope leading up from the road to my driveway. He and his Army buddy were rolling and flipping the tire over and over and we were reported to the HOA by a nosy neighbor. I asked my son to put on his uniform, (not the fancy one) and when he did, NO ONE COMPLAINED...well, he complained, because it was really hot. After the third time of wearing his camo, he took them off and went back to his shorts and tank. Again, no one complained, in fact, several neighbors came by to either thank him or to watch him.

HOAs are not the big bad wolf or the lords that some think they are. They are there to keep peace, regulate, and be sure that nothing gets too far out of hand. If we had been asked to stop rolling the tire, we would have stopped. On that particular HOA, we were located (or situated) on the 10th hole of a great golf course in Indiana. We were not allowed to walk the golf course unless we were members, but we did anyway. I think we were reported twice; nothing happened. They just asked us to not make noise, not to approach golfers, that sort of thing. We adhered. It's not as if we were banned, fined, or cast out. Most of these places have reason; they use reason.

All this being said, I am sure there are some horror stories out there about HOAs and how they completely restrict you from doing what you want to do. This is Halloween and one of the HOA rules in a neighboring association, not ours, is that kids from the association can trick-or-treat, but not others. They literally pass out passes to wear on their costumes. That's a bit too much, I would have to have something to say about something like that, but the underlying reasoning is valid. It is a more uppity posh hood and they don't want it to be trashed. During the Pandemic they even shut the gates and had a sign that read *"No Trick-or-Treating is to be done in the HOA due to health reasons"*. (That was 2022!! A year after 90% of the lifts.)

There you have it, my opinion. I would rather be in an HOA that was respectful and flexible than to be in one that is not, or to not be in one. It just makes sense to me. Whether or not it makes sense to you is a you-thing. You decide. Have a bright and cheery experience or go home...well, you know, move your home.

The Junk Drawer

Almost every house has one. I have two. I know, I know, I'm one of those overachievers, it's true. I have two kitchen junk drawers. I put more "*useful*" junk in one of the drawers and less useful things in another. I have no idea how I actually choose to separate them, except that when I first put the item into one of the two drawers, I must make some sort of mental decision about whether I'll use it again, when I may use, it or if it just isn't bad enough to throw out...yet.

I'm planning my exit strategy a bit early, and in doing so I'm taking notes as to what I will take with me when I move. I will likely not take much of anything from the junk drawers because my daughter will need whatever is in them when I do leave. I say that I have no idea what she'll need. What I have done is go to Pinterest and see what the experts (if there are junk drawer experts) say about organizing the messy chaos so that I can either narrow my needs down, throw out what I don't really need, or maybe just .... God forbid, do away with having a junk drawer; but I'm not sure that's even possible.

My new place will be so well organized that people will think I'm actually OCD. I'm not, but my place will be neat. I'm buying literally everything the Pinterest gurus say I need. I'm excited about it. I'm getting drawer spacers, cabinet dividers, modules to put things on, space-saving wire things to hang things on, and I'm just too excited about it. I have about 50 food containers and I'm taking them with me. I'll need more baskets...I love little kitchen storage baskets.

I found a few things to help me organize my refrigerator too; a ziplock storage holder! WHAT? Yes, it's true. One thing I saw that will save space in the freezer, is to put your meat into ziplock-type bags, flatten the meat, then stack them. Boom! I will likely only have 4 mugs, 4 plates, 4 saucers, and cutlery for 4. I'll likely have only a few kitchen towels, mitts, etc., as well, since it's just me. I'll have a washing machine; I can wash the towels. I'll even probably just do my own dishes....just sayin'.

I looked into my first kitchen drawer and made a list of several things I have. We all have these things in our junk drawers. Pens, pencils, Sharpies, tape, wrapping ribbon, twine, scissors, a tape measure, pencil sharpener, nail file, batteries, measuring tape, bookmarker, watch, chain, flash drive, cards, dice, sewing kit, highlighters, wire, glue, a ruler, a lighter or two, and some other stuff. You get the picture. In the OTHER drawer, the one I say has the useful things, I have screws, tools, a hammer, more scissors, more glue, a corkscrew, electric hand blender blades, a small socket set, and a knife sharpener...and other stuff.

I know you can relate. I bet as you were reading that you added to the list, and you thought *"Yep, that's me"* a few times. I don't have a spool of thread; my friend pointed that out to me. I don't have a pocket knife either. I've decided to get a little toolbox when I move and keep a small set of tools in it. I'll get one drawer organizer and put the junk stuff in it, but I'll use the toolbox for the other. It will be kept in the garage or under the sink. Good plan. I'm making plans for a house I'll buy in about six months. My plans have plans. My notes have notes.

I've also been Pinteresting things today to see if they work. I put baking soda and peroxide on my old baking pan for 15 minutes and nothing happened. I'll add vinegar to it tonight and let it soak overnight to see if it does any better. I hope it does. I mean, I could also go out and buy new pans. It's OK...I can do that. I just haven't in something like 20+ years, that's all. I did recently break my 25-year-old crockpot liner, the crock bowl part...shattered into about 12 pieces when I was washing it. All three of my kids have volunteered to buy me a new one for my birthday. You gotta love kids who know you THAT well.

My birthday is in about four weeks. I'll let them decide who will buy what. I need:

- Crockpot
- Over the sink dish rack
- Drawer organizers for spices, junk drawer, cutlery
- Pantry baskets
- Refrigerator organizers
- New journals

My kids are the best...the BEST....I would never ever trade them or sell them. I like them very much. Well, that's about it. Just making plans to make plans. Someone has to; those drawers are not going to organize themselves.

Hiding in Plain Sight. (Little Yellow Dog)

It can't be easy being a two-legged dog in a four-legged world. Poor Faith, I can't take her anywhere without curious questions, people stopping us every 10-15 seconds to ask the same questions that the last group of on-lookers just asked. She's good with all the attention - sometimes it's me that has to take a breather - Faith just sticks out her tongue and smiles!

We live in a suburb of Oklahoma City, the city is named Edmond, and we're doing our best to help the state celebrate our 100th year anniversary this year - really cool things happened in Edmond in the past 100 years. Recently Edmond has been making news because of a little dog that just happens to live in the neighborhood - we've been here quite a while, but I guess she's just now being seen. They call that hiding in plain sight. Faith probably doesn't even know she's been in hiding. With winter weather, storms, traveling, (getting lost on airplanes and having the media tell the world you live in Orlando could have something to do with it) and of course just chilling under the bed - Faith's been noticed more recently than she has been in the past, that's all.

This afternoon (74 degrees and sunny) a few boys in the hood were playing hide-n-go-seek in the various yards that surround our little cul-de-sac street - one bouncing, long haired kid took his refuge behind my refuge...our garbage can, one of those big green dumpsters that the city gives you and then demands that you find a way to hide it out of sight so that the homeowners association doesn't come down on you - when did we agree that they could anyway? Whatever -

the kid was hiding behind a dumpster in my yard when Faith, who had been visiting another neighbor (to her great surprise), decided to out the boy by skipping her 37-inch frame over to him at warp speed...barking! He was freaked!

The kid was torn between turning himself in, and possibly losing the game, or staying and getting an up close and personal view of my kanga-dog now rapidly approaching him; tongue out, barking voice, no arms - walking upright - yes, he HAD seen the dog on Montel and Ripley's, but he NEVER expected to see her in ....her own yard, just two doors down from his! OUT! He's out! The other boys got to the central tree first, and called him out! Hahahha...the dog won! When the boy called back to his friends that it was unfair they just laughed at him - *"She's on our team!"* they shouted back - *"She's always lived there, we knew that"*. Well, now he does.

I took Faith to the post office a couple of days ago where she's always meeting new people. It's always the same: *"Have I seen that dog on Oprah? You live here?"* They ask me if I live in Edmond because I have a post office box and I guess they realize you have to live in the immediate area to rent one - I do live here - and have! No, we're not from California. We're not from NYC - which is the first choice of most passersby because of the 10 trips we've taken I suppose - and we're not from Florida...which so far has seen more of our sunny faces than any other state in the union besides our own Sooner State.

Yes, you've seen her on Oprah. You've seen her on Ripley's. She's been on Montel, Maury, David, Ricki, in magazines, newspapers, on stage with over a dozen rock bands - she's been in circus performances both in person and on television, she's been on Animal Planet, Animal Radio, Animal Attractions, PBS, AOL, CNN, MSNBC, and every local station known to men - but she lives in plain sight - and I might add, not too glamorously - she spends 90% of her time under the bed! That's right people - the World's Most Photographed Dog is a cave animal after all. Who knew she was so .....normal? (God did!)

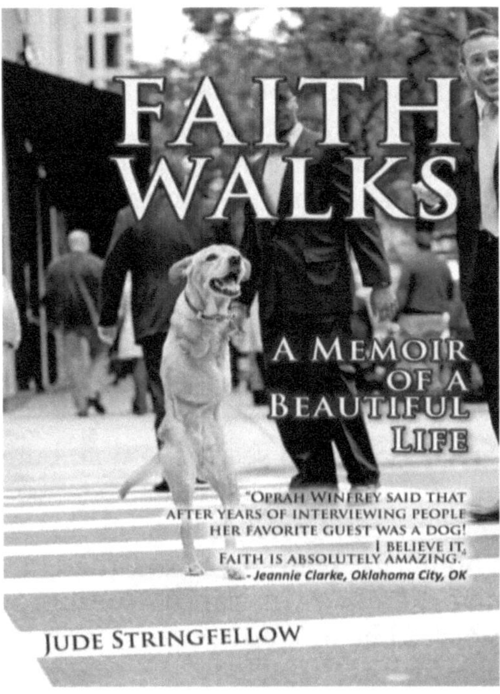

Faith Walks is available on Amazon.com

Focus!

I've been unwilling to admit it, but I do finally need to wear reading glasses and that fact really bothers me. I'm going to be 62 in November, which in and of itself amazes me. I didn't know 62 even existed when I was younger. I thought you died before that time; for sure only really old people were over 60. Well, turns out that I was wrong. I'm still very young, and I don't mean "*young at heart*"; screw that, I'm young. I don't feel old, I don't do old-people things, I don't complain about my body aches...and now dang it, I need glasses to read.

I don't need glasses to see, I see fine, but when I read I need them. I can see things in the distance, it's the close-up things that I can't really focus on, so what do I think I can do about it? Well, turns out there are some pretty interesting exercises you can do to improve your eyes and the muscles and/or veins, or whatever it is back there in your brain, that can help you see better. It's working, so I'm going to keep doing it. I don't care if people laugh at me. I'm having fun.

Here is what I do now. I sit up straight because somehow sitting up straight helps you no matter what it is that you're doing. Without moving my head, I look forward at something pretty far away, and then I look at something really close, maybe my thumb or something. Then, I do it again and again and again. Next, I keep my head immobile, but I look as far as I can to the right, then the left, then the right, then the left for about 10 sets.

After the left/right thing, I do it again looking upward and downward, not moving my head. I do this about 10x and then I close my eyes. I rub my eyes lightly, and I heat up my palms by rubbing them; then placing my palms over my closed eyes. I repeated the exercise a couple of times. The whole thing takes maybe 5 minutes and I can feel it in my eyes for sure. I think it's working. I know I still have to use the glasses to read the fine print, but it does feel better than it did two weeks ago when I put them on all the time. I'm using them less and less now.

Anyway, that's what I have, and that's what I'm doing. You don't have to do it, and you may think it's crazy, but let me just say, I don't know if it's fail-proof because we do get older, and things do fall apart, but why not try and make things better if we can? We stretch, we move around, we keep our bodies moving, why not do the same for our eyes. You can do the same thing with your chin too, your teeth and jaw, you open, close, go to the right, the left, etc. You can stretch your jaw, and you can feel better about yourself; it really does make you feel more in tune with your own body.

Hey, it's your body. You may as well like what you have to the point of doing all that you can to make it the best body you can have. Just sayin'...do it if you want, I do, and I love it. Maybe in a few weeks, I'll report how it's working. I'm also trying to focus on what goes into my body and how I exercise. I've been in an ongoing battle for years with this one; I am so normal when it comes to being normal. Maybe I'll find a way to be successful instead!!

Why Must it be a Hassle? (Because it's ME!)

I came so close to having an average and normal day once - - but that was so long ago, that now, the normal is so far from average. I woke up this morning feeling bloated and I had no idea why. The lemon-lime water I've been drinking for three days is definitely doing its job; let me just say that. I think I've pooped 10 times in the past three days and yes, I can say I'll keep drinking this stuff. If it's cleaning me out this good, I don't want that to stop anytime soon. Bloat gone! All is good.

I decided to make breakfast for myself. I do that from time to time. I grabbed the flour, the butter, the baking powder, and the milk, and I made myself biscuits, only to find out afterward that we were out of all the jams and jellies because my kid cleaned out the fridge and she threw them all away...she does that. Notice would have been GREAT. OK, no worries, I'll use the honey - nope. She took that to work. People, I had to eat my biscuits without gravy since I didn't make sausage or bacon. I used maple syrup.....First World Problems.

Then, just because I live here, and it is the way that it is, the communal washing machines decided to both quit at the same time. Now, I know it's a major First World Problem, but we have to be honest about it; they were old. They needed to be replaced years ago. For both of them to quit at the same time seems really suspicious to me, and I'm going to put the blame on my crazy neighbors because I know I didn't do it. There's a 3rd washer that we use if we have to, and I had to. It took 1 hour and 43 minutes to do the one load. Tell me you live in an old complex, without telling me you live in an old complex.

The clock hadn't struck 8:30 a.m. yet, and there was a fraud alert sent to me on my debit card by my bank. I love my bank. They take such good care. The problem was that another hacker decided to take $99.00 from my account when I purchased something online. CRAZY how that works, because the company I bought something from had ZERO clue that they were being used as a mule; it happens. I hate it, but it happens. It's happened to me about four times now. The bank closes my card, and issues me a new one, then I have to write or call the places that take money out on a monthly basis to let them know I have a new card number. GEEZ.

While I was blaming a neighbor; another neighbor came out of his apartment to tell me that one of our other neighbors had been in a really bad car wreck. She's a Lyft driver, so I thought maybe she had passengers too. She did not, so that was good; but she's not expected to live, and that's really sad. I truly hate to hear these types of things.

Before lunch, my publisher wrote to me to let me know that the book I tried to release (Faith Walks) has a spine width that is .511 and it should be .481; they want me to redo the cover. WHAT? The book was in production at another publisher and printed for Amazon sales for 12 years, but suddenly it's the wrong size? And did you see the difference? Literally .03 inches!! NO. Just use it the way it is! I don't know if they will but I asked them to. Then, I redid the thing when I didn't get a response from them, but the thing is, I had to edit the PDF the original publisher sent to me, and I couldn't open it to make that change. I had to redo it through CANVA and when I did, I had to adjust things and it didn't turn out the way I wanted.

Not only did it change a few things; but I made a mistake on the back and I already uploaded it!! I have to wait for them to reject it before I can upload the corrected one. If they don't reject it, I'll have to resubmit it, and that takes another 2 or 3 days. I can't imagine them even thinking it's OK to say it's .03 inches off in the spine so we're going to not print it, even though it's been printed over 50,000 times, and yes...it has been printed over 50,000 times, so yeah, there is NO REASON to change it.

I went to the store to get the cat litter, cat food, and dog food, and there was only one cashier with about four of us in line. Again, First World Problem; so I waited. I said to myself, it's OK, you'll survive this. I was doing really well until the lady buying whatever she was buying was looking for her cash, she didn't have enough, so she went for a card, but it was declined. I thought about my card, so I kept patiently waiting...for another five full minutes. C'mon, call another cashier at this point. I didn't say anything, but my mind was squawking!

The man in front of me asked her if she could call someone and she said they had all quit or just not showed up today. There wasn't even a full moon, so I don't understand. I was finally checked out, but you guessed it, her drawer wouldn't shut so she couldn't ring up my purchases. We had to wait another several minutes for someone to come up to the front from the back; someone with more authority than the first lady had. BREATHE....so I did.

I picked the kid up from work, we went home, we got to our front door, and found that the managers had taken off the number plates of all the doors, and had taped off everything. I guess they're going to paint. Notice would have been great...another First World Problem. I began counting my blessings and saying them out loud. It always helps me when I do that. I have a home, I have food, I have water, I have a car, I have gas, and money to pay my bills. I have three great kids, 2 grandkids, and a few animals. I have written 9 books, I have an education, I have friends who know me and they still love me. I am a very blessed woman...but you know what, more than all that, I have Jesus in my soul. That makes all the difference in this world and every other world to come.

We're gonna have issues. We're gonna have problems. We're gonna face nasty situations, bad people, and just stuff....but we don't have to face it alone, and that is the best news I can give you. On the flip side, Michael's had candles on sale 2/$7 and they all smell like Autumn....this week, next week I'm sure they'll have their Christmas candles out, but for now, it's Flannel and Football, baby!!

Photo Credit: Pinterest.com

American Confidence

We Americans have it so easy, don't we? We're expected by so many, to have the confidence of 10 "*normal*" people. (What's not normal about being sure of yourself?) We walk through things like it's nothing. We approach matters with our heads up, staring adversity straight in the eyes! Well, some of us do, I suppose, but the thing is, we've been forced to be so edgy folks; we have to deal with pulling into, pulling out of, walking around, walking through, and surviving all these gas stations! Hell, those places will find a way to kill you if you're not on your A-game the entire time!! This doesn't take place in the UK or other places; we are dodging cars, trucks, people, tankers, workers, and others...we're apt to wrangle someone into making a competitive sports game out of it. (We'd win)

We do have confidence I suppose. I know I do. I was born with a healthy amount of it, and I got it from both my dad and my mom. Dad never said a word about his plans, but he always got things done. Mom made things very clear as to what she wanted and how it would be carried out; it was always carried out. I don't think I ever had a day in my life when goals weren't set and goals weren't met. That's how you do it. That's what's behind all this expected bravado! We just do what needs to be done, and when times get tough, we hunker, we don't quit or give in to the pressure. Why would we?

When I was in the UK, specifically in Scotland, I would walk into a cafe and notice that there wasn't a sign asking me to wait at the front. I usually did anyway, long enough to get the attention of the wait staff, I'd nod, and then take a seat. I wanted them to know I was there so I could be served. I wasn't trying to be rude, mean, or demanding. No, we're more commanding if anything; there is a difference. I didn't want to be there 15 minutes before someone noticed I hadn't ordered. It never failed, I got waited on immediately. I also told them when I ordered that I'd be ready for my check about 10 minutes after I got my food, or they could leave it at the same time they dropped the food off; that just makes it easier. Again, I don't have to wait for them to get around to finding me. I had a waiter go home once and I didn't get my check for about 45 minutes. That's not service. That's carelessness.

I am often asked by my Scottish friends (and those who stare blankly at me while I'm there) if I consider myself arrogant because I ask pointed questions, or because I stand under the shelter at the bus stop when the queue is clearly outside of it. No, I'm not being arrogant, I don't want to be wet. There is enough space for EVERYONE really, and we know who was there first. We can wait to board the bus. I'm just not into being rained on if I don't need to be. I rarely carry an umbrella. Maybe I should, but it gets in the way, and they'd think me much more than arrogant if I used it as a weapon in times of necessity.

No, I'm about the least arrogant person I know; I do know who I am though. I know my limits. I know my likes. I know my dislikes. I also know what I'm capable of doing or saying. Being self-aware (and even self-approved) doesn't make a person arrogant; it's rewarding to know that I like the company I keep when I'm alone. I can get into the best of moods when I'm with me. I can often be found talking to myself for that very reason; I agree with myself more often than I don't, but when I don't, I simply blame my English blood, and I declare independence and move forward. I have been known to put myself in my place!

It has been ingrained in me to do what I believe is right and to do what I know I can achieve. I do ask for help. I am also there to help others, and they don't even have to ask most of the time. I see they need something, so I volunteer. That often makes them think I'm purposely butting in; well, maybe you needed that! Maybe you weren't making it and it was so very quite obvious, so yeah, I stepped up and there you have it; you're welcome. It's not rude, it's not overbearing. It's me being there to assist and if you need me to, I'll drag your ass where it is you need to go. Again, you're welcome. It's it better to say thank you than to think the person who has your back is trying to gain from it? I don't need anything. I have Jesus.

So yeah, next time you're in the UK, or anywhere in Europe really, or in Scandinavia, I hear it's just as likely to happen there as well, and you see someone waving at you for no reason whatsoever....just nod, say hello, and maybe wonder to yourself which college football team they root for because it's very likely that if someone waved at you and spoke to you in those places that person is from my home country. I'd even venture to guess that person is from the South, rather than the North. Go ahead, play the card you're dealt! Ask! Ask them if they watch college football, and who their favorite team is. If they look you in the eyes and smile, then come back with *"Boomer Sooner!"* you'll know you're in good company, and if there's a tornado in the sky, you'll be safe as long as you're with that person.

Just sayin'.

Such a Spoiled American

I spend hours and I mean HOURS on the computer looking at the pretend houses I will someday buy when I move to Scotland. I know I shouldn't hope, wish, and dream, but hey, it's just the thing(s) I do to both entertain my brain, and to keep me motivated for if and when the time does come. I need to be so ready. First, and you should know this, houses in Scotland are NOT, not, not like they are in Oklahoma. You can find houses like they have in Scotland in other parts of the UK, but you're not going to find them over on this side of the pond for so many very (spoiled) interesting reasons. Let's go over a few, shall we?

Houses in Scotland (for a great part of the equation) were built between the years 1929 and 1959. So many of these *"two up - two down"* houses are exactly what it sounds like, smaller homes built with two main rooms (usually bedrooms) upstairs and two main rooms, such as a living and kitchen, downstairs. Yes, there is a bathroom and it could be on either floor. I shouldn't have said *"bathroom"*, I should have said *"shower room"* or *"wet room"* because unless there is an actual bathtub in it, they don't call them bathrooms! These houses were built KNOWING that an entire family of 4-6 could be living in them, and they only have one bathroom. These houses were built KNOWING that there would or could be a family of six living in them and they don't have what I call a normal-sized refrigerator. You can't make this stuff up.

The kitchens do have a front-load washing machine in the kitchen itself, but not a dryer, as most Scottish homes don't have a use for one. They hang their laundry out on the green line or if it's raining (and it's usually raining) they hang their clothes up on a rack that suspends from the ceiling. This rack could be found in the hallway, in the kitchen, in a bathroom -- heck, it could be in a bedroom! I've seen dryers in bedrooms, refrigerators in bedrooms, freezers, and/or three beds in a bedroom. I've seen carpet that looks as if they lost the bet on hideous hotel carpet gambling, and I've seen rooms without closets as well. You heard me, bedrooms without closets (or wardrobes as they are called). The really big huge Oh-My-Gosh-Are-You-Freaking-Kidding-Me thing is that Scottish homes don't have screens on their windows. Nope! They don't.

Some of the homes have an under-the-stairs storage area where you could possibly stash an extra toilet, but there isn't enough room for a little sink. That's OK, I will do that! The person can walk to the kitchen to wash their hands. There will be two toilets in my house. There will be a bathtub in my house. There will be real live screens on the windows, and YES, there will be an air conditioning unit installed and all the rooms will be ducted to that central unit. Most of the houses have radiators in each room, sometimes two per room for heat. They have NO air conditioning whatsoever, and I've not seen a window unit anywhere either - - that means it either doesn't get hot enough, or it doesn't stay hot very long. I get that. I do. I read up on the temperatures, but I'm not living in a house hotter than 72 degrees. It's not happening. YES, I am that spoiled.

I'm told the terrace houses are rather insulated, and that's good to know, but I've seen some really tacky looking wall paper (I am not sure we Americans have seen wallpaper other than what's on our phones, since the

1980s) and I've seen the most interesting fireplaces without actual fireplaces because fires in and around the main cities have been outlawed due to too many older homes going up in flames and taking neighbors with them. Google it. I'm not kidding. I don't have to have a fireplace. I'm good with just the fake thing that looks like one. Some people use it for decor. I think I'll take mine out and have the area transformed into a little shelf or something useful. I'll Pinterest that.

Let's talk hedges. EVERY house on nearly EVERY block has some sort of hedge around it. I don't like hornets and hornets love hedges. Sorry neighbors, yes, I'm going to annoy you further by taking out my hedges. Don't worry, I'll put up a nice tall privacy fence so you don't have to see what I'm doing on the other side. What will I be doing on the other side? I will likely be hanging upside down on my aerial hammock, or sitting in my hot tub with a fizzy water! (LaCroix, Bubly, Perrier) The back yards (gardens) in most cases are about 22 feet by 60 feet and they either have a gate at the back or they don't and you can't access them any other way other than through the house. My fence will have a gate! I say that. I can't very well put in a gate opening up into the neighbor's garden. We'll put a pin in that one for now.

Refrigerators. I talked about them before. The *"big"* ones in the UK (Scotland for sure) are the size of a rather small apartment fridge, not the dormitory-size, or the mini fridge, but the size of say, a tiny apartment that you can't turn around in the kitchen size, that's about the size of their average basic *"big"* refrigerator. Most of the houses either have that one or two smaller dormitory-sized units. I assume one is a freezer, I could be wrong. There are really tall and skinny units, they are more modern and I wouldn't mind one of those, which could actually work out. I just have to have a good freezer. I do buy things in bulk such as meat and frozen fruits. I did ask about that once. I was told that you cook frozen food when you buy it, there is no need to store it. If you didn't intend to cook it, you don't buy it. That's an interesting concept.

The attic! Oh yes, the attic. This is so very interesting and very very different from what we have here in the States, particularly in Oklahoma. Our attic access here is in the garage. We open the hatch by pulling down the rope, and we unhinge the ladder to climb up, and usually, the thing isn't finished out, but we can scoot boxes around on boards we've laid over on top of the beams. Makes so much sense, right? Not the same as it is in Scotland, and they have it right. They do it better, I think. The access is in the hall or a bedroom.

You do still pull down the hatch, and you do still unhinge the ladder. HOWEVER, from what I have seen in nearly every single unit I've looked over, the entire attic is finished out top to bottom, and you can stand up and walk around in it as if (as if) it was another bedroom! That would be because IT IS ANOTHER BEDROOM for the kids when they are in their younger years and have no issue running up and down the shaky ladders! Apparently, they leave the ladders down at night, and they put them back up when the kids come down to go to school. Gotcha! NOPE.

The attic in my house may very well be a bedroom or a guest room, but I will have the engineers come out and put in a little spiral staircase in a closet, extra area, bedroom, something so that the folks who come to visit me won't fear that I'll trap them inside my attic. At least the attic will also be ducted and hooked up to the central A/C. I may even add a skylight because I'm cool like that. My attic will be a place of beauty! Something to be admired. If anything it will at least be functional and part of the house. If I do only use it for storage, I will not have the extra staircase added, but I will have it connected so

266

my things are temperature controlled and not getting all hot and moldy. YUCK.

I'll show a floor plan and an exterior photo for you to look at and admire. If you're from the States you'll just (as I did) shake your head and think to yourself *"OK, well that makes sense, there are more people so they have to build upward"*. That was my thought process anyway. You can fit two Scotlands in Oklahoma, and yet there are twice as many folks in Scotland than there are in the Sooner State. We have just under 3M I think, and they have close to 6M, something like 5.8M. It makes perfect sense to build UP. You should see the blocks and blocks of apartments in Edinburgh and Glasgow! Oh, and most of them, even though they are four stories tall, don't have an elevator! You walk! They call it a lift, and yes, you just walk up the stairs and down the stairs. Also, if you're on the ground floor that's called the ground floor. If you're on the next floor above the ground floor, they call it the 1st floor whereas we will call it the 2nd. That can be confusing.

All in all, I'm looking forward to the next chapter of my life. I'm going to try to be as Scottish as I can be, but yeah, I'm not giving up my fridge, my dryer, or my A/C. I don't think I'll have to bend too many arms and I bet I have more friends over in the summer who will appreciate the flow of air and the buglessness of my window screens. That's right. I don't really like bugs. I can say that with confidence. I don't mind them living in their space, but they don't need to be taking up residence in mine! Call me spoiled. I don't mind because I know I am.

Be Prepared. It's a Choice

I'm going to try and be positive while writing this blog, but to be honest, I'm just over here shaking my head and wondering why folks will show up to a scheduled Zoom call completely unprepared. We were told, (told, told, and retold) that it would be required to have a desktop or laptop, two monitors, a headset with a mic, as well the ability to download a certain program. We were told. Let me try to get that through, we were given at least 3 separate emails letting us know that before the Zoom we were to have these things in place.

I get it if a person can't afford the desktop, the laptop, the monitors, whatever is needed. I do get that, I've been there a dozen times myself, but it is required. I have had to tell my kids so many times that we can't afford this or that; if you can't, you can't and you move forward or try to find a way. It may be that you have to wait until you can afford it before you can participate, but to show up to the Zoom where 50 others are ready to go, and not have what you need, is the epitome of not being ready. It doesn't mean that a person is a bad person; they're not being selfish or rude, they are just not ready. People, we have to be ready. We are required to be READY.

I'm thinking that being prepared for whatever can happen in life is a learned thing; we are to be taught. We need to be taught. This means we have to be willing to be taught. We do that by showing up, listening, following directions, and asking questions. Listening is extremely important. If we're not ready to listen, to gather the intel, to understand the situation, we're not going to be ready or able; we may only be willing. Why am I going through this rant?

I'm on a Zoom training session with about 50 folks. We've all been waiting for this particular class for over a month. Through a series of emails, we were told we needed to have certain components of equipment, we were told to download a certain program, we were told to show up at a certain hour, and we were told we were required to have a camera as well as a headset with a microphone. This is 2023. This is NOT something we don't know; however, we simply have too many lazy folks who just can't get their act together, or they don't put an urgency to what is required.

Don't blame me for being direct. Don't blame me for speaking the truth. Don't blame me for being frustrated and disappointed with the generation(s) who think it's OK to be late, OK to be slack, OK to be less than what is required or expected. Why should 14 of us wait for the other 36 who aren't compliant? I remember in 2011 when I was asked to interview enough folks to meet the criteria so Xerox could hire them for open enrollment. We needed 80 folks. I had to interview 600+ to get 74 because so many folks were unwilling to be drug tested. Seriously? Those that did pass that test were woefully unprepared for the first day due to either not being able to wake up, show up, or do what is expected of them.

I didn't want to say it, so I'll let the instructor's words do the job for me. The instructor, who openly stated his age to be 46, said that out of the 50 people who were to show up and do the work as expected today, 48 did in fact show up, but 11 of them were late. He stated that 11 others were early, and the rest were literally signing in exactly at 8:00 a.m. CST. He commended those of us who were early, and made the statement that of the 11, 9 of those people were "*Boomers*". There were no "*Boomers*" to show up on time or late. He then went on to say that there were too many folks under the age of 40 who either didn't have the withal to show up, sign in on time, or to have whatever was required of them. The 9 "*Boomers*" to a person, had their equipment ready, their download ready, etc. He was making a specific point. I think I'm willing to make it as well.

We may be older. We may be "*over the hill*" but most of us can still climb it without having to check our social media, take a selfie, and call a friend to ask for directions as to which way we were supposed to go up that hill. The generation just below mine is mostly responsible, but the one below that is disastrously late, and they don't give a rip to be apologetic because they don't actually think that their behavior is out of line. This, as they say, is our future. Welcome to a disorganized mess, is all I can say if that is what the world at large wants to accept.

I'll give you ONE MORE example before I go. During the scheduled training the instructor gave us all a break so the ones who were not downloaded, prepared, and/or set up could do so. He said, "*Be ready, come back at 9:30*". When that moment came, there were six (6) people who took their break rather than taking the 20 minutes to set up what needed to be set up. When he drilled them about it, they said "*You told us to take a break*" I am NOT kidding you. This is where we are folks. Do we blame these people, or do we blame their parents? I bet you can't blame their grandparents!

GEEZ LOUISE!!!

Waffle House. The Southern Camelot

If you're from the South you get it. If you're from anywhere else, you have to come here to get it, but Waffle House is the best restaurant, the most *"American"* restaurant there is. Fight me, if you think I'm wrong. I'm not wrong. You haven't experienced America if you've not been to a Waffle House (pick one, any one of them) at say 2 or 3 in the morning for a bit of food, and a whole lot of WHAT THE HECK IS THIS?

It's been a minute since I've been to one, but after watching a few videos of what's been going on at these places, inside these hallowed squares, I think I need to venture back to one of the yellow-roofed master chef experiences; it could be a calling. I'm not sure. It could be that I just can't believe all the things (crap) I'm missing by sleeping in my bed at night, and not hanging out with the Wafflers.

A few of the more recent videos I've seen involve the staff (they are all specially trained, by the way) either dancing, singing, and/or twerking while cooking, they are also deflecting chairs, throwing dough, spilling coffee that didn't taste as good as perhaps one customer thought it should; they are tearing it up! People go in now to video, to upload stories of what they see and witness on TikTok to see who can get a better Waffle House video. No kidding. It's really addicting to watch.

I know that in the 80's I used to go to the Waffle House after performing as a stand-up comedian. I would go in around 2:45-3:00 a.m., maybe get a big breakfast, maybe just some water with about 10 lemon slices, which could be considered 4 lemons. I'd be the one dancing, but the staff would always join in with me. We'd have fun then, and that was 40 years ago. Times have changed a bit, I don't remember there being any mean brawls, which are being reported now. I remember laughing, dancing, one-upping, and meeting people you have never seen before because they were on their way to Dallas or something.

Matthew Mitchell, the Southern comedian on YouTube just posted a really fun video about the staff at all Waffle Houses being trained in martial arts as well as culinary specialties. He's not wrong. He's like *"We'll teach you to chop, cut, poke, punch, and then we'll teach you to cook too!"* He's not wrong. Kid Rock has a history (2007) of being arrested at a Waffle House. More than a lot of folks have been killed at a Waffle House; it's just a magnet for such behavior, and probably (no doubt) because it's always open. I know that Denny's has a slogan of *"Always Open"* but Waffle House is right there. They don't close. They stay open during pandemics. They stay open during tornadoes. They stay open during hurricanes. It literally took FEMA to close them down in some instances. People were not happy about it either. (There are more YouTubes about that as well.)

People get engaged at Waffle House. People get married at their favorite Waffle House. People have funeral and wedding dinners at Waffle House. It's just a thing here in the South. I saw a worker leave her post as a cashier to help a kid do his homework once. I saw another worker go into the back kitchen area and bring out a bottle of ketchup that was about to be thrown away. She asked the patron if he wanted to get some of it using a knife or something. The entire restaurant was out of ketchup, the manager had sent a kid to get some more, but the worker was like, *"Let me see what I can do"*. This is the South.

Write and Publish Your Book – Almost Free

I say "*free*" and what I mean by that, is that it didn't cost me any out-of-pocket money to write and then publish my book. It was literally free, but you do have to have a computer with Word, and you do have to have internet access. I'm not talking about 100% totally free, but you don't have to pay a big-time publishing company, or even a small boutique publishing company to publish, format, and/or design your book. You can (with a bit of patience) do it yourself. I'll explain.

I'm going to use "*Murder Book*" as an example because I have paid for every other book I wrote prior to *Murder Book*, to be formatted, edited, published, and then printed and distributed. You do still have to pay if you want to promote it, but I bet there are ways to do that by word-of-mouth, and other formats such as Tik Tok, and Facebook; the list is endless.

OK, so you want to write a book, and you've got a story to tell. Great, get your computer, and be sure you have a word processor loaded onto it. I use Word by Microsoft; others may use Google Docs or any other format. I prefer Word. I really preferred the older versions, but then again, the new versions probably have more capabilities when it comes to the actual formatting of the book. It's a trade-off. I wrote Murder Book in about 2 months' time. I started it in genuine in June, but I had started a bit before that, just sort of playing around with outlines and such. We'll say I wrote it in two months. Then, I called around, hunted the internet for places to just take the document in Word, which was 83400 words or so, and to just format it using a 5"x 8" book, and I needed a cover for it too.

I ran into three major problems. (1) Either they could format it and not do the cover, or (2) they could do the cover, but didn't want to format the book, or (3) they could do both and they were really expensive. I tried contacting folks on Fivver who were talented, experienced, and needed a good reference, as they are usually cheaper. I found GREAT people, but some of them seemed REALLY shady. I had a gal promise me to do the formatting for $10 and that just seemed crazy since I had paid an actual professional publisher over $700 for the same service a few months back. Why or how could she do it for $10? Turns out I was being RIPPED OFF by the publishing houses. I can do EXACTLY what they did for zero cost! NOTHING.

The lady who wanted to charge $10 told me how. I sent her $10 by the way. I don't count that as part of my book prep, it was more or less a thank-you. She appreciated it. She told me how to do the format, which two videos on YouTube to watch, because they were really close, but a little different; she felt it was good to point out their ideas and methods were really good, but they do have slightly different results. I watched, I learned, I took notes, and then I applied my new knowledge, and guess what, it worked. I managed to format my book in less than 30 minutes. I can do the next ones much faster, but I was learning how, and even 30 minutes isn't bad. I waited four weeks for one publisher to get my book formatted and sent to me for approval. I did it in 30 minutes!!

You write your book, and you save it as a PDF. Then you go to Microsoft tools and you input all your needed measurements. I'll actually make a blog soon with all the directions. That will make people happy. Anyway,

I wanted to know if I had the ability to possibly make a cover that I liked as well. Turns out I do. I watched about four or five videos, and the ones I found most helpful suggested that I go to Adobe and download it for a month (free trial) and then go to Canva and do the same. Canva has a 30-day free trial as well. I went to Adobe Stock, and I downloaded 10 free photos that I may want to use in the future for books. I think I screwed them up when I downloaded them as I resized them. Don't do that. I may have to do another free month using another email address to get the same photos but in their original size.

Once you download the photo you want you upload it into Canva, AFTER you download the KDP book cover format template, which also is free. You just have to find it. If you use the Canva book design tool they tell you where the sites are, and there are more than just KDP, but I know they do 5"x 8" books, so I went there. You have to do a bit of research, trial, and error, practice, and have patience, because you have to get the spine width to fit your book size. My book has 395 pages. It is 83400 words, and I am using regular paper, nothing fancy. You'll find that fancy adds width. So, once you have figured out your sizes, you add that to the Canva template, and you upload your photo for the cover.

The front cover is what you're uploading, the back cover is handled differently. You choose your texts, you put them in, you choose colors, you change fonts, but remember if you use a font that is not open-sourced, you may have to get a license to do that. That can cost you, so remember to also do your research to find the fonts you need and want. There are thousands that are free, you'll probably find many you can use. When you get the front cover done, you read the instructions on Canva to show you how to upload the solid color for the back, stretching it over the entire border of the template. If you don't stretch it the distributor will kick it back saying the size is off by fractions of a fraction of an inch, but it matters. COVER THE DANG TEMPLATE.

Done. You have created your book in Word, you have saved it in Adobe as a PDF, uploaded it into MS, and formatted it, you've researched to find out how to change your chapter styles, your headers, your footers, your numbers, heck, you've even done your freaking cover for FREE!! WOW! The next thing you do is upload each, two separate files, into your Ingram Spark account under new titles. I use Ingram Spark, you can use KDP or whoever you want. Ingram Spark is not charging to upload a title. It used to cost $50 for the book and $50 for the cover, but they had a bit of competition recently, and they dropped those charges. Woot!! (again, if you want to promote the book it will cost you, but writing it and getting it to the point of distribution doesn't have to cost you.)

I paid $1250 for "*Faith Walks*" to go from my computer to being a book. I paid the same or close to it for "*Of Kilted Pleasure*" and for "*Jude's Almost Daily Blog Book*". I paid about $700 for my less than 100-page poetry book. NOT AGAIN. "*Murder Book*" looks as professional as any of my other books, and I did it for NOTHING. You can't count the cussing, fussing, screaming, or wall-kicking moments that I had. I will be so much better with "*Pinball*", in fact, I've already downloaded the cover for "*Pinball*" and about four other books I will write. I know they will all be about the same size, so I used that same template. If they are not that size, I'll simply fluff and stuff until they reach that size. I'm happy with my newfound creative side.

Was it easy? HELL NO. But, I did learn a great deal not only about book creation but also about myself. I won't format for others, but I will do what my associate did for me, I'll tell people which YouTube videos to watch, and where to find the right templates. I'll list the steps below. Let me know if you're wanting to write a book and publish it for NOTHING. I'll send you in the right direction if I can. Woot!!

Ingram Spark: www.ingramspark.com

Canva: www.canva.com

Adobe: www.adobe.com

Silly Decisions (Some Make)

Without going into so much detail about the ins and outs of independent claims adjusters, how they work, what they do, what they can expect to be paid for doing it, and so forth, I will say that I come across those who just don't understand the game -- but they are the EMPLOYERS; they should know better.

Independent Claims Adjusters are just that; we are claims adjusters who have for reasons of our own, decided to be independent rather than captive. Captive can be good if it pays well, the hours are good, and the employer isn't hanging over your shoulder to be sure you're actually working. The truth of the matter is, most adjusters are either remote or field, not in-house or staff, and they work - - ready for it? INDEPENDENTLY...on their own. They don't need someone reminding them what it is they are supposed to be doing.

That being said, no one is first an independent without first being trained. How do you get properly trained if everyone wants you to have experience before you start? Good (no, great) question. Here's the answer; there are literally dozens of companies who will hire people fresh out of the gate but usually during CAT or catastrophic events such as big storms, hurricanes, tornadoes, wind and hail, etc. Once they hire someone who doesn't have the experience another company would prefer, the hiring company uses these folks as the undercoat for their experienced adjusters. It's a harder harsh way of being trained perhaps because the hours are extreme, but the fact is, people will and do hire inexperienced people, train them, and then either release them due to lack of work, or the person themselves will leave and find a company paying a steady-eddy salary with less hours and less micromanagement - - until the next CAT season!

See, with CAT seasons, a person can make upwards of $34 an hour, to begin with and then another time and a half after the first 40 hours. Most CAT employees (at least the adjusters) work 72-84 hours a week. The money begins to stack up rather quickly. Do the steady-eddy captive sorts really, in their WILDEST dreams, think that an independent will remain captive when CAT comes? Not going to happen, unless they can negotiate a better salary, more time off, etc. You've got TPA or third-party admins now offering 15-18 days of Paid Time Off, holiday pay, etc., but they still pay about $50-55K a year; which won't touch what 1099 independent can make. There are independents, and many of them, clearing over $200K a year. Who in their right mind would think that person will remain with them as a captive?

I just had an interview, not 15 minutes ago, with a captive company wanting to pay me $55K and they had the withal to explain to me that they really needed someone with more actual experience. Well, OK. I agreed. They probably do NEED and WANT that, but it comes at a hefty price tag. The person they'll find and put into that slot will be someone who lied about their experience on their resume so they can be hired. When they get the job they'll claim they were trained a completely different way, but hey, they're willing to be trained the company way...of course, they are; they have NO experience. When they get it, say in 6-8 months, they'll leave and work for the first CAT opportunity that comes along or they'll choose to find a company that pays more for the 8 months experience they have. Simple facts.

Anyway, I was cordial. I was kind. I asked specifically what they were looking for, and they told me, and I explained I wasn't qualified at this time. I did however, take the opportunity to briefly explain why it is that they will likely find someone who lied, train them, pour money, time, and effort as well as hope and trust into that person, only to have them leave even as soon as September when CAT season is in full swing. Or, I explained, they can hire me, and I'll stay. I don't need as much as others want and/or think they need. I was raised by a woman who felt that ethics and loyalty were valued measurements of a person's character. We'll see what they choose. I'm 99% sure they'll fall flat, but hey, I did try to warn them.

If you don't know about CAT seasons and independent adjusters, you may want to check it out. I'm currently licensed in 5 states, and about to get another one soon. I may not have it all yet, but it doesn't take a rocket scientist to figure out that I'll be hired as soon as the first real CAT hits - - so why would I want to jump ship then and go back to work for the people who (a) didn't have the insight to hire me in the first place (b) wanted to treat me as if I had little to no experience (c) would only give me $55K a year (albeit the bennies are good)? The answer? I don't need a lot of money, I prefer 8a-5p work, M-F, and I want to say I have a job, this is what I do. I could use the extra hours to write books!

Some people are silly, I suppose. They'll learn. It really is ONLY a matter of time.

Cats are Weird. (That is All)

We have an ironclad rule in our house; if you are seated and a dog is on your lap you don't have to move or do anything. You can order people about the house, making them do things for you, but you can't for any reason disturb the dog. I suppose there are reasons, but they are few and very very rare. You don't disturb the dog. The same rule does not and never will pertain to cats. Cats are not worthy of the loyalty and devotion I offer to my dog(s) because they themselves are neither loyal nor devoted to me. Cats are weird. We can all (mostly) agree on that one thing.

So, to prove my point further, that cats are weird, I will tell you about Bilbo and Sam. Bilbo is MY cat. He's not quite two years old, but he's about twenty pounds. He's a big boy. He's a grey and black Tabby. He was given to us by a military friend who had another military friend who was being deployed. We end up with animals for all sorts of reasons; this is not new. Sam, on the other hand, was an adoption from the city shelter when my daughter Laura felt that she just HAD to have a cat to go with her other cat Frodo. Sam, by the way, is Sam Wise, he's Frodo's friend, right? See how this works? Frodo, Sam Wise, and now Bilbo. We are THAT family.

Sam and Bilbo get along so much better and more often than anyone gets on with Frodo. Frodo is more or less a loner and by that I mean he only speaks to Laura. He tolerates me. He doesn't even come running when I shake the treat bag if he can't be bothered. Frodo is thin.

Bilbo and Sam are so not thin. They always run when the treat bag shakes, and they wait on it as well. They are simply not thin cats. Sam is another Tabby, but he's yellow; he is also at least twenty pounds. Frodo may squeak out 8-9 pounds if he's lucky. He's a Burmese grey/blue. He's very thin naturally.

This morning, as they do, the *"boys"*, meaning Bilbo and Sam, were in their usual position(s) of one dominating the other and looking THAT way. I usually click my tongue and shoo one or the other off of the other, and they resume in another room. They also lay around the bed(s) kissing and licking one another, presumably cleaning one another, but I really think they may actually be in a relationship. I'm not going to ask. I just continue to shoo them when I see them being what I would deem inappropriate.

We also own horses, so I have things lying about the house that goes with these animals. I have a crop whip, a shorter one, that I use on the dog to keep him from walking into my room. He makes a mess. He doesn't really ever get hit with the thing, he just sees me holding it or picking it up, and he walks away like a good dog. This is NOT the behavior that either of my *"boy"* cats (Frodo is a boy too, but he doesn't give a hoot about anything for any reason). Bilbo sees the crop is lifted and he eyeballs my hands, watching me and waiting for me to either use it or put it down. Sam tries to get under it. Sam likes being smacked with the crop whip. I never hit him hard, but that's how he is...he likes it. He's just so...well, inappropriate.

This morning I was typing, just working, and my Bilbo comes over to let me know he was available for cuddles should I be in the mood; I am usually in the mood to cuddle my cat. Sam saunters up to us while we're cuddling and he paws at Bilbo as if to say he is the only one allowed to show affection to him; so I cuddled both of them at the same time, which is always fun. Two fat cats squirming to get out from under the loving squeeze, you know. Sam sees the crop whip on my desk and begins pawing at it, asking me to lift it. I do. He stares at me. He wants me to lower it. I do. He stares at me. He wants me to strike him in the rear with it. I do. He loves it. He rolls over and invites Bilbo over to cuddle. I stop. I walk away. I find a dog.

Cats are just weird. That is all.

Frodo (laying down) Bilbo (sitting)

Get Serious About Getting Naked

You and I both know that any given day, usually every single day, we all get naked at some point during said day. If we're honest with ourselves we should be getting naked so we can take a shower and/or take a bath and it's that bath time that I'm about to talk to you about. I just needed to get your attention long enough to drag your eyes over here to read what it is that I'm rambling on about today. I've been on a writing streak lately, and if you're gonna streak, you should be naked. If you don't get that you don't get that, but if you do, it was hilarious!

You may or may not care to know this, but I am one of those wild and crazy women who take a bath every single day of the week. I don't care if I end up taking a shower too; that's OK, I'm good with getting naked a couple times a day, nothing wrong with that whatsoever, but it is going to happen at least once, because I refuse to wear my clothes in the bathtub. That's just silly talk right there. Nope, this girl is buck naked when she bathes. Let it be written, so let it be done.

When I do take that daily bath I fill the tub with not just the hottest water I can stand (girls are so weird) but I also put in over a cup full of white vinegar, about an ounce of sweet almond oil (I say an ounce, I've very rarely measured anything in my life) and I empty about a 1/3 of a regular box of baking soda into the tub as well. But wait, I'm not finished, I also use a good amount of Dr. Teal's Lavender foaming bath Epsom salt as well - - to say I spoil myself is beyond an understatement. I am the worst and the very best to myself. I don't drink, smoke, do drugs, party, or collect things, so my baths can be a bit expensive, it's OK.

I think the manager at Big Lots had to laugh at me today when I replenished my bath supplies. I took a big orange basket and filled it with 8 gallons of white vinegar, 16 boxes of baking soda, 4 bottles of Dr. Teal's Lavender foaming bath, and yeah, I bought a bag of shortbread cookies too; a girl's gotta eat something. The cashier asked me if it was a party at my house tonight! LOL...I told her I'd ask the dogs and cats if they had something planned because I don't. I just get myself naked and soak out all the heavy metals, stress and anxiety out of my entire system over and over again day after day. I swear, I have no worries at this point, and the last time I remember stressing I was still young enough and able to make children. I haven't been stressed in a minute or two.

I don't even know when it was that I began filling up the bathtub in such a strange and unusual way, but nearly every time I get hugged at church or touched by someone who hasn't touched me before (that came out completely wrong) I am always complimented on how soft and smooth my skin is, and I've even had people lean into me and ask me what perfume I'm wearing because they can smell the light cast of vinegar and almonds I suppose. I usually say it's something I picked up at the store a while back. I'm not lying. If they licked me they'd probably taste the baking soda and give me a stare or two. So far I've not had anyone do that; which could in and of itself be a sad thing. I'll have to blog about my feelings concerning not being licked in another blog...not today. (You can't see me on the floor trying to make it back into my chair from falling out of it laughing at myself.)

Who knew getting naked could be so fun? Who knew getting naked could be so good for you, and it feels really good too. I mean after you've eliminated all the yucky toxins in your body from just walking around in polluted air every day, you need to get the smoke out of you, as well as the smudge and smog, the stuff falling into the air from being sprayed on plants, crops, in the clouds. You can't be in the urban areas without literally being exposed to so many dangerous chemicals at the micro levels. I'm not kidding you when I say that this works. It works. I said it again, and I wasn't kidding then either. This bath concoction works. You don't have to make your water hot as Hades, I just do that because I like to do that; most people (including me) will add cooler water to temp it down a bit at times. Does it work in cooler water? Sure. I've just never ever been a cold-water fan. Even when it's really hot outside I don't do the whole icy water therapy thing - - I'm more of a Tropical Temp fan when it comes to water. Think Sea Turtle, not Polar Bear.

There you have it. You have the best idea now for what to do with yourself next time you get naked. I mean, I can't tell you what you should or shouldn't do when you are, but at least now you know what can be done. Don't forget, and this is sooooo very important, don't forget to wipe the tub out when the water is fully drained. You don't want to slip on the oil the next day when you shower. I guess I do usually get naked twice a day; I use a big fat cup to pour the bath water all over my head about 100 times so yeah, my hair gets rather oily and I let it stay that way during the night and wash it in the morning. I don't do that if I'm not going anywhere but I do most days. You may or may not care to know this, but I don't blow dry my hair. No need. I let it dry on its own. Now that you have that tidbit of information you'll understand why it is that I look like I've just slicked my hair back on an off day if you catch me walking the dog. Just smile. No need to ask now.

Go ahead. You can do it. Get naked! Take time to defret yourself. The Bible says you shouldn't fret. I say you can only fret when you're playing your guitar - - otherwise, there is no need. Soak it out.

Irn Bru. (Not a Fan...Sorry)

If you've been to Scotland, you've seen Irn Bru. You may not have realized what it was that you were looking at, but you had to have seen it. It's everywhere!! You can call Irn Bru a soft drink, but you can also call it a replacement liquid for antifreeze and not be too far off from the truth. OK, I'll be serious for a minute and say I'm joking, I don't really want anyone to use Irn Bru as a replacement for their winterizing, but at the same time, it tastes what I think radiator fluid would actually taste like. NO, I don't have any actual experience with drinking that. No emails, please.

When I first went to Scotland, I naturally wanted to try literally everything that was typically Scottish. All tourists do what tourists do. When someone comes to Oklahoma, they want to see the Zoo, they want to see our football teams, they want to take in a BBQ and a rodeo. It's what you do. So, there I was, in the first convenience store that I happened into, and I saw the bright orange bottle being sold in the soft drink aisle (actually, it was an end cap) and I bought a bottle. To my surprise, the convenience store wasn't like a 7-11 or Quik Trip here, it wasn't that overpriced, and you don't pay the extra 8-9% tax when you get to the register, so the price of 80P was that, 80! Not quite a quid. I don't know what they sell for now.

I didn't pop it open and down it right there; I remember my friends saying it was better when it was cold, so I took it to the hotel and I put it in the little fridge. When I say little fridge, I mean, "*Oh. My. Gosh. That's terribly small.*" I can't shake that part of the UK; it's just there. Tiny, tiny refrigerators. I put the Irn Bru into that box, and I let it sit for a few hours. When I came back from my first day of touring and being a typically obnoxious visitor, probably asking way too many out-of-the-question questions, I decided to settle down with my first authentic bottle of Scotland's "*other*" national drink. I'm not a whiskey drinker, so this was my jam...except no, it was not.

I was SO underwhelmed by the taste of the favorite drink in my adopted land that I was upset with myself for feeling the way that I felt. I tried it a second time. I thought maybe I had just been...you know, unprepared. Nope. The second time it hit my tastebuds was not any better, and it was this time that I absolutely realized that the sugar content must be something only a toddler would do; but then again, I realized that someone thought it up, someone else agreed, and they made it. They made it, they continue to make it, and they distribute it....everywhere.

I was told that the Irn Bru I had in 1982 is different than the recipe they have now; this is because a man complained about it being bad for the national health of Scotland. This particular man must have some pull; he was popular enough to garner the attention of the powers that be to literally change the recipe to force the A.G. Barr company in Cumberland to dramatically decrease the sugar levels in their own patented soft drink. I don't actually like sugared drinks, and I'm from the South. I don't put sugar in my tea, which I think is actually considered a sin where I come from, but nevertheless, I'm one of the VERY few who would prefer Irn Bru with less sugar. (That is if I could get past the actual taste.)

When in Rome! PLEASE, don't let me discourage you from going to Scotland and trying the Irn Bru. You may love it. You may end up buying so many bottles and trying to get past Customs. I don't know. You may think it's the best thing EVER, but I just think it looks pretty (it's orange), and it should remain sealed and in its little bottle; they have cans too, but you can't see the liquid inside the cans. I think, if I remember my history, that the drink was developed around the same time that Coke was invented, and it may or may not have been used for medicinal purposes. I can see using it to start a campfire...or warding off evil spirits. That being said, the locals say it is the best hang-over drink and that it will bring you straight back to reality!

For years the makers of Irn Bru tried to keep the ingredients a complete secret, but the bigger distributors (mainly the US and Canada) demanded to know the full list of ingredients before allowing it to be sold in our respective countries. I've seen it in a few stores, but I've never stopped and looked at the packaging to see if the ingredients are listed. I do remember reading on the package that the drink could have an adverse effect on children's behavior! WHAT? Yes, that's always good to know; good to share! Gotta love their honesty. If you do try it, and you don't like it, it's OK. No one will be sad about it. No one will try to convince you that you're wrong. You like what you like. If you love it, you could find a few new friends with really cool accents. Just sayin'.

Murder in Edinburgh (Working on it)

I am about to murder someone in my book(s) and he will be gloriously found, while a detective who has been called upon to investigate is cautious to both not betray his own involvement in past events, and do his best to unearth the clues leading to the conviction of the murderer (or will it be a murderess?)

My books will be in a loose chronological order, there will be some flashing back, there will be some overlap, and there will be some future telling. I'm in the middle of the mix now, and diving (delving) into as much of it as I can without doing too much damage to the living soul of the manuscript. I tend to let the dead tell me more than they could have when they were living. It's not the murder, and it never has been for me, it's the cover-up and the disposal of the body(ies) that make my books more interesting; at least for me.

Currently, I am the only one reading my book(s) because I've not published anything dealing with the murder books at this time. I've written several, but I don't like what I've done with most of them; that's the trouble with writers. We can't stop the ink once it gets a good flow to it. I reckon it may be that way for a few painters as well. I dare say there have been a few who should have called it quits but just couldn't release their brush! I fully comprehend the concept. I'm going through the pale now, fleshing out words and transforming my vocabulary at the same time. I am using the handy-dandy Thesaurus to create a new connotation here and there, if not to change the entire meaning now and again. My thing is, I really like double meanings, so if I can bolt a word rather than slay one, I will do that. I want the thing to rivet, not destroy. I want the concept and the premise to damage, not obliterate.

Right now, I'm reading a more contemporary novel involving murder in Edinburgh, Scotland, which is where my murder (well, the murder I'm writing) takes place. I am using words, thoughts, concepts, ideas, and innuendo, as well as closely relating many of my passages to meet and even marry those of other authors. This method will both reiterate that the styles and context agree and that they have been widely accepted. No need to reinvent the wheel, but you know I'll never cross or toss a line. I'll never plagiarize. I'd sooner bleed my last.

For instance, my detective will not be caught dead in a proper coffee house drinking a smooth yet bitter cappuccino, but he will visit the public houses for what he refers to as a "*Cup of Joe*"; I wonder how many readers know the reason why it's called Joe? I'll explain in my book, as it has been often explained in others. That's the sort of thing I do. I reiterate but never take. Here's a nugget; did you know that the cappuccino was invented around the 1700-1720 timeframe? Interesting. I'd love to study a bit about how they got the milk to froth; steam of course, but I'm interested still in finding out more. My readers will know. I'll find out and let them know. For now, they'll have to Google it I suppose. I know I will.

One of my murders will take place in a close on the Royal Mile. I haven't decided which one yet. One of the murders happens in broad daylight, right in front of the worldly world to see; and no one takes notice. Our fine friend Nick Posh will indeed (and in deed) have his work cut out for him as he detects, sleuths, and otherwise investigates the seedy beginnings of the end of a few.

There will be a few. That's another clue - - why stop at two? (OK, I'll stop now.) I'm also writing a poem that will be introduced in the book as well. I'm not sure if the poet dies or if she'll disguise her mannerisms through quill and stain, enough to beg the apologies of others who may have believed her to be less innocent as her hand and mind.

Today, I read of pyrates on the North Atlantic. I read of mystics who fled to the moors before they could be caught, tried, and executed for who and what they were. I read of cannibals, of hungry peasants without enough to eat, and of wild animals roaming the Highlands for centuries. I am breaking down and building up the moments that drain and cascade into my writings. I dream and mend my mind over and over again of the thoughts it has; not wanting to blame Edinburgh or hold her responsible for her crude and cruel past. I am her admirer, but I am also her judge and jury. I will never execute my darling city, but I will expose her. I will not allow her to keep her secrets hidden if they are damned within her soul. She must be saved.

My books (this series) take place between 1920-1940, but in order to accurately understand the men and women of that time I must start about 1000 years beforehand; to create the language, the culture, the barriers, and the breeding. This has been and will be the most amazing journey. I don't have an *"Elephant Cafe"* from which to claim that I have penned the first words of my novels.

I may have to find some really cool place to write a few notes into a notebook so I can claim it and someday they'll hang a plaque to remember the day! J.K. Rowling could have just as easily been holed up in her apartment when she wrote the first words of *"Harry Potter and the Sorcerer's Stone"*. We'll never know the truth; that's not that important anyway, is it? The story of the beginnings of such a great series taking place in Edinburgh's Elephant Cafe is far more intriguing, wouldn't you agree? I'll find a hole in the wall. I'll make it happen. It'll happen. Maybe I'll sit at the side of Ross Fountain, look up at Castle Rock and say this is where I got the inspiration to write all of my stories - - it won't be true of course, but how can any of us know whether or not the story about the Elephant Café is true? We can't.

Photo Credit: (Tony Broonford of Clan Broonford)

I Love Dead People

This is me giving you a bit of an insight into my personality and what it is that I love. I love dead people. Yes, it is true; this woman loves the past, the history of everything, and with history comes (naturally) the deceased. By loving dead people, what I mean is I find myself gravitating to a city or county graveyard where I can walk among the stones, reading them and thinking about the departed whose body is *"resting"* beneath the words shared about them. I read the stones. I think about the person. I make up stories about them. I even pretend we have known each other while they were alive or when we were all in heaven before coming to Earth, you know, the normal weirdness that happens in the mind of a writer.

I can, perhaps, lay the blame of my love for dead people squarely on my mother's shoulders as it was she who first took me to the cemeteries when I was young. She liked to see if she could find the oldest marker, the newest marker, the prettiest marker, the ugliest marker, and things of that nature. It was more or less her hobby, and who is to say if it was odd; I was a kid. I had no idea if it was weird or not. I know that for over 100 years, people have gathered at Edgar Allen Poe's grave to celebrate Halloween with him and/or people who liked his work. I know that's considered odd, but fun. I would do it.

When I was in my mid-20s, I went to the gravesite of Temple Lea Houston, the last son of General Sam Houston; it's in Woodward, Oklahoma. I not only visited his grave, but I also spent the night in the museum, where

295

most of his personal effects still remain. I, in fact, helped to set up the display that they used to showcase his personal and professional wares. That's a wonderful blog; I'll leave the link. When I found Temple's gravestone, I was quite disappointed. It was too new. Yep, it was right out of the 1980s or maybe a bit earlier, but it wasn't from 1905, the year he ceased to be among the living. It didn't fit with the times, and it bothered me. It still does.

Bill Doolin and Elmer McCurdy's tombstones aren't my favorites either. They look like they are trying too hard to be old. Elmer's was set to match Bill's, but neither of them is from the time of the men's deaths. (Albeit, it's true Elmer died in 1911 but was buried in 1977, there's that...another great story.) When you walk the cemeteries as much as I do, you start to notice things, things that maybe others just don't see. I see them. One of the things I see is the blue fake plastic/silk flowers that people buy, and I have a thing about them, too; I don't like them. I've commissioned my friend to steal every blue plastic/silk flower from the graveyard (when I do die), and she's to line my gravestone with them - - all of them. Because that way she can save money and I can have a good laugh.

I find myself doing something else, too; when I look for a place to live in Scotland, I tend to find churches nearby so I can see if their cemeteries are worth walking through. Some places don't even have an old churchyard or kirkyard, and that just won't do. Just as important as it is for me to have a good grocery store within walking distance, I want to walk to a cemetery, MY cemetery, with MY dead people, and I want to meet my new "*friends*" on a regular basis. I have stories to tell and stories to listen to. I have a vested interest in that I am a writer and feel that they can help me fill in some of the blanks when I need to do so.

I don't really care if the person I'm talking to at the time of the meeting was murdered or if they died of natural causes. When I run across a young child's grave, I stop and pray. I usually pray for the families and the sorrow that the child's death caused in the area; as you know, it had to be devastating. We, among the living, can learn a lot from the dead if we just learn to be patient, listen, observe, and maybe do a bit of research. What would we find if we could look inside the coffins? What would we see in terms of dress, attire, perhaps knick-knacks, important papers, jewelry, love notes, and more? I know they may all be just dust by now, but there was a time when... Well, you fill in the blank.

Font Thievery!!

How many of you knew, and be honest, that when you use certain fonts you are supposed to pay a fee for using it? Some fonts are trademarked, and copyrighted, and you can't use them without permission or having a license. It was something I found out today!! No, really, today!! I had zero clue or knowledge regarding the matter before this very day (in fact, about an hour ago).

I am writing another book, and I have joined several online self-publishing groups on Facebook. I know I shouldn't do that, so many people on those things are so freaking weird, but you know what, I have to put up with them, and they have to put up with me. I posted that I was looking for someone to take my Word document of 83600 words and convert it into a print-ready high-resolution PDF so I could upload it onto Ingram Spark to go into the book's exterior. I also posted that I needed an exterior cover created as well. (and both needed to be converted to eBook)

Well, I got quite a few people writing to say one of three things: (1) Some said they could do it, and they shot me a price. (2) Some said they could do part of it, but not the other part. Since I got both parts I was OK with that. (3) Some said I could do it myself. I started thinking about it, and I'm going to do that if I can. It's going to be a bit difficult for this old dog to learn that particular new trick, but I'm absolutely ready to learn.

So, one guy who wanted me to use his company shot me a price of $999. (I laughed) I laughed because I already had four other offers for literally $200, $225, $250, and another for $315. Why on EARTH would I use his service for $999? He then told me I would be paying more because his company had the licenses needed to produce and reproduce all the fonts I would need for my book. That was just the weirdest and strangest thing I had ever heard -- and I laughed again. I mean, it's real, he's telling the truth; but is he?

Turns out there are licensed and trademarked fonts that if you use them you either have to be licensed to do so, or you need permission. Well, as one young man in Scotland knows, (Hi, Tex) I don't ask permission very often, if ever. I do what I am going to do. I may apologize, but I really don't ask permission. So, after digging into the matter I found that there are literally hundreds of fonts that are OPEN SOURCE and the one I'm using now is NOT one of them. I am using Georgia, but it's on this site, and this site has the license to share it. Oh, there you go. Loophole!! Well, there are a few fonts out there that are so close to Georgia that you and I couldn't tell the difference if we used a magnifying glass! I will be sure to use one of them when I download my book into the converter.

The converter has a 30-day trial so I downloaded it, and I'll use it to download this particular book. Then, I'll buy the thing and use it to download the others if I am successful with this one. If I am NOT successful with this one I'll keep reading and studying the methods because others are successful and I will force myself to learn. It makes 100% sense to me to buy a converter for $59 and use it as many times as I want to; rather than paying someone $100 to do it for me.

One woman I found told me she would do the download for $10 and the cover for $5 if I shot her the cover I wanted to use. SO CHEAP. In other words, I go to the app PAINT on my computer, upload a photo, use the tools to add text and whatever and she'll put it together in her converter and trim it up to the size I need. OK. If the new software I'm getting does that I may still give her the chance to teach me. That's worth not only my $5 but I'll give her more to train me. She's really funny too; nothing like me. We don't see eye-to-eye on any subject whatsoever except putting the screws on people who try to overprice their services. When I asked the woman why she charged so little she said she is trying to bring up her reviews, so if she can do 1000 or so books at $10 and/or $5 for covers, we'll give her great reviews. She's not wrong.

Some people are genius! Anyway, I just wanted to chime in and ask you if you knew about the need to be licensed to use a freakin' font of your choice. You may want to think about it before you add it to your website. Apparently, some of these font creators are hell on wheels!! You can go about your business now, I just thought I would break in with a bit of new knowledge. You're welcome.

Know Your Worth

We have had it drilled into our heads since we were very young not to toot our own horns. There's something to be said about it, sure, but there's also something to be known about knowing your own value. I heard someone say once that if you don't know your value, you shouldn't expect anyone else to calculate it for you. They may know you're pretty cool, adequate, or even in most cases, better than average, but if you don't believe you are what you know you can be, then you have no one but yourself to blame when you constantly accept those insults that tend to cut you into pieces. Water on a duck's back, folks; let it go.

Today, I was turned down for yet another position where the company had advertised that they wanted someone with experience, know-how, and the ability to command a team; that's me in a nutshell, but they also wanted someone younger and yeah, if I was absolutely honest about it, they thought my name "*Jude*" belonged to a man. When I met the recruiter face-to-face, the first thing she mentioned was, "*Oh, I thought you would be a man.*" I asked if that was a problem, and she stated that the company was more male-centric. Her word. *Male-centric.* Is that even legal? No, it's not, but it happens.

So, where I wasn't surprised that I wasn't offered the position, I didn't let them cut me down or use redundant paraphrases that have been near extinct since the mid-'90s. Words like "*We're going in another direction*" or "*We were lucky enough to have several people with great qualities and experiences...*" that's when you know they're lying. Most of us who have the experience, knowledge, skillsets, and qualities they're looking for are still employed. The wage they were offering didn't exactly scream *"Career Change"*; no one making that amount would leave, and anyone making more would never have even applied. Shouldn't people be more honest about it? Oh wait...they can't be. They're not allowed to say, *"You know, you're sixty, so...we think we'll pass."* The joke's on you.

The average executive or manager these days who have had a few life experiences stays with a company for between three and five years. Four years is the average, folks. They spend time and money advertising the position. They spend time interviewing, vetting, then training. If they don't have the money to pay the current employee what he or she deserves, they don't have the money budgeted to replace them either. That takes time, effort, and a host of other unbudgeted costs.

Another thing. Companies like to interview and then take weeks to decide if they'll actually fill a position, hoping against hope that while they're waiting for upper management to make a decision, their worthy candidate isn't offered another position. It happens. I interviewed two weeks ago and hadn't heard a peep from the manager; I gave them a call. I let them know I appreciated the opportunity to meet with them and to hear about the opening. The response I received was vague, basically thanking me for my time and wishing me good luck in the future. OK, but the guy you just made the offer to called me about five minutes ago and said he grew tired of waiting on you and went in another direction! (He was my former student and thought I deserved to hear what they said about me during his interview.)

If they call me tomorrow, I'll let them wait two weeks before I make my decision. I'm not in any hurry to work outside of my house. If I can find employment remotely, that's my jam. I'm not dying on the vine, and they need to realize that we old folks have value and worth; we have the stamina and the ethics to be better employees. We were raised on stick-to-it-ness, and we often choose to work overtime without pay just to be sure we did the job correctly or that all the details are covered before we head home. Vintage employees are full, chock full of knowledge, been-there-done-that moments, and we don't always fall apart or throw out the baby with the bathwater. We fix things. We pull up our bootstraps, and we make things happen. We didn't get those trophies for showing up; we earned ours. (Then we put them in the drawer, not on a shelf to be seen or bragged about.)

Yeah, it was a different time. It was hard. It was full of need-to-change, so we made that happen too. We have worth. I have worth. I know I do. I don't have to wait for someone to tell me how great I am. I don't even want to hear it. I don't want someone talking smack about me, and I don't want someone falling at my heels to follow in my big footprints, either. No one, not in a professional or personal relationship, is going to reveal something about me that I didn't already know about myself. I am me, and I have enormous value. It didn't come all at once, nor did it come without pain, suffering, and heartache. I worked for my credentials. I forged my way. If someone doesn't have the insight to consider me a part of their team - - I'm not part of their team. I can find one that doesn't need an adjustment to see what's standing right in front of them.

I don't fit in many boxes; that's true. I am out there; I am contained. I am self-proficient, and I am self-motivated and driven. I don't need a rah-rah committee to boost my ego or tell me that *we're all in this together*; another term that only works when THEY want something. I'm who I am, and I won't change. You wouldn't need or want me to change. If I chose to change, I wouldn't be the one you could depend on, would I? I am who I am, and that's enough.

Hey employers!! Don't ghost people, don't ignore them either; if they aren't what you're looking for, be kind about it. Just do yourself and your company a big favor and don't get caught underpaying your people; some steal clients because of it. Some will sell your tricks of the trade to get what you should have paid them in the first place. I'm not saying I would; but I will write about it and you in my next novel. I'm worth every penny I charge.

Playing AT the Guitar.

Many of you may know that in the early 80s, I had the biggest crush on Edgar Cruz, and yeah, I would have married the man if he had (a) taken notice that I liked him (b) taken the least bit of interest in me, and (c) had he asked. Edgar was and is one of the world's best (and I mean that) flamenco guitar players. He is just amazing; I'll leave you a link to his site so you can check him out on your own.

It was Edgar who inspired me to buy my first guitar and try as I want, I just can't remember much about it. I really can't. I want to say it was a Fender. I know I've owned a few. When you own a guitar you're really supposed to play it too, it sort of works that way, but I think having one in the house was good enough for me. It kept me thinking about my youth, and of course, about Edgar! (OK, if he ever finds himself single again, I may have to approach.) I used to say that Edgar was the GREATEST guitar playing I've ever met, but I have actually met Eddie Van Halen, so maybe I should give Edgar 2nd place since he never taught me how to play.

So, years ago I had a guitar that I really loved. I bought her at a pawn shop when I went in to sell the owner a bit of insurance. She was really old by musical standards, but I didn't think much about it. She was a Spanish guitar, I know that. I named her Stella because I lived in an apartment complex called Lake Stella, and she fit right in with the ambiance of that place. The complex was older, relaxed, just sort of friendly, and in an urban setting, not rural at all. Stella was stolen from me right after I had her cleaned, restrung, and tuned. I am not sure, but I think the owner of the guitar repair store waited until I went to church, and then he snuck into my house. I can't prove it, but a man fitting his description was seen at my apt that day. So sad. I guess he actually knew what I had, and knew I wouldn't really ever use her the way he could. He could have asked! I may have just sold her to him.

Well, I've gone through a few guitars. I gave one to my granddaughter Sailor last year; one that I love so very much. I call him Checkers for a reason. He's a black and white checkered guitar. He's of lower quality, but that's because I didn't want him stolen like Stella was stolen. She was kind of expensive, to be honest. Checkers was right at $100; so yeah, if he was taken I wouldn't have felt it so hard in my wallet. OK, about 2 or maybe 3 years ago now, I was just looking online and found a guy on Facebook who was selling his Yamaha acoustic; I always have acoustic guitars. He was selling it for $100 and I knew the model was worth more than that. The guitar was new, it was never really used, and I thought I needed to go get it. I'm glad I did.

I named the guitar Wallace and call him Wally. I have been playing at him for about 2 or 3 years, not really making anything happen. I just like holding a guitar and playing with it, you know, pretending I know what I'm doing. The dog likes it too. She sometimes nudges my elbow and looks at Wally when she wants me to play him. I love that. Today, I took Wally to Guitar Center in Oklahoma City to be cleaned, restrung, and tuned but I told the guy (Hector) I wanted to stay while he did so I could look around. He agreed and got right on it. It didn't take him 30 minutes and that was in between customers. Good kid. He did a great job.

The guitar tuning and new strings ran $24.99, and I ended up buying two shakers to drive the dogs crazy, and they had a clearance sale on a few things too. I bought my first EVER pair of drumsticks. Why? Do I play the drums? No. I do not play the drums, but I do have dogs and cats, and I love teasing them. I can beat on things around the house, knock them together, and just really be annoying. I like that. For $4.99 I think I got the best deal in the store! I also bought an LP of Simon and Garfunkel.

I asked Hector (he's 19) if he had ever heard of them. He had not. I nearly cried. They had a double LP of Credence Clearwater Revival, and I didn't need to buy it because I have it. I asked him if he had heard of CCR....he had not. I don't know who Hector's parents or grandparents are, but they really failed the man. My kids knew EVERY S&G song from the day they could sing. They knew the Bee Gees, The Beatles, Billy Joel, Elton John, and of course Eric Clapton, Kansas, Foreigner, Journey, and Boston.

Sadly, and I mean this, not one of my children plays the guitar. I absolutely failed them, but then again, I can blame Edgar for not marrying me. If he had we would have had at least two or three kids and they would have in the family band. I can't get any of my kids interested in forming a band with me. I'll have to go solo. That's the only choice I have. At least with the little shakers I can drive them nuts and force them to either join me or leave me alone to my madness. The dogs both hate and love me at this point. The cats don't care. They never care.

Sex, Murder, Cover-Up, Self Defense ("Of Kilted Pleasure")

My book *"Of Kilted Pleasure"* is available on Amazon. Here is the URL. I made it smaller so it would fit nicely. https://tinyurl.com/OfKiltedPleasure So cute. I wanted the book to cost less than $18.99, but they posted it at $19.99. I don't like that, but there's nothing an author can do about it. We're told to double the cost of the print and add another factor so we make our money. I earn about $2.10 per book at the price they've set it at. I hate that. When it's ready for eBook form, I can place the cost at $5.99 and make the same amount. I'll do that for sure. I want the book out there!! I want people to read it.

I'm sitting down with the book now and reading it for myself as if I had never read it before. This seems odd to me, and maybe it does to you as well, but I want to be able to think about seeing the book, buying the book, and just sitting down with it and not knowing what to expect. Of course, I also realize that's impossible since I now only wrote it, but I've read it about a dozen times throughout the editing process.

The first thing I've come across as a new reader is that the author wanted to capture the reader's attention immediately, and she may have gone a bit overboard on the whole sex thing; then again, not really. I've also read other romance books in the Scottish Highlands, and my book is somewhat tame by comparison! I think I'll write another one but have it taking place in the Scottish Borders just to prove that those living in Hawick, Galashiels, and Kelso can hump, pump, and bump just as well as those on the other side of the country. Geez, that was terrible. I'm so sorry!

I will write to as many mental health service companies as possible to let them know about the book because one of my characters deals with anxiety, depression, lower self-esteem, and even isolation issues. He doesn't get over it; he doesn't get cured of it. He works through the individual issues one at a time, and he fights himself over it. He hurts, lives, and is wounded, but he works through these problems the best he can. He seeks help, asks for help, accepts help, and sometimes he just blows up or takes it all internally. He's a very normal man. I want people to know it's OK not to be OK all the time. We suffer and work hard to make things happen when or if we can. If not, we hurt.

I'm very blessed in that I've never been one to suffer from any lengthy ordeal dealing with mental health. I've been depressed. I've been anxious. I've been sad and upset with myself, but it only lasts a bit before I pull myself back to my belief system, and through faith, I work through the harder issues that I know I can't handle on my own. God helps me. I'm blessed to have that faith. I want that for others. The book shows a bit of that. I hope they are encouraged when people with mental health issues read the book. I hope to hear from some of them to let them know they found courage or comfort in my chosen words.

"Of Kilted Pleasure" is more than just a romance novel. It is a historical novel as well. It is a book about life. It is a book about fantasy. It is a book about an escape to another time and another place. It is full of sex, killing, murder, and mayhem, as well as ordinary life, market, church, food, and romance. I wanted to bring it to the forefront of everyone who lives and has thoughts of love and intrigue. The cover-up is a really good one. I think I

like that part of the book the best. As a writer, it's never about the murder or the killing but always more about the disposal of the bodies. That's the fun writing. I think I did it justice.

Let me know your thoughts, and spread the word that the book is available. I need to sell about 30,000 to get enough money to move to Scotland on a more permanent basis...help me do that, please!! THANK YOU. (When I get there, I plan to move to either Fife or the Borders and write another book, or three or six).

Photo Credit: Tom Isaacs

Life With and After Owning a Famous Dog

People assume that because we were on the Oprah Winfrey Show in 2006, we're either famous, rich, or maybe both. Nothing could be further from the truth. Let's start with why we were on the show, shall we? I owned a very famous dog named Faith. Faith was famous for two reasons: she was bipedal and on television. She was born without the use of her two front legs. One was never present, and the other was born twisted and set behind her. I don't do dog health, so I can't give you the reasons. I can say that the vets who looked at her said that the mother dog must have been aged or had some sort of genetic illness to pass that sort of thing down to her puppies at birth. The mother dog was approximately twelve when she had her last litter, the one Faith was a part of.

The mother dog was a full-blood black Chow, and though Faith was yellow, the only way anyone could have known she was half Chow would be to squish her face. When you did that, you could see the Chow; otherwise, she resembled a Labrador mixed with maybe a shepherd of some sort. Faith stood up and walked on her own back legs and was 37" tall when she did so. She weighed just about 27 pounds and was the most alert and feisty animal I ever knew. She was on top of the world every waking moment of her life until she became older; she really was a good dog.

We put Faith directly in the Lime Light on purpose; we wanted to show people that you don't have to look OK to be OK. You don't have to be perfect to be perfect. You can be you, and that's enough. Faith was the best at being the ambassador of love no matter where she went and no matter who she met. We made over 300 flights together, and before that, we traveled by car locally. To say the dog was an international success would be accurate. She was recognized the world over. People flocked to us when they saw us in the airports and on stages. She was a show-stopper. The thing I really liked about her is that she, being a dog, was never judgmental. She didn't care who was petting her as long as someone was.

Taking Faith around the world meant giving up my day job. I was a professor or adjunct professor. I worked for several colleges both on-site and remotely. I was unable to keep that up if I needed to take Faith about, so yes, I made that choice. It wasn't one I wanted to make. I lost a great deal of money, status, and possible tenure, but it was something I felt I needed to do. I think I made the right choice. I know she changed people, and I know they appreciated meeting her and being near or with her. I was reminded over and over again how callous others can be, as I expected to be paid and was often stiffed by colleges, schools, and businesses who would hire us on a Net 30 basis and either not pay or pay us an amount quite less than what we had agreed. It was heartbreaking.

After Faith was unable to do what she did, go where she needed to go and do what she was doing, I made the decision to go back into teaching, but it was not the same. I was teaching at the high school and middle school level, and times had really deteriorated from 2005 when I had left to take Faith around the world. It was unreal how students treated teachers and how the administration wouldn't back the teachers up when necessary. I went back into selling and servicing insurance, and that's what I'm doing now. I was recently released from my job because the agent couldn't afford to continue to pay me. He wanted me to go commission, but that's not what we had agreed upon, and no one in this state wants to use that carrier at this time due to their 50% policy rate increase. No. Salary is the only way to go.

I'll be OK. I have my licenses, and I have experience. I'll bounce back and, in fact, have an interview today to work as a Claims Adjuster for another good company. I'll keep you posted.

You can even be a bit feisty if you need to be.

Me with Faith in 2011

My Two Grannies

So, nowadays people have a multitude of grandparents because of divorce, remarriages, and blended families. I was born in the 60s and my parents were born in the 30s and there wasn't as much of that going around. I had two grandpas and I had two grandmas. Growing up I was privileged to have had a great grandma while I was young as well. I remember thinking she must be 100 years old to have been Grandma's mom! My dad's mom was 15 when Daddy was born. Her mom was 17 when she was born. My dad was 29 almost 30 when I was born, and I was when I thought GGM was 100. Let's do the math. 5+30+15+17= 67. My great-granny was only 6 years older than I am now, and if you take away 8 years because that's when my sister was born, my great-granny was only 59-60 when she became a GREAT GRANNY! WOW. I can't even imagine.

Grandma Stringfellow or Grandma Olivea was a beautiful woman. She was 45 when I was born, and just stunning to look at all the way up until her last couple of years really. She was just as gracious and trim, and she always dressed to the hilt. She was pristine, to be honest, and that went for her house as well. Nothing was out of place, it looked as if it had been "*done up*" as they used to say, by the Merry Maids on a daily basis. She didn't cook that I remember; she may have, but not for me.

We never had dinner at her place because there were too many of us. Dad and Mom had 4 of us. Grandma Stringfellow married at age 14 to a man older, but too much older. They had 4 boys before she was 20 years old. Again, I can't imagine that. Let's contrast.

My maternal Granny, Grandma Edwards, Nancy Melvina Free Edwards, was born in 1894. She was 65 when I was born, making her 70 when I was 5. She was older than my great granny on my daddy's side. When you're a kid that sort of math can be really confusing. Mellie or Granny as we called her because we didn't need to be backhanded for calling her by her middle name; was always (and I do mean always) cooking, cleaning, moving about, and getting ready for something going on at the church. Both ladies were born-again Christians, but my Grandma Stringfellow only attended church, she wasn't really into the social side of it.

Grandma Edwards was the reason people socialized at the church; she was the cook! I was born on Wednesday, and in the church that following Sunday, and in the nursery with my Grandma Edwards rocking my crib. It never really went downhill. She continued to love me wholeheartedly until she went to see Jesus and let me just say I'm sure she still does love me.

Grandma Stringfellow died in 1987 at the age of 70. Grandma Edwards died in 1993 at the age of 99. She had 10 children, 24 Grands I think, and who knows how many other faces showing up for dinner, parties, celebrations, and gatherings. Her house remained spotless too, and there was a reason for it. If we made a mess of any kind we cleaned it up immediately. If we even thought about NOT cleaning it immediately, we were met with a spanking, and it didn't matter how old we were. I remember a cousin once, a foolish child, saying she was going to tattle on my granny for having spanked her. My granny grabbed that girl, turned her back over the knee, and spanked her again, then told her to tattle that one too! She told the little girl, my sweet cousin, that if she didn't do what she was told she would be dragged to the mess and shown how to clean it up and any number of her children and grandchildren would assist in the instruction. She was not wrong.

My Grandma Stringfellow never once, not one single time, told me what to do. She told my dad, and he told me or had my mom tell me. She didn't want to be hated or thought of as being mean. I can tell you this, I liked Grandma Edwards WAY WAY better than I did Grandma Stringfellow and it's because we were kids and she understood that. She corrected me. She instructed me. She cared enough to see that I knew what I was doing. She was pushy, bossy, in your face, and very direct, but she never once mistreated me or caused me to think she was going to harm me. Far from it. She would have defended any of us to her last breath. I think I had two or three actual conversations with Grandma Stringfellow because when we kids would try to talk to her she would remind us that the adults were talking. We were to be in the other room playing. With Grandma Edwards, until I got too big to do so, I sat in her lap and she read the Bible to me and explained it. There's a difference right there.

When Grandma Stringfellow died I can honestly say I was sad for my dad, but I really didn't have any true emotional reaction. When Grandma Edwards died I did. She hadn't been able to cook for three years, so at 96 she fed all of us again, but we let her rest up after that Christmas. When the gates are opened and we all get to the place(s) where we meet people and know them again, I will likely have to look pretty hard to see Grandma Edwards. She'll be "*Mellie*" to us then, but she'll be pretty popular, to say the least. I'll stand in line. I'm good. It's eternity after all, right? I have the time. Can't wait. (I'll hug Aunt Wilma and Uncle Marvin while I wait.)

I Work From Home

I work from home, and I don't ever want to go back into the *"real world"* to make a living. If the truth is told, I shouldn't have to, either. People throw out the current year all the time as if because it is THAT or THIS year, we should be doing this or that. OK, it's 2023, I don't want to have to get up at a certain time, get dressed, put makeup on, drive to work, fight traffic, get to the place, only to find it too cold or too hot, or that see that the others who work there can't be cordial, polite, or civil. I don't want to deal with people coming into the office to ask me something that could be handled in a text, email, or I don't know, by them doing their own due diligence! Guess what, buddy, there's an APP for that! GET IT. USE IT. (I have to, everyone I know has to, and you can too. (I'll go ahead and say, *"It's 2023!"*)

When I work from home I don't get dressed for success, I'm dressed for work. I don't have to impress anyone by slathering on base, eye-shadow, lipstick, or blush. I won't wear mascara for anyone, so there's literally NO CHANCE of that happening. I don't have to, but if I have to, then the boss has to, and every single person in the office is going to because no one is going to tell me that a WOMAN wears makeup. Think about it, I'm a right-wing conservative saying that; imagine if I were a left-wing liberal and the boss or someone else wanted me to wear makeup. I know my politics shouldn't come into it, but what if my religion forbids me to wear it? It doesn't, but that's not the point. The point is I work from home! Not one of my dogs or cats (not even my lizard) has asked me (or expected me) to dress and wear makeup. I still do my job, and I still do it well. There you go.

I work from home. I chose to work from home so I don't have to fight traffic and put myself into lethal situations when idiots decide they're late and can't be bothered to drive like a human rather than a cretin. I can't tell you how many times I have literally counted how many accidents I've seen or passed on my way to and from work all because, or mainly because, someone decided to pass someone, or get by someone, or they decided that they were more important than the rest of us who are abiding by the rules and laws. Why do that if you don't have to? Driving to work takes literally 40-45 minutes each way, and I'm trading that time for NOTHING. I don't get paid for it; it's given away. I'm losing it, and not being compensated for it. If I were to suggest being compensated for it, I would be laughed at. Don't laugh at me, just acknowledge that I work from home.

I work from home and yes, I have dogs. You may hear a dog bark if you call the office number. You can survive that. At least you won't hear a co-worker cussing or the boss freaking out. You won't hear me saying "*I'm sorry, I can't hear you, there's a train going by.*" I mean, I could say that, but there aren't any trains, it's just me and the dogs, cats, the lizard, and my kid. She works from home too. You could hear her, but then you'd think I was at work, wouldn't you? You'd think she was a co-worker, and want to know more about the Australian woman in the background? My daughter is a voice-over actress. She could be a robot, she could be a man, she could be a chipmunk. She could be a male chipmunk from Australia fighting with a robot. She's very talented.

By the way, I work from home so I can make better lunches, and not have to spend an hour away from the office either driving around or pretending that I have something to do so I'm out from under the pressures of co-workers and bosses. I work from home so I can get my coffee when I dang well, please. I can go poop and not have to worry about someone coming in behind me and making faces. I can dance, do squats, lift weights, and study my Financial Advising materials without wondering if I will be seen, heard, or interrupted. If I am interrupted by work, I do my work. It's my job and I do it. I don't take from one boss to give to another. I am the other. I work from home for one boss, and for myself. I work from home because I can get much more done that way. Yes, there are distractions, but not the type that sends me over the moon screaming and wishing I was at home, because I am at home. My distractions are the Amazon man delivering something, or the neighbor wanting to take my dog for a spin because she recently lost hers.

All in all, I am very happy to be an at homer. I literally roll out of bed, take the shower, and dress back in my jammies. I eat when I want to, drink as much coffee, good coffee, as I want to, and NO ONE...NO ONE tells me to smile, and they don't ask me to run an errand. NO ONE ever asks me to just run to the post office, or the bank, to pick up their dry cleaning, their kids, or anything. NOPE. I work from home because it's where I feel most comfortable, free, relaxed, and capable. I do a much better job from home and when the whistle blows and the day if done, I don't have to get into my car and fight traffic again. I make it home on time for dinner, and I have NO angst or anxiety from the trek.

If you think about it, the Pandemic taught us that we don't need to be out and about and mingling with people. So, I guess all of us right-wingers were correct, not that the big pharms or others will admit it; but it is good that we can use their own words against them now. I don't want to be around people who may be sick. They say they're OK, but they say that so they don't lose their jobs. Being home I can work through a cold or fever. I don't have to lose money and my boss gets the work done without having to wait on it. There really are about 10 good reasons to work from home, but the best one I can think of is that I CAN!

UPDATE: Since I've written this blog, I've been home another year, and though I wasn't really *"working"* much, I was training to become a Claims Adjuster, and I wrote five novels in 2023. Woot!! I have been a remote worker for too long to go back into the office, but if they pay me enough to do it I would be foolish not to go. Of course, that pay may or may not include wearing nicer clothes, putting on makeup, and smiling. That's gonna cost a lot more; they'd be better off just letting me roll out of bed in my pajamas with a big cup of coffee; I work better here anyway.

The Hound of the Baskervilles

Being an avid reader, when I was less than ten I remember reading every Sherlock Holmes mystery that I could get my hands on, and that was literally every one of them since I was often hanging out at the library. Yes, I was that kid. You'd catch me walking from 2212 N. Mueller to the corner of 35th and Mueller so I could be at the Bethany Metropolitan Library, and you know, I loved it. It was MY hiding hole. I would find a good spot to sit in, usually up against the wall and on the floor between aisles of reference books since no one ever went there. I would bring my pillow and to my surprise, one of the staff members said I could keep one up there so I didn't have to drag it back and forth with me. What a thought! I did that.

When I was less than a teen I was in the spot where I found such peace, and I had in my hands the hardcover bound book titled *"The Hound of the Baskervilles"*. I remember the story. It was ONE hound. It wasn't the HOUNDS of Bakerville, as some people would call it. My freaking teacher called it that and YES, I corrected her. I know, I'm not really supposed to do that, but I did. I was in the 5th grade when that happened and my mom was called to the office to speak to me. Can you imagine if that were to happen today? A kid corrects a teacher, and then their parent is asked to come up to discuss it? No. That is what is WRONG with our society today. I was in the wrong for trying to openly and publicly correct my teacher. I get that now. I don't know that I got it then. I was right. I knew I was right. My mom even told me I was right, but it wasn't the best practice. It was in fact, WRONG to correct the teacher the way I did it.

What I remember about the entire event is that our school media center didn't have that particular book as it was considered too scary or something for elementary kids. We had other books, but not those written by Sherlock Holmes. That was the year I found out (I was corrected) that the books about Sherlock Holmes were actually written by Sir Arthur Conan Doyle!! WHAT? I knew him. I knew he was a writer too. I just hadn't put two-and-two together until the 5th grade. It was likely because when I went to the library to get the books they were all in the same area (Thank you, Dewey Decimal System), and all the books I was looking at said *"Sherlock Holmes"* on them; so naturally, my ten-year-old brain assumed he was the author. Also, I was flat upset about the fact that Holmes didn't narrate the books, his friend Dr. John Watson did. I couldn't figure that one out either.

So, here we are so many hundreds of years later, and I am still correcting people when they bring up the book in conversation; or they make a reference to it. They almost always say *"The Hounds of Bakerville"* as if Baskerville is a place and there were multiple hounds. Nope. It was ONE big dog, and the Baskervilles were a family who lived in a fictional manor on a fictional moor. It's kind of funny really. I mean, I am wrong, absolutely wrong, about so many things. I'm not as wrong as I could be because I get really really upset with myself when I am wrong, so I tend to fight to my own death about decisions I need to make so I'm not wrong. I kick my own ass, no one else needs to stand in line to do that.

My good friend got it right! I called her and I said *"OK, Sir Arthur Conan Doyle wrote a book about a family who lived on a moor, and one by one the head of the household was either killed by or chased by a big black dog. Do you know the name of the book?"* She answered yes, *"but I didn't know his name was Arthur. I thought it was Conan Doyle."* I did laugh. She did however get the title of the book correct, so we're still best friends. If I turned that around and I had to answer for her who sang this or that song, or what the title of it was, I would be lost in the abyss because I'm not going to get that unless it's a Bee Gee song.

I sat myself down this past week and read the book on my Kindle. I recalled so very little of the book from when I was ten. I really hadn't remembered most of it whatsoever, so that makes me think I now need to go back and read every last thing that Doyle ever wrote. Yes, I do. Did you know, and maybe you don't care, but did you know that before he was an author Arthur Conan Doyle was a medical student and he is a graduate of the University of Edinburgh Medical School? WHAT? Yes, he really was a doctor, and Dr. John Watson is not. Dr. John Watson is a fictional character. I can't tell you how hard I took that information when I realized that neither he nor Sherlock Holmes were real people. Just devastated me. I think I was about 12. I had to question my entire existence at that point.

If Sherlock Holmes wasn't a real person, I asked myself, were the other people in the other books real? That was when I had a long and drawn-out conversation with Sheila Parker; the teacher who lived behind our house. She had kids that we played with, and since she was a teacher, and I had seen her in the Reference section of the library, I figured she might know something about it. She did. She set me straight on fiction vs. non-fiction, and she even told me about TWEEN books and that was fascinating. I didn't do too much reading in that section, but for some weird reason, I loved the Betsy and Tacy books. Geez, now I have to go back and read those again. I have NO clue what they did, but I remember I loved it.

Finka isn't really a hound, and she doesn't live anywhere near England. She's not one of the Baskerville pets, but she is my grand dog. She's adorable, and I needed an excuse to put her picture in the book.

Hugo is 11 months old now. He's not a hound either, but he's black and could be scary if you didn't know him and he was chasing you.

324

Here's a Thought, Be Considerate

Do what you say you will do. If I had to choose a mantra it would be one that I borrow from Jesus, it would be, *"Let your yes be yes, and your no be no."* It's really simple people; if you can't keep your promise to call someone back, or respond to an email, just text them really quick and say so. Just be the person for them that you would appreciate if the tables were turned. I'm only saying this because I am forever and a day being the one who has to either *"take the high road"* or *"be patient"* with others who just can't get it through their heads that being on time, doing what you're supposed to do, saying what is appropriate to say, and you know, DOING YOUR JOB the way it was intended...is the right thing to do. EVERY TIME, not just whenever it suits you.

For so many generations below that of the one I was born in, being on time seems to be a guideline rather than a requirement. The clocks don't stop just because a person isn't utilizing their time in the best way possible. I have a friend, no wait, I have three friends who just can't seem to be where they are supposed to be at the time agreed because they get distracted or allow themselves to be distracted by the simplest of things. I say it all the time, if I'm late, call the police. I am most likely dead. I think I could count on one hand how many times in my adult life that I have been late for whatever it was that I'm supposed to be doing. One hand in over 40 years. We are all given the very same 24 hours in a day. CHANGE your habits if it is in fact your habits that are causing you to be chronically late. Don't say 8:00 a.m. if you mean 8:20 a.m. It's both rude and inconsiderate. There, I said it....again.

I accepted a position once where the boss would say *"I'll call you right after this meeting"* or *"I'll call you right after lunch"*. Several hours would pass before he got around to making the call. I would usually say something to the effect of *"You know, I want your job Boss. You take five-hour lunches! Sign me up for that."* You know he wasn't trying to be negligent, but time just got away from him. HOLD ON TO TIME folks. Make it your bitch, you remain in control if you have half a hope of being the one who can be relied upon. He knew if I said I'll call you in 10 minutes that I'm calling in 9 minutes. Don't go to the bathroom at the last minute if you expect me to call because I will call you if I said I would. If I am going to be one freaking minute late I'll text to let you know it.

I have three children. One is like me. Thank you, Reuben. He gets it. Laura will be late to her own whatever, she's never on time. When I watch or observe her and I point out where it was that she went sideways her answer is usually *"Yeah, I didn't mean to do that."* You may not MEAN to, but you do it over and over. It's a habit. It's just exactly what it is, and you do have control over it; one way or the other. You make choices to be who and what you will be. Caity, on the other hand, is predictable. She will be there at exactly the moment she said, not a minute early, but if you're a minute late she'll let you know. Laura is flexible on your time as well as her time, and Reuben and I have usually walked away after being stood up, but we remember it, and we remind you the next time that you left us hanging.

It's not only about time either. If you say you're going to pray for someone, pray for them. If you say you're going to take someone somewhere, do it. If you say you're going to support someone through this or that program, do that. If you can't make it, do it, or follow through, there may very well be a reason, but be considerate folks, and let the other person(s) know before it becomes a problem

-- when you can. A great deal of people will literally pay $$$$ to life coaches who say the same things I'm saying right now. You have a choice and how you approach that choice-making is again another choice. YOU can be the person you need to be if YOU make a decision to be the person YOU are supposed to be. I can't do that for you. I won't charge you anything for this lesson; it's a gimme.

One more thing before I go. If you have kids start them out young, very very young in fact, teaching them that gratitude is of utmost importance as well as being considerate. Tolerance is good, but so is standing your ground. It's OK to make a point and allow others to make theirs. We don't have to agree with each other, but respecting each other is paramount. OK....I'm done. If you feel the need to share this post or the context of it, please do. More people need to be made aware that being considerate is a good thing. It's a REALLY good thing.

Photo Credit: Canva.com (royalty-free)

CHAPTERS SAMPLES FROM TWO OF MY BOOKS

Chapter One of "*Bay Sorrel Ranch*"

The thought occurred to her, that the first sip of her McDonald's unsweetened tea literally tasted like water from an outside rusty tap being poured over dried out hay that's been left in the Oklahoma sun a bit too long. It may be on ice, but it wasn't something most people would have chosen to cool themselves in the heat of another hot summer day. She assured herself that what she was tasting couldn't be better if she had made it at home herself; which was the one reason she found herself making the one-mile trek to Micky-D's nearly every day. Hay tasted pretty damn good to the woman; it had been simply too long since she had been around it for any real length of time. If she had to make a comparison to it and anything else she would say that the tea seemed like a harbinger of good things to come; earthy, real, not something fake or made to fool anyone.

Juliett Leigh Armstrong, "*Jule*" to most anyone who knew her, was the sort of woman who wasn't impressed with the fancy things in life; even now that her seventh published Highland romance book had somehow "*taken off*" and was as they say "*flying off the shelves*". To be honest, and she usually was honest, Jule would be the first to tell you that she never wrote any of her books with the intention of actually selling even one of them. She did write them with the hope that they would be enjoyed, certainly, but if she and her kids were the only ones actually reading the books, she would have been content.

When *"Tartaned Soul"* sold as quickly and as proficiently as it had over the past few months, Jule found herself searching the net to find not only a good publicist, but also another full-time promoter and manager who could bring about desired results not only in book sales, but also a meaningful tour which could allow her to travel at the same time. Clearly, a win-win for everyone.

Her new manager Michael Maguire lived in Las Vegas, having removed himself from the East Coast area for personal reasons. While the mountains outside of Vegas couldn't hold the same magic as did his wife's longstanding love for the Blue Ridge Mountains of Tennessee, Maguire knew that the wheels turned a little faster in the land of chance. His guidance for Jule, in just under a few months' time, had proven to be literally worth his weight in gold; and Maguire was a big man! Within weeks of their meeting online, Maguire had planned both a seventeen-city domestic book tour, along with an eleven-city international tour including Edinburgh, London, Dublin, Stockholm, Paris, Madrid, and Rome as well as a few more interesting venues. So many expectations, so many sites to explore. Due to his own personal passion and fascination with Europe, *"Mac"* made sure each and every date was spread out over at least a couple of days, giving them time to delve into the sites and history of each gloriously lavish and ancient city they set for venue.

Sixty-eight days abroad meant staying in expensive hotels, being trotted about by book sponsors; all of which were more than happy to bring the newly inspiring author into their stores and professional lives during each leg of her stay. However, as both she and Mac discovered, traipsing about Europe during the rainiest season of the year meant showing up at locations often covered in mud or less than Jule would have wanted to present herself while asking folks to buy one or more of her books. Experiences like this, she knew, weren't necessarily going to be an everyday event, and she absolutely tried all she could to bring about the positive in every solution. No doubt she had no problems finding those silver linings with Mac around, as the man simply oozed out the most upbeat demeanor known on the planet. No one, and she knew that to mean no one on Earth, could ever have accused Mr. Mike Maguire of being anything but confidently and decidedly positive. She told herself she wouldn't put it past Mike to have Type B-positive blood running through every vein in his body.

Mornings in Europe, as opposed to the mornings in the States when they were fetching their coffee, meant standing in queues and being patient about it most of the time. While in Berlin it wasn't necessarily the rudeness of the people that caught Jule's attention, but the fact that the locals literally considered themselves to have the right to push past a tourist to place an order before they headed off to train stations to push past tourists to get to work. She wondered if when they actually got to work if any of the Berliners were apt to push past their fellow co-workers to use the copiers, or to swipe their security badges before someone else could do so. It was just a thought; thoughts pass easily enough. Silver linings! She told herself, find one! While in Berlin the parks and greenways were as exquisite as she could possibly have imagined. *"There you go,"* her mind reminded her heart, *"...there's always something nice you can say."*

Though it had been a few months since her feet had returned to the States from her less-than-whirlwind adventures overseas, Jules hadn't forgotten the agonizing and senseless errand she had needed to take care of even before taking the afternoon to rest from the 18-hour flights including her two-hour lay over in Atlanta; one of busiest and most confusing airports in the world. Upon arriving at her final destination, Jule landed and found her car parked off campus of Oklahoma City's compact airport enthusiastically named Will Rogers World Airport. She came face-to-face with a bright yellowish green envelope dangling lacklusterously from the windshield of her car. The Oklahoma City Police had contacted her via email during her long trip to inform her that the sticky decal sticker on her back tag, the one with the written year on it, had been cut from the tag and was now probably hanging cockeyed on the tag of some illegally or ill-gained vehicle somewhere in the state.

The fact that anyone could just walk onto one of these off-site parking lots was upsetting enough; when she was told there hadn't been any night security at the place in over a month, Jule Armstrong thought seriously about holding the company itself responsible for the theft. After being told that the place had been abandoned, she all but felt that much luckier that only the decal of her tag had been taken, and not the entire car. The off-site parking garage had been the center of a divorce dispute that somehow ended up falling through various cracks in the court system. The gates had been locked, their new locks had been changed, but no one took the time to seal up the open corners of the fence. There were huge holes that gaped open allowing anyone to pass through.

She told herself that had she driven her adorable white fancy 1968 Volkswagen Beetle to the off-site parking facility, her luck may not have been so good. Not that many people gave her newer model Subaru Outback a second look. It had been painted a rather boring Cinnamon Brown Pearl. Why she put herself through that choice in color she couldn't remember; but at least she didn't have to look at the exterior of the car if she were driving it. She thought maybe the price had been lower, but the price of the car wasn't what she was mulling over in her brain at the moment. For a second she remembered that the Beetle was a stick-shift and no one under the age of fifty could probably drive it if they did steal it. Geez, she thought, has it come to this?

"My Bug is precious to me, but not necessarily to anyone else. I learned to drive on it. I've had it since, gosh, 1985 maybe? I was eighteen when I got it, that was November, of...damn, I'm old, I can't remember, but I can come up with it if I really want to. It was November. That much I am sure about."

She laughed, as the lonely younger attendant tried hard to walk away without carrying on anything resembling a real conversation, and not apologizing for any inconvenience.

Because she had agreed to take care of the matter as soon as she returned, Jule felt that it couldn't hurt to give it a good college try. Driving up Meridian Avenue from the airport she was all but guaranteed to find at least one open tag agency that afternoon. Her luck held; the Southside Tag Agency just a few minutes north of the runways was in fact open 24-hours a day, and because she had kept her registration with the little decal sticker's outline and receipt of purchase in the glove compartment, it wasn't hard to find the record of her purchase. She did notice that since she had been in Europe the tag had actually expired, so there were penalties to pay, but at least she didn't have to pay for an entire second year. Who does that, she wondered? Who steals the decals of the car if it's about to expire?

It made sense once she thought it through. In Oklahoma, there are two sticky decals for each tag. One, the one on the left, has the month highlighted, and the second decal, the one on the right, had the year. No one really ever took the sticker on the left; just the one on the right. Damn, just damn. They took the sticker, causing her a little trouble, but since the tag had already expired by the time she landed, maybe someone at the parking garage knew more than they were saying. Maybe they knew she wouldn't be back until after the start of the new year. It made her wonder if the owners or an attendant wasn't making a little something-something on the side; who knows?

Pulling up to her condo and parking the car under the carport still made her feel rather exposed. If they could do it once, they could do it again. Though she had been certain it was the transients or the workers at the park lot who had nicked the tag accessory, she didn't like leaving the butt end of her vehicle open to the public. From this day forward, she told herself, she would take the time to turn her car around and back it into the carport. Pursing her lips and squinting her eyes before finally deciding to do so, she backed the car as far back as it could go so that no one could squeeze themselves into the space and get any elbow room to cut through it again.

She had noticed on the tag itself, that the perp had left a rather large "*X*" where he or she had literally cut the decal from the little grove it sat in. She remembered her son had told her that once she bought the new decal, she needed to take a box-knife and do the same thing, so that if it happened again the crooks would see the "*X*" and know they couldn't get the decal off in one piece. Smart. Clever, and it made sense; but the sad thing was that people needed to protect themselves from theft. Jule Armstrong remembered a time when her younger self, little Juliett, could ride her bike for miles and miles on Halloween night collecting treats from anyone and everyone. Some of the treats weren't ever wrapped because they were handmade. Times had certainly changed; but not for the better. The tag situation was a few months back, but still, she thought about it every time she needed to park her car.

With Autumn creeping up on her, Jule had only two weeks to call the duplexed townhouse, the place she referred to as *the condo*, her home. In the next few days, she would need to hire people, probably a couple of college kids, to help her pack her belongings. She considered hiring students since she lived less than a mile from the Oklahoma University campus. Packing was never fun, but with a bunch of young hearts and good music blasting in the soon-to-be empty halls, she figured she could get the job done rather quickly. A call to the campus student union would secure names and bodies soon enough. Buying boxes at Lowe's and setting it up would be her job; let the kids do the rest.

Spending so many years in one spot left very few spaces in the condo that hadn't been taken up with some sort of memory; be it furniture, accessories, art, or some little thing one of her three kids had given her along her nearly fifty-four years. When she thought about it, she realized she had actually only been a mother for 34 of those years, so the first twenty wouldn't count unless she had been holding onto something from before she birthed her firstborn.

Thirty-seven boxes down and with a few more to go over the next few days, it was time to make good on her promise to herself not to miss the condo, but to make a list of all the things she really couldn't stand about the place so her transition to living in a rather large house on over a hundred acres of ranch land would make more sense and be a bit more comforting than she was feeling at the moment. Good times had taken place in the condo for sure; many with her family, some without. Countless stray kittens had been born just outside her door and in the hedges lining her storage unit. She had even rekindled a sort of howdy-do friendly relationship with the new maintenance man, a retired policeman whose idea of retirement was not to actually retire, but to work until he dropped. Jule could relate. The man had been quite helpful when the last round of the stray cats in her life decided to birth four new faces. It wasn't as if he was a mere stranger – this man was a blast from her past.

Mama cats would somehow manage to dig through the rough branches to find a missing board leading under the storage unit where Jule had placed a makeshift bed for any of them if they so desired to give up their feral ways to bring life into the world with at least a smidgeon of dignity. When the kitties were born Jule could give the mothers a bit of food laced with a slight sedative so she could remove them long enough to bring them all to the wildlife reserve in her city; the one that never asked questions, and never killed a live creature. She knew it was a long shot to do all that she did for the fur babies that considered her home theirs, but it was something she couldn't and wouldn't ever write down on that list of things she wasn't going to miss. About the only thing she would actually miss was the maintenance man; or the way she thought of him. Stephen Mueller had been a part of her life too many years ago. She had all but given up on ever seeing the man again; he had ridden off as it were into someone else's sunset. Here he was now, she wasn't sure she could trust herself not to make an utter fool of herself, so she only smiled when their paths crossed.

Retirement perhaps, had brought him to her homeowners association; even if it would have been early retirement, she knew the man as a youth. She had known of his successful and decorated career as a local law enforcer in the township near her old homestead. It could have been, she argued within herself, that he was the main reason she sought greener and different pastures for herself once she became aware that plowing through dirt on the back of a horse made more sense for a younger girl than it did as an adult. Growing up sent her into the College of Hard Knocks until she realized her pen was her best friend; when once perhaps Steve Mueller could have claimed that role.

Chapter Seventeen of *"Pinball"*

The room was packed, not another soul could fit legally if the fire department had anything to say about the way Dr. Frances Moynihan conducted is lectures. Though a Canadian by birth, Moynihan, as many North Americans were, found himself fascinated by his family tree leading him directly to Edinburgh, Scotland in more ways than one. His father was a direct descendent of the more notable warriors of history, one of which, Robert the Bruce, would become King of Scotland from 1306 until his death twenty-three years later.

On his mother's side, though not as easily traced, the doctor believed himself to be less Celt and more Pictish; going so far as to join a few clubs over the past years, sending them small tokens of support to continue their research. He was French as well, obviously, but he had little interest in perusing that part of his personal history. His father's people were of much less interest to him.

Psychology had been his life's oar, helping him to steer his way through the rougher waters of life. His mind kept his soul at peace, the two often becoming inseparable at night when dreams invaded his deeper thoughts, causing him to self-evaluate, asking questions he would professionally have asked a man like Walter Sanders if he had the ability to do so.

When a man of some opprobrium and honor approached the good doctor following his oration that afternoon, Moynihan thought more than likely, the man was either from one of the social clubs he was a party to, or perhaps he would question the man about how he may join such a club to do the research needed for his own family interest. Neither distinction proved to be true; the man presented himself cordially, extending his hand and introducing himself as Matthew deVille, a doctor of research in the medical area of psychotic thought both with and for the Crown.

"My interest in you, Dr. Moynihan,"

spoke the delicate epicene man before withdrawing his hand, and wiping it clean of any germs which may have been transferred to him through the exchange,

"...is purely academic. I have a patient who I can call 'John' for our discussion today. John is a man of our common heritage, a Caucasian man, who is in his middle ages, not over the age of fifty. He is unmarried at the time, but I believe I would not be too lax in my discord with you regarding rules of silence when it deals with certain patients; this man is one I must discuss in some form or another, in order to better gain an understanding of what it is that I am facing. The man terrifies me Doctor, when he comes into my office I insist that the door to my study be left open so I am not completely alone with him. I would never be alone with him.

"He tells me things that I am not completely sure he himself understands that to divulge such horrific details may pose a problem for me from a humanitarian

standpoint. I do understand my oath of course, but when he speaks of what he's capable of, never saying he has actually committed these acts; he is quite detached from his actions.

"I feel that he may be trying to scare or shock me into a line of questioning only to play a silly game of catch-me-if-you-can, if you understand me. He may have actually committed the crimes, and perhaps he's asking me to help him be caught. I can't tell you; I simply don't know. Can you help me untangle the riddle? The man is most certainly one for the books. He's psychotic in every way possible."

deVille's eyes expressed a sincerity that his initial hand offering did not.

Moynihan paused a moment before asking questions which may have been considered probing, but he assumed the researcher would stop him if he became too immersed.

"Does he tell you he's committed the crimes by explaining or describing them, or is he just asking you to listen to him fantasize about what if, or what could be.?"

Thinking for a paused second, and breathing in a good breath, deVille answered,

"I think he's murdered. He talks as if someone else is doing it, and he is merely watching, giving instruction, or giving his opinion. If a man could do what he says the other has done, no other man could participate without being so detached he would no longer be considered human.

"He's told me that he has taken time with the victims after they've been killed; he likes to 'get to know' why they forced someone to end their lives. He's gone so far to say that he was the one chided, and the other man did the actual killing really. Again, my patient insists that he merely watched; but I simply cannot believe a word he says when he can describe the warmth of the muscles or the wetness of their lifeless body because he's drained their blood from the main arteries.

"Most members of our communities wouldn't know the locations of the smaller and large arteries. Most don't know there are twenty. Those that do know them, may not be able to pinpoint them well enough to drain a body evenly, not the way this man describes. When Reid tells me that he enjoyed the smell of the blood, and the way it pooled, he speaks from experience."

Spoke deVille, realizing of course, that he had accidently released the last name of his patient, hoping Moynihan hadn't been so keen to retrieve the nuance.

"Dr. deVille, I'm working on a research project now where a man has been diagnosed with both Schizoaffective disorder and a form of multiple personality disorder. He has bouts of depression, coupled with anxiety, causing him to want to be stimulated to appease one side of his personality, but he's afraid to try new things; can't bring himself to make the effort.

"He has internal fighting with either himself or another being he believes to be occupying his brain simultaneously, we can't pin him down when we ask him

to unravel it for us; he has different answers nearly every time we ask.

"We, well, I can't give him the credence he seeks because he leads me into several pigeon holes. Is it his game? I don't know. He's being studied by myself and one other and because he knows he's being studied, perhaps as your patient may also realize, perhaps both men are purposely giving false answers to spice the pudding."

Thinking another moment before answering deVille relaxed his stance, and crossed his left foot over his right, a stance Moynihan found to be particularly unmanly, and even uncomfortable.   Leaning into Moynihan in a silly sort of girly way, deVille asked,

"Does your man say he's fed body parts to pigs and hung skins up on cables to dry using salt water from the bay to speed up his process? I mean, the man is purely insane. I don't know if he's willing to be honest or not; but what I do know is I feel that I am either going to have to speak with the police about him, or have someone from one of the asylums cart him out of my room the next time he appears. I live and fear that he's going to draw a gun and kill me just to see the expression on my face."

The man straightened himself before clicking his heels twice, and again offering his hand. Moynihan gave him a nod and politely suggested that in the future, if he were going to extend his hand to greet a man, perhaps he could refrain from wiping the same in the presence of the one who had been courteous enough to return the greeting.

With their shared exchanges of release, Moynihan tried to put the conversation aside. He walked a few blocks to the Bayne's Inn in Edinburgh's City Centre before placing a call to Donald Ramsey's room at the same hotel. Realizing that the American attorney had returned to the States the visitor tried to reach Nick Posh; only to receive the same report.

When mentioning to the clerk at the police station who had replaced Eoghan MacRae after four in the afternoon that he would like to speak with the Chief Inspector, Moynihan was put on hold so the clerk could find one of the on-duty Inspectors he believed could help in the matter. Not willing to involve anyone new in the context of what he knew to be a private situation; Moynihan simply hung up the phone on his end before retiring for the evening.

Chief Inspector Nicholas Montgomery placed a call to the hotel moments later, asking for his call to be placed to the room who had been disconnected. The operator at the switchboard remembered the call, as anytime a call to the police is made a separate note is taken, and she placed the call through to Dr. Moynihan's room immediately.

"This is Chief Inspector Montgomery of Scotland Yard; you called the Chambers Street Police station and either hung up or we were disconnected. Is there something of importance I can help you with sir?"

asked the heavily accented Scotsman before clearing his throat on the other end of the phone.

"Sir, I apologize," started Moynihan, *"...it was me, I hung up. I think I know your name. You're associated with either Posh or Ramsey, is that correct?"*

when the answer came through and clear enough that Monty had in fact been connected with both men, Dr. Moynihan felt confident enough to share all that he could with respect to the visitor he had entertained that evening at the college.

"His office is near Parliament I found, and he's listed as a Crown ally; meaning when someone of higher rank than I wants to see a man about their mental health deficiencies they call upon this Matthew deVille character. He's checked out, I did a bit of research before calling the station. What I can't understand is why he would seek me out to answer his questions when he is the man that the almighty Royalty feel confident enough to go to. He asked me things I felt you should be aware of. He dropped an important name accidently, but it's the name I'm positive I've heard mentioned by Posh or Ramsey, one or the other. He's the man sought in the People of Culloden case that Ramsey was working, the one that paid Eoghan's wife for sex. How the cookies fall in this case!"

claimed the doctor.

"Right, we let MacRae's wife Jane Dunn have a skip on her attempted murder charge when she gave us the address and some of the better times to meet up with this John Reid character. So far, her intel has been spot-on. She's given us a great deal more than what we expected. He turns out to be the other guy we've been chasing, but when he's dressed up as Reid he's clean cut,

stands an inch or two taller. He probably has boot fillers, and he has a fancy soft accent as opposed to his more relaxed and almost derelict undistinguished look when he calls himself by another name.

"If what you're saying is fact, then the man takes himself to the high-end head doctor to tell him what he's done so that he can't be turned in for his crimes. He's putting his eggs in a precarious basket of confidentiality. He's hedging his bets is what he's doing, but how did he get in with the Crown or their people? A man can't just waltz into the Parliament or an office run by one and state his unofficial business; he'd need a in for that."

Monty asked Dr. Moynihan how long he believed he would be in Edinburgh, as Posh was expected back in less than a week's time. Perhaps the three of them could be in a room with Ramsey on the other line, and they could all work out a plan to put a better squeeze on Reid; maybe approaching him when he makes another trip to the flaccid-handed expert.

About the Author

Jude Stringfellow is an American-born Scottish-American writer who likes to travel and write, spending as much time as she can researching and exploring her adopted country of Scotland. Most of her books are either centered around the heathered moors or they include the country if possible.

Stringfellow has written over a dozen books including a poetry book, biographies, romance novels, dramas, and murder thrillers. Her Nick Posh series has been quite popular overseas as well as in North America; with the UK coming in the lead with sales at the time of this print.

Jude spends a great deal of time and effort with animal rescues as well as assisting programs geared at helping people with mental illnesses and homelessness. As a Blue-Star Mom, Daughter, and Granddaughter, she understands the suffering many veteran soldiers go through; it is her passion to continue to do what she can to find assets and opportunities for these individuals. She is involved with volunteer workshops, as well as programs promoting and helping the American soldiers.

Jude is a daughter, a sister, niece, and an aunt. She is a mother, grandmother, and as mentioned, a Blue-Star Mom. She is an animal advocate, a licensed claims adjuster, insurance consultant, educator, and author. As a Christian, a follower of Jesus Christ, she knows her human heart and mind have limitations; but with Christ, all things are possible.

Notes

All of Jude's books are available on Amazon, and through your favorite bookstore hopefully. At the time of this publication, she is trying to format all of her books into EPUB format so that they can be sold online through digital downloads which will be cheaper for her readers.

Thank you for your continued support and kindness. I mentioned a few people in the book who have websites, social media, music for sale, etc. Here are a few links for you.

Steph Macleod – Musician, Singer-Songwriter. You can find his work and musical art on Spotify and his website is: https://www.stephmacleod.music.com

Tony Broonford of Clan Broonford is on YouTube, Instagram, Facebook, X, and TikTok. Look for CLAN BROONFORD (accept no alternatives)

Bethany Christian Trust (Homeless shelter in Edinburgh)

https//www.bethanychristiantrust.com